Aging: An Exploration

AGING

An Exploration

DAVID P. BARASH

UNIVERSITY OF WASHINGTON PRESS
Seattle and London

Library of Congress Cataloging in Publication Data
Barash, David P.
  Aging, an exploration.
  Bibliography: p.
  Includes index.
  1. Aging—History. 2. Aging—United States—History.
I. Title.
HQ1061.B358 1983   305.2′6′09   82-48868
ISBN 0-295-95993-2

To my father-in-law, Morrie Lipton,
who first suggested the idea

Contents

Contents

Preface

You are invited to come exploring. This is your guidebook. You are already packed; indeed, you are already on your way: because you are alive, you age, just like everyone and everything else around you.

This will be no ordinary tourist "exploration" down well-trodden paths. We shall be snooping about in some uncharted terrain—the frontiers of scientific research into the machinery of aging itself. We shall also visit some exotic and little-known places: the land of Abkhasia in the Soviet Caucasus, an isolated valley in the Andes of Ecuador, and the realm of the mysterious Hunzas in Pakistan, at the edge of the Himalayas. These are all (or are reputed to be) modern-day Shangri-las, where age wears a different face and we are compelled to look and ask why.

Not long ago, a fantasy movie portrayed the adventures of a band of intrepid explorers who miniaturized themselves and went exploring within a human body. In a sense, we shall explore aging from that angle as well, examining the body's various organs for the footprints of time, and also diving yet deeper to explore the role of our own cells and even our genes. We shall also extend our exploration across other species, with a look at aging in other things, so as to help us recognize our place in nature.

But our trip is not limited to the here and now. We also travel back through time to experience aging in the perspective of human history, focusing especially on the extraordinary and sometimes even hilarious catalogue of efforts to understand, retard, and even reverse the effects of time on our bodies and minds. In many ways, this part of our tour reveals a cornucopia of the bizarre and zany, eliciting a chuckle from the vantage point of the 1980s. But these remarkable attempts at rejuvenation, holding our attention as they have held the attention of generations past, say something important about our innermost strivings. We even make a journey of the imagination, with a speculative excursion into what things might be like if the human life-span were significantly extended.

When most people think about aging—either their own or that of someone close to them—they typically focus on three major considerations: their bodies, their minds, and their sex lives, sometimes with crippling anxiety about each and with as little information as enthusiasm. Accordingly, we shall devote one chapter to physical processes—what actually happens to our bodies as we grow old; another chapter to mental processes—the psychology and psychiatry of normal as well as abnormal old age; and a third chapter to sexuality—changes in our love life, as the life we love continues on its way.

Aging is not just a biological process, and thus our exploration includes a glimpse at the social side of growing old in America, emphasizing changing attitudes toward this unchanging reality from the early eighteenth century to the present day. Since we all must live in the present, the current sociology of aging deserves special attention and so we linger a bit to look at ourselves. But because America represents only a limited sample of the world's people, we have also undertaken a selected anthropological tour of other ways of growing old, helping to reveal both the diversity and the uniformity of life's passage.

There are several good reasons to join our exploration. Some people climb mountains because they are there; those who want to learn about aging do so because it is intrinsically interesting. Beyond this, nearly all of us have friends or relatives who are old and growing older and, accordingly, whose journey we would like to understand. Some, therefore, will be motivated by the situation of others: modern-day Stanleys whose search is inspired by some close-by Livingston. And finally, there is the personal aspect, the inescapable fact that all of us age. Whether we are aware of it or not, we experience a host of changes in the passing of each dawn to dusk.

Aging is a vast topic, a multi-faceted jewel which must be seen from many different angles to be appreciated, even if it will never fully be understood. It has been the province of many different specialists: physicians, research biologists, historians, anthropologists, sociologists, psychologists, sexologists, and politicians. Collectively, the work of these specialists as applied to aging is known as "gerontology." All too often, however, their findings are unavailable to the interested and intelligent citizen, just as before the advent of mass transportation, guidebooks, and travel agents, the interesting and distant places of the world remained inaccessible mysteries to most people. Aging is not distant, but it too has been strangely inaccessible. On this guided tour, we shall point out the important sights, the Pryamids, Prados, and Grand Canyons of humanity's encounter with age. In our free-form exploration through time and space, we shall also glimpse many little-known wonders, far off the beaten path. If you watch closely, you may even recognize yourself.

Aging: An Exploration

1

Appointment with Age

Youth, large, lusty, loving—youth full of grace, force, fascination,
Do you know that Old Age may come after you with equal grace,
  force, fascination?

—Walt Whitman

We all have two choices: either die young or grow old. When Maurice Chevalier turned seventy-five, he was asked if he regretted it. His answer: "Not when you consider the alternative." As every day passes, we all become more experienced at growing old. It is likely to be your fate and mine, and yet most of us know remarkably little about it.

This book, then, is about aging. It is something that happens to all of us; every year, every day, indeed as you read these words, you are getting older. It is a fact of nature. Yet we sometimes fear it, avoid thinking about it, and may actually resent it, even as we seek to achieve it. It is as fascinating and complex as our attitudes toward it. The pages that follow will consider aging in its many facets: a history of how people have tried to prevent aging and prolong life, including a good deal about mysticism, quackery, common sense, and primitive science; some of the exciting recent scientific theories of what aging is, how and why it occurs, and what, if anything, can be done about it; how the passage of time is reckoned in other living creatures besides *Homo sapiens*; an overview of what actually happens to our bodies and our minds as we get older; and also, of course, a glance at sex. We shall also look at some of the world's unique Shangri-las, places where people for some reason often live to a hundred years or more; we'll examine how other peoples in other parts of the world respond to the universal experience of getting older; and we'll review some highlights of what historians and social scientists have found about aging in America.

3

In short, this book should give you a provocative sampling of the wisdom, foolishness, and realities of aging. It is *not* a clarion call for social action (although certainly such action is badly needed). Nor is it an exposé of nursing homes or a how-to book on "Retirement in the Golden Years" or "Getting All You Can out of Social Security." It won't even tell you how to achieve a Ripe Old Age. Rather, it explores aging as a *phenomenon:* historical, medical, biological, anthropological, sociological, psychological, and philosophical. It is an oddly neglected phenomenon, yet central to our lives.

To be human, it seems, is to be ambivalent. And perhaps nowhere is this ambivalence more clearly shown than in our attitudes toward aging. We seek to live long, yet we dread being old. The thirteenth-century Dominican friar Vincent of Beauvais wrote, "What is old age? A desirable evil, a living death, a strong weakness." Similarly, the Greek poet Menander exclaimed: "Oh burdensome old age! You have nothing good to offer mortals, but you are lavish with pain and disease. And yet we all hope to reach you and we do our very best to succeed." According to Victor Hugo, upon growing old, "one rents a cottage with a balcony, on the edge of the abyss."

Despite the simple, undeniable fact that we all grow old, age has a curious way of taking us by surprise. In a sense, age is even more mysterious than death. Depending on our beliefs, we may view death as simply the end, or perhaps our soul's entry into heaven or hell. In any case, the change is abrupt and clearly marked. By contrast, becoming older and finally, being old, involve gradual, imperceptible transitions through which we are transformed into a different being while yet remaining ourselves. Finally, we might ask, like Louis Aragon, "Why, what has happened?" and answer, "It is life that has happened, and I am old." Or we may feel like the playwright André Gide, "I have to make a great effort to convince myself that I am at present as old as those who seemed to me so ancient when I was young." Of course, denial may play a big part: "I will never be an old man," claimed financier Bernard Baruch. "To me, old age is always fifteen years older than I am."

My grandfather once commented that the hardest thing about growing old was seeing his children become middle aged—I assume that he was better able to see it in his children than to recognize himself changing with time. Marcel Proust wrote of his reunion with people he had not seen for many years:

> At first I could not understand why I found some difficulty in recognizing the master of the house and the guests. . . . The Prince had provided himself with a white beard and, as it were, lead soles which dragged at his feet. A name was mentioned to me, and I was dumbfounded at the thought that it applied to the blonde waltzing girl I had once known and to the stout white-haired lady now walking just in front of me. We did not see our own appearance, our own age, but each, like a facing mirror, saw the other's.

One response to aging, then, is to deny it in oneself while freely granting it to others. Some people go so far as to refuse to deal at all with the possibility (indeed, the certainty) of their own aging, and studiously ignore anything that smacks of age. To them, old persons are "memento mori," unwelcome reminders of their own eventual death.

Certainly, there is a mindless, relentless, perverse insistence in the passage of time itself. And although we may sometimes appreciate its curative power, especially when injuries or sadness must be overcome—healing all wounds, and so forth—time is more often viewed as a grim reaper, a gaunt gray figure with a vicious scythe.

Henry James once pointed out that it takes an entire lifetime just to learn how to live, "which is absurd, if there's not to be another in which to apply the lessons." Is old age worth spending one's whole life to achieve? People have revered it, reviled it, sought to achieve it, yet dreaded and even resented its arrival, and once "there" they have expected reverence, beseeched pity, gloried in adulation, wallowed in despair. The great Irish poet W. B. Yeats, in a letter to a friend, wrote, "I am tired and in a rage at being old. I am all I ever was and much more, but an enemy has bound me and twisted me so as I can plan and think as I never could, but no longer achieve all I plan and think."

We have received no end of advice on *how* to grow old, ranging in extremes from Dylan Thomas' "Do not go gentle into that good night. / Rage, rage against the dying of the light," to Dante's suggestion that we "gently slip cheerfully into the arms of God. . . . And even as the good sailor, when he draws near to the port, lowers his sails, and gently with mild impulse enters into it, so ought we to lower the sails of our worldly activities . . .

5

so that we may come to that port with all sweetness and all peace." There is something quaint and unreal about such imagery, especially to the modern ear. And yet, as we shall see, Dante's counsel of inner peace via higher communion is reflected in the thought—and behavior—of many Eastern peoples, as well as in some recent theory in sociology and psychiatry. Meanwhile, to no one's surprise, medical science is more likely to rage against aging itself—and lately, it has been finding some weapons with which to mount a direct assault.

For the present, as well as the immediate future, however, aging is very much with us. And the Western mind is caught in a conflicting cross fire of intellectual traditions. On the one hand, we have the Greco-Roman view that aging is a great misfortune and accordingly, "whom the Gods love, die young." This view was developed clearly by the ancient poet Mimnermos: "Brief is the fruit of youth, no longer than the daily spread of the sunlight over the earth; but when that spring-time of life is passed, then verily to die is better than life, for many are the ills that invade the heart." Not surprisingly, the English romantic spirit that inspired an ode to a Grecian urn also shared the Grecian attitude toward growing old. Thus Lord Byron wrote:

Oh, talk not to me of a name great in story—
The days of our youth are the days of our glory;
And the myrtle and ivy of sweet two-and-twenty
Are worth all your laurels, though ever so plenty.

What are garlands and crowns to the brow that is wrinkled?
'Tis but as a dead-flower with May-dew besprinkled:

By contrast, age is consistently glorified in the Middle Eastern tradition, including the roots of Judaism and Christianity. The Arabic word "sheikh," or leader, originally meant "elder." The Biblical patriarchs of the Old Testament are all said to have lived over nine hundred years (including Methuselah, of course). The exaggeration is not coincidental, but rather it reflects the respect accorded age. If these were great and wonderful people, beloved by God, then according to the early Semites, they must have lived to a very great age. The Bible reminds us that "the hoary head is a crown of glory." And it should come as no surprise that the Jewish community has traditionally had some of the best old-age homes, or that Browning gave these famous words to his Rabbi Ben Ezra: "Grow old along with me! / The best is yet to be, / The last of life, for which the first was made."

Aging, in reality, almost certainly falls somewhere between the horrors of the Greek mind and the glories of Middle Eastern tradition. Nonetheless, when we think of old age, it is often in stereotypes, notably two extreme opposites: either the repulsive character, the dirty old man, the helpless doddering fool; or the dignified and venerated sage, who has risen above the trivial dross of day-to-day affairs and embodies wisdom, strength, and perfection. We fear the former and adore the latter; and yet, the effect of either stereotype is to remove the old person from the realm of normal humanity. Either by their degradation or their exaltation, the stereotyped elderly stand apart.

Victor Hugo, whose literary productivity continued into his eighties, glorified age in his heroes: "His beard was silvery like an April stream. . . . For the young man is handsome, but the old superb. . . . And fire is seen in the eyes of the young, but it is light that we see in the old man's eyes." From Merlin the Magician to Tolkien's Gandalf the Wizard, we see the recurring image of the wise, pure elder. "His hair and beard and robe were white," wrote novelist Ursula Le Guin in her description of a supremely good arch-wizard in her *Earthsea Trilogy*, "and he seemed as if all darkness and heaviness had been leached out of him by the slow usage of the years, leaving him white and worn as driftwood that has been a century adrift."

Fourteen-year-old gurus may gain national attention and even some followers, but their particular interest comes from their being anomalous: we expect that God's messengers will be old. Psychoanalyst Carl Jung identified basic recurring themes of the human unconscious; among these "archetypes" was the Old Man. The Jewish and Christian God, of course, is no youngster either. Jung would argue that this view of God makes contact with a deep-seated need to venerate age. Perhaps in so doing we project hopes for our own old age; perhaps we reveal our primate heritage, much as gorilla bands are led by elderly, despotic, silver-backed males. In any event, our attitude toward the aged is so ambivalent that it hurts: "Don't trust anyone over thirty" was a slogan of the late 1960s, and yet, despite the anger and apparent sincerity of these words, youth and even the middle aged seem to harbor a hope and need for the idealized, aged leader.

7

In one episode of *Gulliver's Travels,* young Gulliver learns that in a distant land certain people, the Struldbruggs, are born with a star on their foreheads, indicating that they will live forever, whereas most of the population grow old and die. Gulliver is entranced, not only by the good fortune of the Struldbruggs themselves, but also by their mortal contemporaries: "Happy people, who enjoy so many living examples of ancient virtue, and have masters ready to instruct them in the wisdom of all former ages!" But Gulliver finds that instead of being learned and lofty, the Struldbruggs are dejected, vain, opinionated, loveless, without teeth or hair, without memory, and hence unable even to read (since they can't get from the beginning of a sentence to its end without forgetting where they started). Because their native language has gradually changed over time, as all languages do, and they have been unable to keep up, they are unable to communicate with their own kind. They live as foreigners in their own country. Similarly, the eighty-two-year-old French lady of fashion Ninon de Lenclos commented in 1702 that the elderly "have that melancholy privilege of remaining alone in a new world."

It may be, as Dr. Ethel P. Andrus once noted, that "old age is not a defeat but a victory; not a punishment but a privilege." The old person has triumphed over all the forces of the universe that assault the body integrity of us all. And it may be that we all crave to think well of age. But, like Gulliver, we are sometimes disappointed in the Struldbruggs we meet. In fact, old people themselves don't always paint a very rosy picture of their situation. Said Chateaubriand: "It is a torment to preserve one's intellectual being intact, imprisoned in a worn-out physical shell." And Freud, at age seventy, wrote: "It may be that the gods are merciful when they make our lives more unpleasant as we grow old. In the end, death seems less intolerable than the many burdens we have to bear."

In her book *Nobody Ever Died of Old Age,* an otherwise sympathetic portrayal of aging and loneliness in the United States, Sharon Curtin commented:

> Aging paints every action gray, lies heavy on every movement, imprisons every thought. It governs each decision with a ruthless and single-minded perversity. To age is to learn the feeling of no longer

growing, of struggling to do old tasks, to remember familiar actions. . . . The body seems to slowly give up, randomly stopping, starting again as if to torture and tease with the memory of lost strength. Hands become clumsy, frail transparencies, held together with knotted blue veins, fluttering in front of your eyes and reminding you of growing infirmity.

Who can say where accuracy ends and self-pity begins? The following comments by an old woman may show that she has come to believe all the nasty negative stereotypes America has of its old. On the other hand, maybe what she says is all too true. Certainly, if she feels this way it is true for her, regardless of why:

What is the sound I make when I am old? Shuffling for sustenance, napping for strength, dressing for no one, waiting for one certain visitor, I am a diminished me. No capital I. No self to fling free, a bird sailing skyward. There is only a small i, shriveled within the layers of the years. Somewhere in the early sleepless morning, when daylight still brings flicker of promise, I lie young on my scarcely wrinkled bed and am warmed by the feel of husband-hands caressing me knowingly or of child-fingers on my face or of friend-touch on my hands. But these moments pass. Daytime brings no warmth, and at last I rise because I have always risen and go to prepare myself for a day which stays too shortly and a night which comes too soon. I am an island, barren, surrounded by the waters of my plight.

Not a pretty picture, and if we were to go into the economic status of today's elderly, it would look worse yet. Mountain climbers speak of certain "objective hazards" of their sport: avalanches, lightning, falling rocks—obstacles that the universe provides, and over which people have little control. Similarly, growing old has its objective hazards—changes in body and mind that happen over time, come what may. As we shall see, the exact nature of these changes is not nearly as clear as we might expect, but the fact of them is as clear as the wrinkles that are, or will be, on your face.

There are also, of course, the "subjective hazards" of aging— not only the way we view our own aging, but also the way others view it. Attitudes toward aging can have a profound effect on the process as well as the people who undergo it, and for the last hundred years or so, the American attitude has become less and less generous. One of the earliest, most outspoken, and influential gerontophobes was Thoreau: "I have lived some thirty

9

years on this planet, and I have yet to hear the first syllable of valuable or even earnest advice from my seniors. They have told me nothing and probably cannot teach me anything." And again: "Practically, the old have no very important advice to give the young . . . they are only less young than they were." However, this is the same Thoreau who suggested that the young man collects wood to build a bridge to the moon, and then finally an old man builds a shed with it!

In his last years Michelangelo called his great statues "mere puppets." Is this the objective grandeur of old age, in which any human accomplishment shrinks to insignificance compared to one's widening perspective on the infinite? Or is it simply the ultimate tragedy of it all, an angry, shrinking denial of oneself and everything else that comes inexorably with the passage of time?

Our view of old age, then, is a welter of contradictions, perhaps because old age itself is a contradictory experience: by definition, if we are old, we have lived for a long time. But the longer we have lived, the less living we have left, and once we become really old, the less liveliness we have. George Bernard Shaw lamented that youth was so wonderful it was a shame that it was wasted on the young.

And yet, age is not without its defenders.

Despite his unflattering picture of the Struldbruggs, Jonathan Swift wrote that "no wise man ever wished to be younger." At sixty-three, Cicero defended age (and the Roman Senate) in his essay *De Senectute:* "States have always been ruined by young men, saved and restored by old." He adds: "If there were no old men, there would be no civilized states at all." In fact, old people (particularly men) have typically enjoyed a good deal of power, and the fruits of living to a ripe age have often been sweet indeed—at least to a privileged few in virtually every human society. To the sixteenth-century Italian nobleman Luigi Cornaro there were certain very practical benefits of living a long time:

> Men endowed with fine talents ought to prize a long life very highly . . . a refined and talented man . . . if he is already a cardinal, when he has passed the age of eighty he will the more likely become pope; if he is a public official, how much greater is the possibility of his being called to the highest dignity in the state; if a man of letters, he will be looked upon as a god on earth; and the same is true of all the others, according to their various occupations.

Cornaro also argued that death comes more gently and peacefully in extreme old age, without the agony of life's passage among the young.

Goethe, speaking of oak trees, but metaphorically of people as well, noted that "a century's struggle with the elements makes it strong and powerful, so that at its full growth its presence inspires us with astonishment and awe." He was nearly a century old himself at the time. Astonishment and awe; tried, true, and proven; leathery, gnarled, and tough; wise, experienced, strong, and powerful—all these images can go naturally and well with old age.

Benjamin Franklin's influence at the constitutional convention was certainly due, in part, to the simple fact that he was in his eighties at the time. Even if the body declines, this can be offset, and more than offset, by greater wisdom, balance, and experience. Writer Garson Kanin tells of the old, retired electrician who was called in desperation by the mayor of a large eastern city, when modern computers were unable to locate the cause of a widespread power blackout. The old man, who had helped install the original power plant, quickly found the difficulty, tapped the right wire, and restored power to the city. He then presented his bill for $1,000: $.02 for actually doing the tapping, and $999.98 for knowing where to do it.

❧

"The rich," said F. Scott Fitzgerald, "are different from the rest of us." And Hemingway is said to have replied, "Yes, they have more money." Similarly, the old are different from the rest of us: they have lived longer. Aging is intensely personal. It is our unique transaction with time. But it is also something we all share. The first discovery of a gray hair, the shock of approaching contact between hand and scalp, seeing our children grow up, being expected to cease working or making love, being unable to eat peanut brittle—each of these little jolts of awareness is visited upon us very privately. And yet, they happen to everyone else as well. We are all growing old, and at exactly the same speed.

When do we start to age? Some claim that life is mirrored in each day: youth as dawn, maturity at noon, and then the long afternoon of old age leading into night. It could be argued that we start to age after passing our "prime," sometime around the middle of life. At first, aging augments; then, it detracts. But we lose about one hundred thousand nerve cells every day, even while we are "young," and these are never replaced. Similarly, we progressively lose taste buds, hair follicles, and sensitivity to high-pitched sounds. In fact, perhaps we begin to age when we begin to live, at birth, or maybe even sooner. A woman's eggs, at least, begin to age even before she is born: humans are born with about 400,000 "oocytes," cells that may ultimately develop into eggs. These have dwindled considerably by age twenty-five, and all are gone at age fifty. But, three months *before* her birth, the average female fetus possessed 6.5 million of these hopeful eggs. Something happened along the way—they got old, and so in a sense do we.

Part of the strangeness about aging comes from its unreal quality. Our bodies may age, but not the *I* inside. "The heart does not grow old," wrote Voltaire. "But it is said to dwell among ruins." It is probably significant, therefore, that we may speak of the child within each of us, not the old man or woman. Yet, of course, the old person is imminent within us, just as the child is a memory. Maybe the strangeness of old age as opposed to childhood lies in the simple fact that we have already been children before we can ever become old. Our primary personality associations—our own certainty of "who we are"—are established when young. It is during early childhood that we become aware that we exist, independent of the rest of the world, distinct even from our parents. And when we look around and discover ourselves, we find that we are young. Small wonder, then, that we are later surprised to find ourselves becoming something else: old.

We can bring the past—our youth—into the present and even project it into the future. It is much harder, however, to cast a mental net forward in time, capture an image of ourselves as old, and use that image to interpret the present. And yet, why are we surprised by a fate that is natural, universal, and inevitable?

In fact, we are not young one minute and then suddenly old the next, accosted by age as by some back-alley mugger. The human brain is particularly sensitive to rapid changes; we "get used" to gradual shifts and hardly notice their occurrence. That's why it takes an infrequent, intermittent visitor to notice how much our children have grown, or how we have grown older.

The changes, although gradual, are nonetheless real, and not entirely unnoticed. "We grizzle every day," wrote Emerson, "I see no end of it." Maybe there is no end of it, except for death. But at least it is something we all share.

At one point in Plato's *Republic,* Socrates is found to say, "I consider that the old have gone before us along a road which we must all travel in our turn and it is good we should ask them of the nature of that road, whether it be rough and difficult or easy and smooth." The old person is a prophecy about the younger, and the road he has traveled stretches out ahead of us all. Unlike most journeys, however, it is not the arrival that really matters, but rather the trip itself. It has been said, for example, that middle age arrives when we stop counting how long we *have lived* and begin reckoning how much longer we *will yet live.*

The Greeks claimed that an unexamined life is not worth living. It seems that as human beings we cannot help examining the fact that our life changes as it goes. In the pages to come, we shall explore these changes, scout the road ahead, and try to provide some basic information that may make the journey less surprising and more enjoyable.

Throughout history, human beings have made desperate efforts to hold off aging and its end, death. So far, these efforts have not been successful. Although public health and medical science have reduced the chances that any of us will die prematurely (that is, before we approach the maximum life-span for humans), there is good evidence that not one year has been added to that life-span. However, great strides have been made in understanding the intimate biology of the aging process: what it is, how and why it happens. In chapters five and six, we shall investigate some of these findings, with possible implications for the eventual extension of life itself. Before that, however, let's pause in chapters two and three to recall the often bizarre history of how, like Peter Pan, mankind has tried to avoid its appointment with old age. It is a story that often repeats itself, in different guises.

In the preface to his 1934 novel, *Appointment in Samarra,* John O'Hara quoted a passage from Somerset Maugham. It seems that the servant of a wealthy Baghdad merchant had been shopping in the marketplace when he met Death. He was frightened by the terrible face that Death made at him, ran home trembling, and begged his master for a horse so that he could flee Baghdad. The merchant agreed, being a kindly fellow. Accordingly, the servant left immediately, for the city of Samarra. Later that day, the merchant met Death and asked indignantly why he had threatened the innocent servant. "That was not a threatening gesture," Death replied. "It was only a start of surprise. I was astonished to see him in Baghdad, for I had an appointment with him tonight in Samarra."

2

Rejuvenation, Part I

From Gilgamesh to Quackery

During the First World War, in the midst of the bloody Battle of Belleau Wood, an American sergeant yelled to his troops, "Come on, do you want to live forever?" Presumably, our good sergeant meant to rally his men to risk their lives, but in fact if most of the world's people were asked this question, the response would be a resounding "Yes!"

In this chapter and the next, we shall examine the peculiar and persistent history of humanity's efforts to prolong life. Bear in mind, what may seem downright silly to us now, was generally very serious at the time. In fact, few things have captured the human imagination as forcefully as the notion of living longer.

Probably the oldest written epic of our species is the story of Gilgamesh, recorded on Babylonian clay tablets about 3,700 years ago. (If that doesn't seem old enough, consider that the story almost certainly comes from Sumerian civilization 5,000 years old.) Gilgamesh, it seems, was a demigod of enormous vigor and accomplishments. He was a warrior-king who delighted in dismembering his enemies, deflowering his friends, and generally living in the manner prescribed by today's ever-present beer ads: "with gusto." But the gusto of Gilgamesh became a bit excessive and so the gods created Enkidu, a rather unkempt fellow with the strength of a hundred.

Straightaway, Gilgamesh and Enkidu had a good knock-down, drag-out fight, from which they emerged the best of friends. The two buddies then teamed up, slaughtering evil ogres and subsequently killing a great bull, sent by the Goddess of Love, who had been spurned by Gilgamesh in favor of his hell-for-leather bachelorhood. At this, the gods were offended and responded by causing Enkidu to sicken and die. Gilgamesh was so appalled and shaken by his friend's death that after mourning Enkidu he began to mourn for himself, becoming obsessed about the unbearable fact that he too would eventually grow old and die. So off he went to seek immortality.

Along the way he met a character named Utnapishtim, who advised that in order to master death, Gilgamesh must first conquer death's cousin, sleep. He would have to stay awake for six days and seven nights. However, Gilgamesh did not quite make it, whereupon he then tried Utnapishtim's second suggestion: to dive to the bottom of the sea and retrieve a particular thorny plant that grew there and would rejuvenate anyone who had grown old. Gilgamesh took the plunge, plucked the plant, but then made a fatal error. On his triumphant way back home, he stopped briefly for a swim in a clear pool—presumably to wash off the sea salt. When he had finished, he made a shocking discovery: a snake had swallowed the marvelous rejuvenating plant.*

All his efforts for naught, Gilgamesh was disconsolate. Eventually he returned home, resigned to the fact that he would grow old and eventually die. But his failure to defeat old age and death also brought with it an affirmation of life, since he was finally left with the sound advice of Siduri, a divine barmaid of some note:

> Thou, O Gilgamesh, let thy belly be full;
> Day and night be thou merry;
> Make every day a day of rejoicing.
> Day and night do thou dance and play.

Ecclesiastes echoes:

> Whatsoever thy hand findeth to do, do it with thy might; for there is no work, nor device, nor knowledge, nor wisdom, in the grave, whither thou goest.

Gilgamesh resolved to eat, drink, and be merry, for eventually he would grow old and die. Having exhausted the alternatives, he now accepted his mortality.

---

* Apparently, then, the Garden of Eden was not the only place where mankind was done wrong by a snake. But at least Gilgamesh's bane got something out of it—you see, having eaten the rejuvenating plant, snakes acquired the ability to shed their skin, thereby becoming younger at each molt and living forever. Can any of us say the same?

The beer ad suggests living with gusto. And why? Because "you only go around once in life." Gilgamesh would agree.

✀

The promise of longevity, even immortality, is offered by many of the world's great religions. Christianity would certainly qualify as a death-denying creed: "I am the resurrection and the life, saith the Lord; he that believeth in me, though he be dead, yet shall he live; and whoever liveth and believeth in me, shall never die." By contrast, whereas the New Testament promises eternal life after death, the Old Testament is more concerned with here-and-now. Rewards for righteousness in the Old Testament include extended lifetimes while still on earth. For example, Genesis 5:9–29 lists the patriarchs who lived before the flood, and their ages at death: Adam, 930; Seth, 912; Noah, 950; Methuselah, 969; and so on. After Job finally recognizes his utter baseness and insignificance, he is given respite from his sufferings, and finally the ultimate Old Testament reward: "And after this Job lived a hundred and forty years, and saw his sons, and his sons' sons, four generations. And Job died an old man, and full of days." Thus, while the New Testament suggests that we live an exemplary life in the hopes of eternal afterlife, the Old Testament points directly to serene old age as the reward of righteousness.

Old Testament practicality may have even helped in pioneering efforts at age prolongation. The ancient Israelites seem to have been the first to explore "Shunamitism," an innovation that may be seen either as a would-be antidote to old age, or as one of its possible perquisites. It seems the Israelites were greatly worried about their aging King David. They feared that he might die from being unable to maintain his body warmth; he was always cold, no matter how many blankets were piled on top of him. So, a young damsel, Abishag the Shunamite by name, agreed to sleep beside the chilly king and add her nubile warmth to his cold bones. The Book of Kings begins as follows:

Now King David was old and stricken in years; and they covered him with clothes, but he gat no heat. Wherefore his servants said unto him, let there be sought for my Lord the King a young virgin; and let her stand before the King and let her cherish him, and let her lie in thy bosom, that my Lord the King may get heat. So they sought for a fair damsel throughout all the coasts of Israel and found

17

Abishag the Shunamite, and brought her to the King. And the damsel was very fair, and cherished the King, and ministered to him;

Apparently Abishag won David's heart, or at least his appreciation for her age-retarding qualities, because when the old king
finally died many years later, he bequeathed her to his son Solomon, who also partook of her beneficent charms.

It is claimed that Shunamitism does not involve sexual relations between old men and young ladies, just sleeping together.
According to the Book of Kings, David and Abishag did not
"know" one another. Still, the prescription has remained popular from that day until the present. The Dutch physician Hermann Boerhaave suggested that the old burgomaster of Amsterdam might regain both his strength and his spirits if he would
only sleep between two young girls. We can only wonder how
strongly the good burgomaster's arm had to be twisted.

An erect penis has often been associated with youthful vigor,
and as we shall see, sexual restoratives have traditionally been
seen as rejuvenating agents. Surprisingly, there may even be some
truth to the notion—aged rats given the opportunity to mate with
receptive, young females, live longer than others who are forced
to remain celibate. Maybe sex is irrelevant here, and the important factor to the old rat, as to Solomon, was simply the appearance of a new interest. In a famous experiment in industrial psychology, it was found in the 1960s that increasing the lighting
improved work performance in a major factory. The really interesting finding, however, was that *decreasing* the lighting also
improved performance! In fact, what mattered was simply change
itself. The beneficial role of change, of stimulation for its own
sake, has been dubbed the "Hawthorne effect" for the county in
New York State where the factory was located. Perhaps King
David and the burgomaster of Amsterdam discovered the Hawthorne effect long before the industrial psychologists.

In any event, we should not discount entirely the effect of a
new, young, and attractive sexual partner, at least on male sexual performance, if not on his longevity. It is a known biological
fact that male animals show enhanced potency when paired with
a new female, as opposed to the relative monotony of monog-
amy. This is consistent with sociobiology—the evolutionary view
of social behavior—since for males, more copulations may well
mean more offspring, whereas the reproduction of females is
limited not by the number of times they mate, but rather by the

success of those matings and the subsequent parental care provided. For our purposes, it is significant that having a new partner does not seem to increase the life-span of either man or woman. For instance, a young gigolo may flatter the vanity of an aging matron, making her feel more desirable and hence younger; but a younger lover does not seem to actually subtract years. Nonetheless, such experiences may well add life to one's years, if not years to one's life.

But perhaps sex really does promote longevity, at least among males. A study of the mortality of British clergy during the 1930s showed that, for whatever reasons, Anglican ministers had a mortality rate that was 31 percent lower than the average for British men at that time. Similarly, other Protestant ministers enjoyed mortality rates that averaged 26 percent below the national average. The only exception to the generalization that clergy live longer was found among Roman Catholic priests, whose mortality rate was 5 percent *higher* than the British average. Presumably, their celibacy rate was also higher.

Despite Shunamitism's clear sexual possibilities, it appears that much of the early rejuvenationists' fondness for virgins was not so much lecherous as genuinely and naïvely quaint. For example, consider the following proposal from one "Lama," a sixteenth-century Italian alchemist who offered to turn old men young (along with lead into gold):

A small bedroom well-shuttered should be prepared, and five small beds, each large enough for just one person, should be installed therein; then have five young virgins, that is, under 13 and in good health, sleep there. In the spring toward early May, a hole should be made in the bedroom wall, through which should be passed the neck of a long-necked vase, whose glass body should be exposed to the fresh air. It is not hard to see that when the little room will be filled with the breath and expired substance of these five young virgins, the vapors will travel continually from the neck into the body of the vessel where, because of the cool air surrounding it, they will be condensed into a very limpid water, that is, a tincture of the most admirable efficacy and which one quite properly might call an elixir of life, since, by means of several drops of this liquor administered at the first symptoms of a sickness which threatens to become acute, it attacks and breaks up the disease-causing substance until one's animal strength returns and chases it from the sick body by means of an invisible perspiration.

Even today, in modern Japan, old people often seek to enter the public baths immediately after young men or women, believing that "youthful humors" pass from young bodies into the water, and from there into their old bodies, thereby reinvigorating them. It is a rather gentle and indirect route to rejuvenation.

Actually, the evidence for humans suggests that too much sexual excitement, like cigarettes, "may be hazardous to your health." Although intercourse only rarely precipitates fatal heart attacks, *sex with someone new* may not only be exciting, but dangerous as well. In fact, a study of persons dying of heart attacks during sex showed that of thirty-four such cases, twenty-seven were involved in an affair at the time! (Presumably, less than 27/34 of all love-making by potential heart-attack victims is not adulterous.) Nonetheless, part of the appeal of May-December marriages—at least to the December male—may be the short-lived improvement in his sex life, regardless of whatever effect such a pairing may have on his span of life.*

❧

Westerners may be surprised to learn it, but many practices of the Chinese philosophy/religion of Taoism were directed specifically at prolonging one's life-span. The ultimate goal was to become a "hsien," an immortal. Not surprisingly, however, the road somewhat resembled the wild and heroic path traveled by Gilgamesh, at least in difficulty, if not in content. For while the exploits of Gilgamesh were just that, exploits in which the hero sought to overcome the obstacles in his environment, the Taoist adept was expected to seek triumph over *himself*—certainly, a difference in emphasis that is consistent with the differing Eastern and Western view of humanity's place in the universe.

For the Taoist, the ideal diet was austere, to say the least: the ultimate goal was to avoid producing any foul body excretions. This was achieved by living on air and one's saliva (a medical oddity reminiscent of the mythical Polynesian island where everyone made a good living doing the neighbor's laundry). Since even would-be hsiens needed somewhat more sustenance en route to this calorieless paradise, these hopefuls were expected to live for extended periods on only berries and roots, avoiding especially all meats and grains. Great emphasis was also placed

---

* Recall the noble lines from *Porgy and Bess* regarding Methuselah's extended life-span: "But who calls that livin' / When no gal'll give in / To no man what's nine hundred years?"

on breath-holding, with the expectation that the successful hsien eventually would live by recycling his own air, much as the human embryo was believed to do. So, the Taoist adept practiced holding his breath for progressively longer periods. When he could hold his breath for the period of a thousand normal respirations, it was said he would become immortal. Of course, people can greatly prolong their breath-holding ability by practice; snorkelers and pearl divers train themselves in this way. But Taoist neophytes interpreted the tingling and mild euphoria that results from prolonged breath-holding as signs that they were succeeding in diverting their breath to the secret recesses of the body where it would eventually retard aging and propel them toward immortality. Western physiologists, however, simply call it anoxia—oxygen depletion, which, if prolonged, can cause unconsciousness and a life-saving resumption of breathing. We do not know how many erstwhile hsiens were saved for normal old age when they blacked out, whereupon prosaic breathing reflexes betrayed their more cerebral longing for hsienhood.

In the Taoist drive for immortality, not everything was as austerely stoic as a breathless, foodless life might suggest. Sex, at least, was allowed. In fact, it was encouraged. However, as we shall see, it was sex of a most unusual sort.

The Taoists believed that immortality could only be achieved by preserving one's supply of "ching"—which may be defined as energy, essence, spirit, and semen. Typical sexual relations do just the opposite. The male enters the female with an erect penis, vigorous and full of energy, health, and good spirits. Some time thereafter, the penis is withdrawn, somewhat wrinkled, shriveled, small, and almost penitent. Something has been lost; one's ching has been depleted.

Accordingly, the Taoist sexual ideal favored the opposite transformation: for ching to be increased rather than lost, the penis should be inserted when flabby, then withdrawn while still vigorously erect. The result? Ching has been transferred from the woman to the man, instead of vice versa. In the process, of course, the man should diligently refrain from ejaculating, since this would involve unforgivable loss of one's ching. *Coitus reservatus* became the Taoist sexual recipe. Not surprisingly, the male Taoist ideal called for the woman to reach orgasm, thereby transferring more of her ching to the man. Since any one partner is limited in how much ching she could provide, Taoist sexual prescription called for sex with as many different partners as possible:

> He who is able to have coitus several tens of times in a single day and night without allowing his essence to escape will be cured of all maladies and will have his longevity extended. If he changes his woman several times, the advantage is greater; if in one night he changes his partner ten times, that is supremely excellent.

The ideal sexual partner, according to Taoist teaching, was a young woman between fourteen and nineteen years old; if at all possible she should not be over thirty, and never over forty. Furthermore, she must not have thick skin, a deep voice, hairy legs, or a cool body. Since even the aspiring hsien was not quite yet a saint, occasionally his self-control would fail, and his precious ching escape. But even then, all was not lost. Taoists were taught to squeeze themselves tightly between the anus and testicles during any errant ejaculation. This prevented the semen from escaping to the outside, by diverting the flow to the man's bladder. Thus was one's ching preserved inviolate, and for one's self alone. (It is interesting to note in passing that this procedure is employed as a purely contraceptive technique by several different human societies.)

Taoist tracts are clearly sexist. The doctrine of ching preservation was entirely a male strategy. Presumably, ancient China was bestrewn with young women, robbed of their ching by selfish males who vehemently refused to give up any of theirs. Or at least, not without a fight. Taoist sexual teaching, if extended logically to both sexes, would seem to generate something less than connubial bliss; presumably, women seeking to accumulate ching would desire intercourse with as many different men as possible, all of whom should ideally—from the woman's perspective—be generous with their ching. But, as we have seen, men were taught to be stingy with their ching, much as their women might desire it. It seems obvious that two ardent Taoists would be ill-matched bedfellows. Ideally, perhaps, Taoist men should associate with numerous nonaspiring women, each of whom would be generous with her orgasms (i.e., her ching) but would not insist on his. Similarly, the ardent Taoist woman should find non-Taoist men who would altruistically donate their ching to her.

Back in the real world, Taoists during the first few centuries

A.D. also practiced an ancient form of group sex at the new and full moon. This was known as "uniting the yin and the yang," and scandalized both Buddhists and Confucians, since no social barriers were recognized during these holidays, somewhat reminiscent of present-day Brazilian Mardi Gras.

Don't be misled, however, into thinking of early Taoists as wanton lechers. Sexual intercourse was necessarily preceded and followed by extended periods of rigorous prayer and meditation. Alcohol was strictly forbidden, and sex was prohibited on at least two hundred days of each year, because of various taboos. For whatever reason, Taoism is no longer a vigorous movement, and its life-prolonging precepts are now part of history.

Nonetheless, as we shall see repeatedly, aging has often been associated with loss of sexual prowess, especially decrease in male potency. In this regard, the Taoists anticipated much contemporary thinking, and their writings provide some of the earliest explicit recognition that for many men, the penis is the barometer of aging. For example, see how the Chinese writer Chin P'ing Mei described the effects of a secret, supposedly age-retarding substance:

> The first engagement will leave you full of vigour,
> The second stronger than before.
> Though twelve exquisite beauties all arranged in scarlet wait your
>   onset,
> You may enjoy each according to your fancy,
> And, all night through, erect your spear will stand.
> In a hundred days, hair and beard will know its power,
> Your teeth will be strong, your eyes more bright.

P'ing Mei was a renowned alchemist of his day.

Alchemy, as we all know, was a flourishing concern during the Middle Ages, and it gave birth to modern chemistry. It is less well known, however, that alchemists were no less motivated by hopes of turning old people young than of turning base metals into gold. In fact, the two goals seemed logically related: the sought-after philosopher's stone would perfect everything according to its nature, turning lead into gold, and the old and sick into the young and healthy. In other words, "Longer Living Through Chemistry." Since gold is imperishable and untarnishable, turning substances into gold was equivalent to making them immortal. In fact, it was widely believed that human immortality could be achieved by consuming gold made into the correct elixir—the so-called "aurum potabile," often derived either from drinking gold tinctures directly or by drinking out of gold vessels.

To those who doubted his chemical successes, the great Taoist alchemist Ko Hung recited these "facts":

> Pheasants change into big oysters, sparrows into clams, earth insects get wings, water frogs flutter and fly, moles become birds, putrid grasses become fire-flies, the iguanas become tigers, snakes become dragons; therefore, how could these transformations (lead into gold, old men into young) then be untrue?

How, indeed?

Over in Europe, fires burned and concoctions bubbled, as the worthies sought the secret of eternal youth along with infinite wealth. In 1737, one year before his death at seventy, Dutch physician Hermann Boerhaave wrote:

> O Alchymist's hope, how you charm our minds and with what promise you comfort us! To hold to an unfailing bodily health, a constant vigour and tranquility of mind, to preserve these into a green and rugged old age . . . The old grandam regains a merry suppleness, the long-dry juice of her youth returns. . . .

In search of that promise, medieval European alchemists hunted for the quintessence, the "fifth essence" beyond the basic four of earth, air, fire, and water. The Greeks also had believed in it, but to them the quintessence was beyond human reach, residing in the heavens where it conferred immortality on the stars. Of course, the rejuvenating quintessence has never been found, although men have sought it for the past one thousand years. And the search continues. Interestingly, there was a brief time, around 1100 A.D., when even the skeptics thought that the marvelous substance had been found at last. Through the recently discovered process of distillation, a new liquid was revealed. It was "water," yet it burned; it was cool to the touch, yet hot to the taste; it miraculously kept meat from rotting and yet its effects on the human spirit were even more remarkable. This short-lived "quintessence" was, of course, alcohol.

%

When Sophocles, the great Greek tragedian, was in his eighties, his relatives brought suit against him, claiming that he was no longer competent to manage his money and property. At the time, he was writing *Oedipus at Colonus*, now acknowledged as one of the finest plays of all time. As his defense, Sophocles read part of the unfinished manuscript to the Athenian judges. He won the case. As it happens, *Oedipus at Colonus* is one of the few works in our literary heritage that celebrates a very old person. It also contains this criticism of those who seek to avoid aging and its consequences:

Who craves excess of days
Scorning the common span
Of life, I judge that man
A giddy wight who walks in folly's ways.

As we have already seen, there have been many such "giddy wights." Any objective viewer would have to agree that excess of days has long been one of the major cravings of the human race. Historian Gerald Gruman has identified three major themes which reflect humanity's yearning for victory over aging: the antediluvian theme (literally, "before the deluge"), the hyperborean ("beyond the forests"), and the rejuvenation quest. Of these, the antediluvian promise may have been the most persistent, despite its general disregard today. The idea is that once upon a time, long ago, people lived much longer than they do today. For example, although the Bible prophesies threescore years and ten as the normal life-span, it also records the nine hundred plus years supposedly allotted to the patriarchs. If we could only somehow regain the state of grace these ancestors enjoyed before Noah's great flood, the argument goes, then we would regain their life-spans as well. This seemingly naïve idea motivated much thinking between the Renaissance and the nineteenth century. Certainly it is consistent with the long-standing notion that history is circular and that some day we will relive the Golden Age of our ancestors.

Just as Methuselah personifies the "antediluvian" ideal, "Shangri-la" is the epitome of hyperborean wistfulness. In James Hilton's novel *Lost Horizon*, there exists a far-away place, hidden in the Himalayas, where people do not age. It is a persistent and compelling dream, this notion that somewhere, over the rainbow, there lies a special magical land where remarkable things take place. We willingly suspend our disbelief for lost continents inhabited by dinosaurs and places such as Shangri-la, where time stands still. In fact, this is a dream that crosses many cultures; myths abound of an "abode of the blest," where people enjoy extraordinary longevity. One of my favorites is the ancient Indian legend of the Utturkarus, in the northern part of that sub-continent, where the magic Jambu tree confers one thousand years of life. The landscapes are of precious stones, and beautiful maidens literally grow on trees! Dreams of Never-Never Lands are appealing, perhaps especially to middle-aged, would-be Peter Pans—whose motto is not so much "I won't grow up," but rather, "I won't grow old." Although the hyperborean dream may well be as unrealistic as its antediluvian counterpart, we shall see in chapter 11 that people do, in fact, seem to live longer in several rather out-of-the-way places. This may not be the stuff out of which hyperborean legends are made, but at least close. And, what is more important, these modern-day Shangri-las are real.

Finally, we come to Gruman's third category, the rejuvenation theme. In its most general form, this is the idea that people can actively *do something* that will either prevent aging, or reverse aging after it has occurred. This is by far the most widespread notion and, of course, it includes the Gilgamesh quest as well as the Taoists' sexual machinations and the strivings of medieval alchemy. With the rise of modern anesthesia, rejuvenationist procedures began to emphasize surgical intervention. As we shall see, such attempts have now largely been given up, but not without a lively history. By far the most common rejuvenation efforts have centered on the quest for a special substance, a quintessence that could be eaten, drunk, or (more recently) injected.

A less well known episode in the saga of Jason and his argonauts occurred when the doughty hero returned from his long voyage, bearing his new sorceress-wife, Medea, along with the Golden Fleece. Jason was dismayed to find that during his long absence, his father, Aeson, had grown weak and feeble-minded in his old age. Jason begged Medea to use her magic arts to subtract some years from his own life-span and give them to his father. She refused, but elected instead to send her personal dragons on a new quest. They obtained the following substances, with which Medea proceeded to concoct a wondrous, rejuvenating broth (according to Ovid): "Pebbles from the farthest Orient, hoarfrost gathered under the moon, wings and flesh of the infamous horned owl, entrails of a werewolf, the skin of the Cynphian water snake, liver of a long lived stag, the head of a crow nine centuries old, and a thousand other things." Medea stirred the brew with a dried-up old olive branch, which immediately grew leaves, flowers, and even olives. At one point, her pot spilled over, and the cracked, dry earth sprouted an instant jungle of flowers and life. Aeson drank and was rejuvenated.

Modern-day Samoans prescribe a root broth to guarantee a healthy old age, whereas the Kwakiutl Indians of the Pacific Northwest recommended bathing the face in urine and then washing in salt water. The Yukaghir people of Siberia were careful to keep at least a few lice on their bodies, to prolong life. And the Hopi Indians suggested ice-water baths and—shades of modern America—running.

A further sampling of rejuvenation ideas among nontechnological peoples might include the following.

Berbers (North Africa): always tell the truth; a frequent liar will age so quickly that he will even beget bald-headed children.

Dieri (Australia): avoid gray hairs by avoiding your mother-in-law.

Eskimos (of Labrador): be brave; "he who encounters head winds will live a long life."

Palaung (Burma): be virtuous in one's prior incarnations; it follows, therefore, that the attainment of old age indicates one's virtue the last time around.

Ancient Hebrews (Palestine): "Honor thy father and thy mother, that thy days be long in the land."

Hopi (American Southwest): don't worry; "it is not well to count the years, it makes one old."

Ainu (northern Japan) and Iroquois (eastern United States): respectfully request that one's ancestors grant longevity.

Hottentot (south Africa): say "live to old age" whenever someone sneezes (interestingly, many Americans say "God bless you," and Germans, "Gesundheit" under the same circumstances).

Despite this diversity of rejuvenationist effort, before modern medicine entered the battle in the late nineteenth century, most efforts were of the Medea type—the secret, special potion. And despite Medea's predilection for such animal ingredients as crow's head and stag's liver, most of the world's potions emphasized plants.

Of these, the mandrake had special importance. It is actually rather unassuming, a member of the potato family, native to southern Europe and the Middle East. It has mild narcotic pow-

27

ers, and perhaps, most importantly, a forked carrot-like root, producing a very vague resemblance to the human body. (The likeness is, in fact, no closer than that of certain star clusters to bulls, lions, crabs, hunters, etc.) In Genesis, Jacob used mandrake to ferment his aphrodisiac wines. He must have been careful in harvesting the mandrake, however, since it was said to shriek piercingly when pulled from the ground. In fact, the shrieks of a mandrake supposedly could drive a person insane. The recommended harvesting technique, for this reason, was to tie the leaves of the plant to a dog's tail, stuff cotton in one's ears, and then kick the dog.

Only slightly less celebrated than mandrake as a rejuvenation drug are the orchids. It is not clear why orchids ever received this attention, although a hint may be provided by the Greek word for testicle: *orchis*. Perhaps the bulbous orchid root was fancied as resembling a human testicle. In any event, one of the most storied rejuvenating substances, "salep," was simply powdered orchid root. A medieval treatise by one Hieronymus Braunschweig reported that it "causeth great heat, therefore it giveth lust unto the workes of generacyon and multiplycatyon of sperms." Once again, of course, we see the equation of supposed sexual renaissance with a reversal of aging.

There have been many other similar substances, but for a final example take "soma," a mysterious, never-identified plant that nonetheless was much beloved by Hindu herbalists. To profit from it, one had to consume only soma juice and nothing else. The result was supposed to be an increasing weakness and loss of weight, until, by the eighth day, the fingernails, teeth, and hair fell out. Eventually, however, perseverence and faith were rewarded, since after seven weeks new hair, nails, teeth, and muscles grew in, and the soma-drinker became "in no way inferior to the combined strength of a thousand rutting elephants." (For this last, we have the word of the great Indian physician Sushrata.)

Despite the importance of herbal remedies as anti-aging devices, any review of rejuvenation quests would be incomplete without mentioning the fabled fountain of youth. The idea is an ancient one, probably well fixed in the human psyche, even before Ponce de Leon. Thus, the association of bubbly, active life-giving water with rejuvenation and anti-aging seems natural enough. And furthermore, Freudians have no difficulty interpreting the importance of fountains. But the specific history of the fountain of youth idea is less clear. According to Eric Trimmer, author of *Rejuvenation: A History of the Idea*, it probably involves a shadowy, mysterious, and almost certainly mythical character known as Prester John (also sometimes known as Presbyter, or Elder John). A story prevalent in Europe from the twelfth to the fifteenth century told of a powerful Christian king somewhere in the Orient—India, Persia, Abyssinia, somewhere. He had defeated the infidels in Mesopotamia. He was marching at the head of a glorious army to liberate the Holy Land (but was unfortunately blocked at the Tigris river). He ruled over seventy-two kings and had a remarkable domain, including various exotic features such as ants that dug for gold. He also had a fountain of youth.

The renown of Prester John (or the gullibility of Medieval Europe) was such that Pope Alexander III wrote him a lengthy letter in 1177. The letter was never answered. Nonetheless, some myths seem to thrive best in the absence of any confirmation, and the fountain of youth seems to be one of these. Actually, the European world was well prepared to accept the notion of an age-defying fountain, since Alexander the Great was said to have drunk from a fountain of youth during one of his campaign exploits, whereupon he was restored to the age of thirty. (Since he eventually died at age thirty-three, he can't have shed very many years at this particular fountain.)

During the Renaissance, Europeans were flexing their intellectual and creative muscles. Great advances in science, medicine, the arts, literature, and geographic exploration all followed from the happy discovery that people could, at least to some extent, work their will upon nature. And the process was self-reinforcing, since new progress (which was itself a result of optimistic enthusiasm for what human beings could accomplish) led to further optimism, and thus more progress, and so on. So it was in this time of confidence and hope that Ferdinand V of Spain sent Juan Ponce de Leon to the New World in 1513, in optimistic search of the fabled fountain of youth. Historians now seem agreed that the primary motivation was actually gold rather than rejuvenation. Certainly, Ponce de Leon was no starry-eyed dreamer; he was a tough, battle-scarred adventurer who, as all American school children know, wound up discovering Florida. Although he failed to find the fountain of youth, even the worldly

Ponce may have wondered about it for a time, since Florida is in fact blessed with many beautiful clear-water springs, and Ponce apparently discovered several of the most lovely: Wakulla, Manatee, and Silver Springs. We can only imagine his thrill of anticipation as perhaps he dangled a toe in one of these springs, and then carefully sipped a few drops cupped nervously in his hands. Ironically, although Ponce's rejuvenation quest went unfulfilled, it has been followed ever since by millions of North Americans, who also seek to discover in Florida some relief in their old age, if only warm weather and a good suntan.

Ponce de Leon aside, Europeans have long had a quasi-mystical faith in the restorative powers of water. Lucas Cranach's sixteenth-century painting "The Fountain of Youth" shows old and decrepit souls being carried on shoulders, carts, and wheelbarrows to what looks like a large wading pool, and then emerging at the other end as young, robust, and attractive men and women who partake of an elaborately prepared feast of celebration. (A close look at the lower right corner reveals a just-rejuvenated couple ducking into some fortuitously placed bushes, suggesting once again that hearty eating is not the only dalliance associated with youth.)

Actually, bathing had long been popular as a luxury among the European upper class. The Romans are estimated to have used over three hundred gallons per person per day. But the Catholic Church took a dim view of public bathing during medieval times: "The baths are opened promiscuously to women, and there they strip for licentious indulgence, for from looking, men get to loving, as if their modesty had been washed away in the bath." Nonetheless, baptism is firmly in the pro-aquatic tradition, and many a saint is said to have performed miraculous cures at holy springs. After the Reformation, many of these holy wells became the wishing wells of today.

Water cures for aging and its disabilities have remained popular among Europeans. One of the best-known proponents of all time was one Vincent Priessnitz, a semi-literate nineteenth-century central European peasant. In his youth Vincent "cured" his own sprained wrist and later, broken ribs, by immersion in water followed by a simple poultice of wet bandages. He subsequently developed a spa at Graefenberg, where rich Germans seeking to regain their lost youth ate very heartily and then subjected themselves to immersion, showering, and wet-wrapping in spring water that averaged about 50 degrees Fahrenheit. By the turn of the century, an elaborate therapeutic rationale had been established for "hydrotherapy"—basically, it was supposed to keep the body's pores in a state of cheerful openness, somehow purifying the blood and with it, all other body functions. Kaiser Wilhelm I went regularly to spas at Ems and Gastein, and lived to be ninety-one (in spite of it?). Water cures remain popular to the present day, especially in West Germany and southern France, where the emphasis has shifted from cold, bracing water to natural hot springs which are often spiced with a penetrating sulfurous reek. Not surprisingly, this also is claimed to aid in rejuvenation. Perhaps the unconscious logic is that subjecting oneself to the smell of brimstone in the here-and-now will delay a similar appointment in the hereafter.

When it comes to rejuvenation based on the powers of liquids, however, many people might prefer Benjamin Franklin's celebrated suggestion. He was writing to a friend while serving as American ambassador to France, commenting on the supposed and celebrated revival, by the sun, of flies that had been previously "drowned." Franklin wrote, "I should prefer to any ordinary death, being immersed in a cask of Madeira wine, with a few friends . . . to be then recalled to life by the solar warmth of my dear country."

❧

Not all efforts at rejuvenation have involved such aggressive intervention as special potions, sexual calisthenics, and semimagical water cures. In fact, one of our oldest traditions speaks of "moderation in all things": the great Platonic mean. Even renowned healers like Hippocrates and Galen emphasized that age is natural, unavoidable, and cannot be "cured." Ibn Sina, a respected Persian physician, born in 980 A.D., is better known to the West as Avicenna. His advice: "The art of maintaining the health consists in guiding the body to its natural span of life . . . it is not the art of averting death or of securing the utmost longevity possible to the human being."

There is a wide range of human goals concerning aging. Some, like Gilgamesh and the Taoists, sought immortality, pure and simple. Others, symbolized perhaps by Ponce de Leon, sought rejuvenation, a reversal of the aging process, although not necessarily eternal life. Yet others, the most moderate of all reju-

31

venationists, sought a more modest goal: not to live forever, or even to shed years from their mortal frame, but rather to postpone the ravages of age, achieving a long and happy life, if not an eternal one. Of these, the most famous was Luigi Cornaro of Padua. After living a wild and dissipated life for his first thirty years, Cornaro was advised by his physician that unless he mended his ways, he would never see fifty. Cornaro reformed himself with a passion, eating lightly, exercising regularly but in moderation, and taking great and continuing delight in the beauty of his rural surroundings. In 1550, at age eighty-three, he wrote his *Discourse on the Sober Life,* one of the extraordinary bestsellers of that time, which went into numerous printings and became required reading in the intellectual salons throughout Europe. A second *Discourse* followed at age eighty-six, a third at ninety-one, and a fourth at age ninety-five. He died at ninety-eight years of age, robbing (or sparing!) us all of a fifth discourse. Cornaro also wrote a comedy at age eighty-three, commenting that most others write tragedies at that time of life, if they write at all.

Cornaro can be seen as a mainstay in a very respectable tradition: the "hygienists," who emphasized that maximum health and happiness can be achieved not by heroic intervention, but simply by taking good and sensible care of oneself. (Cornaro was also a wealthy and privileged Italian nobleman, who could afford to do just that.) It might seem that after the revolutionary discovery of "germs" by Pasteur, Koch, Lister, Semmelweiss, and others, the hygienists would have achieved wide support. But in fact the opposite occurred, at least initially. With the recognition of bacteria, protozoan parasites, and, finally, viruses, simple hygiene did not seem aggressive enough. Nonetheless, many more lives have been successfully prolonged by public health measures such as separating sewage from drinking water and improving nutrition, than by open-heart surgery or even the "wonder drugs" such as penicillin. In a very real sense, the hygienists and Cornaro were right. Many physicians are now coming around to their unexciting but reasoned position. It may well be true, as Cornaro claimed, that "a man can have no better doctor than himself." Better health and a more likely, if not more pleasant or postponed, old age are almost certain to result from not smoking, avoiding excessive fats, reducing stress, and getting regular exercise.

On the other hand, there will always be those who argue for the Gilgameshian life of intensity, gusto, risk, and flair: those who claim that a life of moderation doesn't really help one to live longer—it just seems that way because such a life is so boring. The Roman poet Lucretius emphasized that life, however prolonged, will always remain insignificant compared to how long we shall be dead:

> What is this deplorable lust of life that holds us trembling in bondage to such uncertainties and dangers? . . . By prolonging life, we cannot subtract or whittle away one jot from the duration of our death. . . . However many generations you may add to your store by living, there waits for you nonetheless the same eternal death.

᠀

As we shall see in the next chapter, the battle with age has spawned a great many sincere efforts at remedy, which are now recognized as failures. As we shall see right now, it has also spawned a large number of out and out quacks.

The ultimate rejuvenationist quack was undoubtedly James Graham, a P. T. Barnum-type huckster who reigned supreme in London during the 1780s. In his Temple of Health, an eighteenth-century amalgam of Playboy Club and European Health Spa, Graham lectured regularly and showed off his "Goddesses of Health," beautiful, young, scantily-clad women, as models of what his followers would soon attain (if female) or would soon be able to enjoy (if male). Among the twelve different medicines he provided to his templegoers—at great cost, of course—was Aetherial Ambrosial Quintessence, which, according to his handbills, was made in his "Adepti-Alchyrical Medico-Electrical and Philosophic Apparatus, infinitely superior to anything that now is or ever was in the World."

As if that was not enough, according to one of his handbills Graham's Electrical Ether was prepared as follows:

> . . . in the great metal globes on the dome of the Electrical Temples of Health and of Hymen in the Apollo and other apartments . . . to be acted upon by the celestial fire. The essence is purified by filtration upon a new principle, which prevents all possibility of the finest and most volatile parts evaporating. The globes are entirely lined with metal on the in- as well as the outside. They are twelve in number, each containing full thirty-six gallons. The glass vessels too are covered with metal, enclosed in curious magnetic cases, and their stoppers are pierced with glass tubes and thick metal

rods, which end in a multitude of points, from which streams of the electrical fire etc., are continually pouring in upon the aether and aromatics, in luminous and most glorious streams.

Graham also added a "Grand Celestial or Magnetic-Electrico Bed" at the extraordinary price of 50 British pounds per night. From his description, it may even have been worth it:

> The Grand Celestial Bed, whose magical influences are now celebrated from pole to pole and from the rising to the setting of the sun, is 12 ft. long by 9 ft. wide, supported by forty pillars of brilliant glass of the most exquisite workmanship, in richly variegated colours. The super-celestial dome of the bed, which contains the odoriferous, balmy and ethereal spices, odours, and essences, which is the grand reservoir of those reviving invigorating influences which are exhaled by the breath of the music and by the exhilarating force of electrical fire, is covered on the other side with brilliant panes of looking glass.

> On the utmost summit of the dome are placed two exquisite figures of Cupid and Psyche, with a figure of Hymen behind, with his torch flaming with electrical fire in one hand and with the other, supporting a celestial crown, sparkling over a pair of living turtle doves, on a little bed of roses.

> The other elegant group of figures which sport on the top of the dome having each of the musical instruments in their hands, which by the most expensive mechanism, breathe forth sound corresponding to their instruments, flutes, guitars, violins, clarinets, trumpets, horns, oboes, kettledrums etc. . . .

For a time Graham was successful, even wildly successful. Not only did he earn a great deal of money, but he actually developed a satisfied clientele, who claimed to be rejuvenated by his treatments. It is interesting to note that along with his obvious, phony hucksterism, James Graham also preached good, sound hygiene: exercise, moderate diet, basic cleanliness. This might have contributed to his success, but probably not significantly. We might suppose that his exorbitant prices worked against him, but in fact the opposite was probably true: by exacting large fees, Graham may well have gained the confidence of his clients, predisposed them to think well of his treatments, and actually even made the treatments somewhat effective.

There were probably two factors at work here, characteristics of the human mind that profoundly influence the body. We shall encounter these two again and again as we examine numerous "rejuvenating" treatments that actually seem to have little or no basis in biomedical fact, and yet have many satisfied customers. They are the *placebo effect* and *cognitive dissonance*. Placebo comes from the Latin "I shall please," and that's what it does. Its best-known example is the sugar pill. Placebos are medications or treatments that have no scientific basis for working but which are given to a patient nonetheless, in the hope that the patient's trust and confidence in the cure will somehow be of benefit. We might think that the sole benefit of placebos comes from the satisfaction a patient gets from receiving the doctor's attention and from receiving a "medicine." But in fact, placebos *actually do work,* by mechanisms that are almost completely mysterious.

About 35 percent of all placebo treatments are successful; somehow, they really do cure. These cures include relief of 50 percent or more of the pain experienced by cancer patients. Even such a purely physical thing as warts can be cured by placebo— simply painting a patient's warts with a brightly colored but inert dye and then telling the patient that the wart will be gone when the dye wears off. Incredibly, this "mind over matter" procedure is as effective as any other technique, including surgical removal. Noted psychiatrist Jerome Frank comments that "apparently the emotional reaction to a placebo can change the physiology of the skin so that the virus which causes warts can no longer thrive." When patients with bleeding peptic ulcers were given a distilled water injection and told that it was a potent medicine, 70 percent showed a distinct improvement. Finally, the powerful placebo effect can work for ill as well as good. Thus, noted physiologist Walter Cannon found that the reputed ability of native witch doctors to cause death by voodoo is in fact often true. That is, if the victim believes it, he or she may actually die from such reverse placebos.

Given that the power of positive (or negative) thinking can have such immense effects on the human body, it is not really surprising that many quacks have flourished in the field of rejuvenation. If the would-be rejuvenator can be personally convincing, smooth, and appropriately flamboyant, with just enough abracadabra to impress the gullible, then real cures can often be effected. This is not to say that a ninety-year-old can literally be transformed into a thirty-year-old; however, the placebo effect may actually help with arthritis, high blood pressure, gout, and a variety of afflictions associated with old age. Perhaps most

prominently, it can help with sexual problems. Sexual performance, especially in males, is often equated with youthfulness,
and its diminution, with age. As we shall see in chapter 10, by
far the greatest part of male sexual problems associated with age
are psychological rather than physical. So, the stage is set for
placebo rejuvenating treatments to confer a real improvement in
one's potency, and then to be hailed as a bona fide age retardant.

So much for the powerful and often underrated placebo effect.
What about the other consideration: cognitive dissonance? Most
of us don't like dissonance; we are more comfortable when things
"go well" together. In particular, we don't like to consider that
our behavior is in any way dissonant with our own self-image.
As a result, human beings have a well-developed capacity for
self-justification, explaining to ourselves and others why our actions actually "make sense," however silly or incorrect they may
actually be. By doing so, we avoid or reduce cognitive dissonance, within ourselves.

What does cognitive dissonance have to do with James Graham and his Electrical Ether or Grand Celestial Bed? Just this:
having spent large amounts of money as well as time patroniz-
ing the rejuvenator, most people would find it very difficult to
admit to a lack of improvement. Most people see themselves as
sensible, not foolish. To admit that they have been bilked would
be dissonant with this nearly universal self-image. Therefore,
patrons of any rejuvenating scheme will be strongly disposed to
emphasize the positive and to overlook any negative results. If
the treatment is carried far enough, such negatives might even
disappear. And of course, this makes it all the more likely that
the treatment will be proclaimed—and in fact, to some extent
actually be—a success.*

---

* It is interesting to note that even after Graham's remarkable emporium closed
down, its irrepressible proprietor enjoyed another fling with financial and popular rejuvenating success, this time via "earth bathing."

3

Rejuvenation, Part II

Yogurt, Cell Therapy, and the "Erector Set"

The late eighteenth century seems to have been a heyday for rejuvenation elixirs. Thus, in the 1790s, operating at about the same time as James Graham, William Brodum marketed his "Nervous Cordial" and "Botanical Syrup." These were said to counteract the "well-known" consequences of masturbation when young—weakness in old age. At one time, sixty-eight stores in England were selling Brodum's concoctions, as Englishmen sought to expiate the sins of their youth.

Schemes and concoctions such as these are in no way limited to the distant past, however. During the 1930s, the "Vitalizer" was marketed successfully in the United States, until its creators were prosecuted for using the mails to defraud. It was simply a flashlight attached to a small metal rod and activated by a cord; insert the rod in one's anus, turn on the flashlight, and "electric force" surged through the body, bringing strength and youth. An elixir known as "El Zair" was also available at this time from a rather unexotic address on West 16th Street in New York City. It was supposedly made from substances that "could only be producred in certain lofty and almost inaccessible mountain ranges in Africa." The mixture was produced by "an English scientist of considerable note," following directions given in a secret Arabic manuscript. The ingredients had to be harvested during certain unspecified phases of the moon and only with appropriate incantations. When properly prepared and administered, the elixir would grow hair on bald heads, make women fertile, cure tuberculosis, and "clear away the deeper seated waste matter" that causes old age. Its real makeup? Epsom salts dissolved in vinegar.

37

Despite the absurdity of El Zair, the claim that curing constipation will also "cure" old age brings us to one of the early efforts on the part of Western science to come to grips with aging
and its biologic causes. The major figure was Élie Metchnikoff,
a Russian biologist who worked primarily in France. Metchnikoff was no quack. In fact, he shared a Nobel Prize in 1908 for
the discovery of phagocytosis, the process whereby white blood
cells attack and destroy invading bacteria. Metchnikoff also developed a rather convoluted theory of aging through "auto-
intoxication." The crux of it was that aging is caused by the
accumulation of toxins from waste matter stored in the large
intestine. He pointed out (incorrectly, as we now realize) that as
we go from fish to reptiles to birds to mammals, we find progressively shorter life-spans, which in turn are correlated with
progressively larger colons. Metchnikoff made the novel argument that defecation is a dangerous activity for animals, since
they are susceptible at that time to being surprised by a predator.
The main function of the large intestine is to reabsorb water and
certain other materials from fecal matter before it is eliminated
from the body. Accordingly, Metchnikoff suggested that the exceptionally large colons of birds and mammals permit them to
avoid predators (since they reabsorb more material and thus de-
fecate less often) but at the cost of being poisoned by their own
waste products, which necessarily remain in the body for a longer
time. The ensuing "intestinal stasis" supposedly generates toxins that damage other body cells, whereupon these damaged cells
are destroyed by the body's phagocytes—like an army of Sorcerer's Apprentices gone wild and turned against the body they are
supposed to protect.

Metchnikoff suggested that one solution to this problem—and
hence a solution to old age as well—was to drink lots of yogurt.
He noted that bacteria which produce lactic acid tend to inhibit
the putrefaction of food, and furthermore that the inhabitants of
the Balkans, who drank a lot of yogurt, were also reputed to live
to a great age. Metchnikoff therefore proposed that by consuming large quantities of yogurt, which is made by lactic-acid-
producing bacteria, a substantial increase in longevity could be
achieved.

Metchnikoff's theory was widely accepted during the early decades of the twentieth century, and indeed the modern mystique
of yogurt as a "health food" may date from that time. In fact,

very old people often do experience reduced intestinal motility and, as a result, some tendency toward constipation. Accordingly, it is tempting to view intestinal sluggishness as a *cause* of aging, rather than a *result*. Some authorities even recommended more drastic recourses than eating yogurt: Sir Arbuthnot Lane, a prominent London surgeon, diagnosed a so-called chronic poisoning emanating from the lower bowel. Patients thought to be suffering from "Lane's disease" underwent surgery to remove part of their large intestine. Sir Arbuthnot called it "abdominal spring cleaning" and performed his surgical "cures" well into the 1930s.

We now recognize that aging is not caused by intestinal toxins. It is actually quite easy to eliminate all the bacteria residing in our large intestine; in fact, this happens regularly as an unwanted side-effect of broad spectrum antibiotics such as keflex, erythromycin, and penicillin. The result is not rejuvenation, but rather, diarrhea. Ironically, the best cure for this medically imposed condition is to reinfect the denuded intestine—by eating yogurt!

The saga of scientific anti-aging efforts focuses next on an extraordinary Frenchman with a tragic end, Dr. Charles Edouard Brown-Séquard. Born to an Irish-American sea captain (Brown) and a French woman (Séquard), Brown-Séquard had a distinguished career as a physiologist and neurologist. Like Metchnikoff, he was no quack. He authored over five hundred research articles, held prestigious medical posts in the United States, England, and France, and is today considered one of the great pioneers in endocrinology, the branch of biology and medicine concerned with the action of hormones. By 1889, he was a legendary figure in European scientific circles, holding the chair of Experimental Medicine at the Collège de France. That spring, word leaked out that Brown-Séquard had begun work with some sort of endocrine extracts and that he would report his preliminary findings at the June meeting of the Société de Biologie in Paris.

Excitement ran high as the imposing, 6'4" Brown-Séquard began his talk. "I have always thought," he said, "that the weakness of old men was partly due to the diminution of the function of their sexual glands. I am seventy-two years old. My natural vigor has declined considerably in the last ten years." He then proceeded to describe, in detail, his progressive sexual impotence and declining physical strength. He further explained that on 15 May, he had mashed the testicle of a young dog, passed it through filter paper, and injected the resulting pinkish liquid into his own leg. Shortly afterward, he repeated the procedure with guinea pig testicles, and then did it yet a third time. He reported that after the injections, his physical strength increased dramatically. In his own words to the Société: "I have rejuvenated myself by thirty years and today [here, a triumphant pause] I was able to 'pay a visit' to my young wife."

The impact of this report was enormous and immediate, due only in part to Brown-Séquard's tremendous prestige. In addition to his very personal revelations, the fact that he had experimented directly on himself lent an especially poignant credibility to the whole undertaking. Finally, it should be noted that the average age of members of the Société de Biologie at that time was seventy-one. It is unlikely that the personal implications of Brown-Séquard's possible discovery were lost on the distinguished—and perhaps somewhat extinguished—membership.

The French newspaper *Le Matin* began raising money for an Institute of Rejuvenation wherein aging Frenchmen would be restored to youth via the *Méthode Séquardienne*. Brown-Séquard threw himself totally into the effort, creating an extraordinary Rube-Goldberg-type device with belts, pulleys, dials, and other paraphernalia. Bulls' testicles went in one end and the means to instant rejuvenation was supposed to come out the other.

However, the next few years were not kind to Brown-Séquard. Unfortunately, his initial results could not be repeated. A German medical magazine eventually wrote that "his fantastic experiments . . . must be regarded as senile aberrations." A Viennese newspaper commented testily, "The lecture must be seen as further proof of the necessity of retiring professors who have attained their threescore and ten years." Shortly afterward, his wife left him for a younger man, and Brown-Séquard died, a laughingstock, at seventy-nine.

What had happened? It seems very likely that Brown-Séquard had honestly reported his findings, but that he had misinterpreted his own powerful placebo response as a major anti-aging discovery. It should be mentioned that Brown-Séquard did not attempt to profit personally from his "discovery." Furthermore, his work probably did result in isolating small amounts of the male sex hormone, testosterone, more than thirty years before it was analyzed and synthesized by Adolf Butenandt, a German biochemist. So, Brown-Seéquard was a brilliant man fumbling in the dark several decades ahead of his time. In so doing, he stumbled on his own wishful thinking, encouraged in no small way by world-wide enthusiasm for a miracle rejuvenator.

Brown-Séquard was the first of several investigators—some bona fide scientists, some get-rich-quick frauds—who entered the anti-aging field during the early decades of the twentieth century. They all shared one thing in common: emphasis on the role of sex glands to restore male potency and thereby to achieve rejuvenation.

Author Patrick McGrady called this group the "erector set."

Most prominent of the erector set was undoubtedly Serge Voronoff, wealthy scion of a Russian vodka manufacturer. Voronoff practiced medicine in Paris, and before the First World War he had served as personal physician to Abbas II, Khedive of Egypt. Abbas maintained eunuchs to guard his harem and Voronoff noted that these castrated men seemed to age more quickly than intact men. (This observation has since been confirmed.) Voronoff went on to draw the connection between testicles and age: perhaps having intact, youthful testicles would retard aging in men whose bodies had otherwise become old. He differed from Brown-Séquard in emphasizing that an entire additional testicle should be made available to aging men, rather than just a chemical injection. Furthermore, he insisted that the testicle should come from an animal more closely related to human beings than were Brown-Séquard's dogs and guinea pigs. Best of all, of course, would be a human testicle.

Voronoff began advertising for human donors. "Restoring the productive force of a Pasteur," he wrote, "is well worth a slight mutilation of a robust laborer [that] . . . in no way diminishes the donor." Much to the good doctor's dismay, however, only two young men volunteered. And not only that, they had the nerve to demand enormous sums of money for their precious organ. Voronoff sniffed that at such rates, only the wealthy could afford to walk around with someone else's testicle. So, he shifted his focus to the next best species, chimpanzees. France, Britain, and Belgium allowed vast numbers of wild chimps to be shipped from their African colonies to Voronoff's luxurious villa clinic on the Italian Riviera. There, the hapless apes were relieved of their testicles while many of the world's wealthiest men were in turn relieved of large sums of money for the privilege of having a chimpanzee testicle implanted in their scrotum. During his career in the 1920s, Voronoff may well have earned more than $10 million.

For a time, Voronoff was an international hero. The Encyclopaedia Britannica asked him to write on rejuvenation. Speaking of the aging process, Voronoff claimed:

> The only remedy is to graft a young testicle, whether that of a young human being or an ape, by which the tone-giving substance is provided, so as to increase the vitality of all the cells which are weakened but are not yet atrophied and therefore still able to renew themselves, and thus effectively to renew the whole organism.

Despite his popular and financial successes (or perhaps because of them), Voronoff was not treated kindly by his scientific peers. And as time went on, he increasingly merited their disdain. Voronoff presented talks at several scientific meetings in which he displayed "before and after" photographs of his patients. The photos were obviously retouched and evoked jeers from his audience. Shortly before his death, Voronoff had to face another much more horrible fact: not only did his patients not live longer, many of them wound up actually living less long and substantially less well—along with their testicles, Voronoff's chimps had donated syphillis to his patients!

If Serge Voronoff was of questionable scientific repute, at least he started as a legitimately trained physician. Not even this redeeming feature can be found in Voronoff's remarkable American counterpart, John Romulus Brinkley. Sporting a bogus medical degree, Brinkley eventually earned about $12 million transplanting goat testicles into aging Americans. Story has it that his career began when he and a patient, the latter complaining of impotence, were watching some rutting goats in a nearby field. "You wouldn't have any trouble if you had a pair of those buck glands in you," suggested Brinkley. "Well," responded the patient, "why don't you put 'em in?" So he did. Within two weeks, the patient's sex life was humming along and one year later he sired a baby boy. Its name: Billy.

As Brinkley's fame grew, he didn't limit himself to the rich. In fact, Brinkley offered three separate plans, geared to different budgets, including a "poor folk's treatment." "Come to Dr. Brinkley," he exclaimed. "I can cure you the same as I did Ezra Hoskins of Possum Point, Mo." He also offered an "average man's treatment" and, finally, "the businessman's treatment." For an extra $5,000, he would even provide a human testicle, guarantee that the graft would take and furthermore that it would come from someone younger than thirty-five years.

Many of Brinkley's patients died of peritonitis, which Brinkley claimed was not related to his surgery. But the sad fact remains that his procedures were not very antiseptic, and it is likely that he was responsible for several unnecessary deaths. Brinkley was eventually prosecuted in the United States, whereupon he escaped to Mexico and continued to advertise from his 1,000,000-watt radio station, XENT. He was certainly flamboyant—driving a Stutz Bearcat, piloting a Lockheed Electra, and cruising about in a 150-foot luxury yacht. He even ran for governor of Kansas three different times, and the last time he nearly won. An American phenomenon.

Voronoff and Brinkley, like Brown-Séquard before them, were simply wrong. Testosterone may have certain short-lived beneficial effects, but these quickly disappear. There is no evidence that longevity is enhanced or aging retarded. As for the testicle transplants, it is worth remembering that modern medical science requires a full armamentarium of immuno-suppressant drugs just to induce a patient's body to accept a graft *from another human being*. It is almost inconceivable that a goat or chimp testicle would "take"—even assuming that it would do any good. And yet, these members of the erector set had satisfied customers, at least for a time. Regarding his newly acquired goat testicle, no less a personage than Dr. J. J. Tobias, chancellor of the University of Chicago Law School, crowed, "I'm a new man. It's one of the great things of the century." The likely explanation: placebo, plus cognitive dissonance, since after spending large sums of money and undergoing substantial health risk as well as possible ridicule, such patients may be naturally inclined to emphasize the positive. Nobody wants to seem a fool.

A final member of the erector set deserves mention: Viennese physiologist Eugen Steinach. It had been known for some time that certain plants, such as coleus and spinach, can be kept in prolonged juvenile vigor by simply removing the reproductive parts as they appear. Apparently, energy diverted from reproduction is thus available for growth and maintenance of the body, resulting in greater health and longer life. In 1920, Steinach discovered that male laboratory rats lived longer and appeared more healthy when their sperm ducts were severed—that is, when they were given a vasectomy. The "Steinach rejuvenation operation" was a very popular surgical fad until the 1930s. Steinach's procedure may appear to be the exact opposite of Brown-Séquard and Voronoff, but actually it isn't. All these approaches reckoned on a supposedly life-prolonging and sex-stimulating effect of the male sex hormone.

Steinach simply reasoned that if the sperm-producing function of the testes was blocked, then the glands would increase testosterone production by way of compensation. They do not, and the Steinach operation was finally recognized to be a failure—although, once again, not before many satisfied patients initially pronounced it an unqualified success. For example, the great Irish poet W. B. Yeats noted that both his sexual and his poetic juices were waning during the sixth decade of his life. He insisted on the Steinach operation, despite the warnings of family and friends. Maybe it was scientifically and medically worthless as a rejuvenator, but Yeats's vasectomy put both his penis and his pen back into good working order, at least for a time.

If the discussion thus far seems to have emphasized rejuvenation of *men*, it is because that was in fact the main emphasis of most early rejuvenators—perhaps because they were men themselves. It may also be that the close association in many people's minds between male sexual potency and youthfulness provided a convenient focus for rejuvenating efforts. The fact that male potency is so sensitive to placebo effects doubtless lent an initial luster of success to such efforts. However, women have not been entirely ignored: Clayton E. Wheeler, a mail-order fraud rejuvenator, catered to women. He found that whereas men were only impressed with such aggressive procedures as surgery and testicle transplants, women preferred milder treatments, as via injections and suppositories. He eventually suicided on his yacht when prosecuted by the federal government. More recently, Royal Jelly, or Apiserum—a substance produced by worker honeybees—has been marketed, with the claim that it provides the same life-sustaining benefits to women as it confers on the queen bee. No mention is made that for women to receive a proportionate amount, they would have to use several bushel baskets per day.

❧

When it comes to modern rejuvenators with medical competence, one name stands far apart from the rest: Paul Niehans of
Switzerland.

His work has been on the fringe of science, never accepted but
never fully refuted either. In fact, Niehans' work has never really
been evaluated by the medico-scientific community. Nonetheless, and although he was (and still is) considered a quack in
most circles, there are passionate supporters of Niehans in the
United States today and numerous European practitioners of his
particular rejuvenating technique, so-called "cellular therapy."

Niehans retired in 1965, after establishing a major clinic called
La Prairie, near his home at Vevey, Switzerland. Up to his death
in 1971, he was tall, handsome, distinguished, and thoroughly
aristocratic. The following selection from Patrick McGrady's *The
Youth Doctors* conveys an impression of the Niehans residence,
and also some insight into his mystique:

> Niehans lives ten minutes from the Vevey railroad station, and every
> cabdriver knows his home. It is magnificent, white, a two-story
> affair overlooking the lake on the south and underlooking the Alps
> in every other direction. Majestic, billowy cypresses line the path
> from the road up to the door of Sonnenfels, which means "rock in
> the sun" and formerly belonged to Emperor Haile Selassie.
>
> A maid answered the doorbell. With a tiny key she unlocked a
> mammoth iron grille door with the gold initials PN wrought into
> the upper half. My steps echoed across the white Italian marble
> floor of the foyer, until I reached the magnificent needlepoint car-
> pet of the waiting room. Vast Gothic chairs upholstered in deep
> Burgundian reds matched the drapes. On the walls were a Van Dyck,
> a Dürer, and a painting attributed to the Sienese School (supposedly
> Niehans' favorite): a portrait of the Holy Family which art scholars
> have photographed in great detail.
>
> At his left hand is a large bronze medallion portrait of his grand-
> father, Frederick III of Prussia. One of the carved chairs across the
> room is a gift of Alfonso XIII of Spain. Two swords lie on a small
> table. One belonged to his grandfather . . .

Early in his career, before he assumed the mantle of a rejuvenationist, Paul Niehans was a swashbuckling young army doctor
who volunteered his services on the battlefields as well as in the
bedrooms of the upper class during World War I. Even before his
development of "cellular therapy," Niehans did unconventional
and controversial work on tissue transplants. A celebrated case

in the late 1920s gave him the reputation of having added 9½ inches to a dwarf's height in one year by implanting a slice of pituitary. Although positive verification of this story is lacking, it is known that when Niehans then visited New York City shortly afterward, another dwarf camped on his hotel doorstep, loudly demanding the same treatment. He was followed the next day by three dwarves and a giant. One day later, the contingent had grown to twenty-five dwarves, four giants, and several midgets. At this, Niehans was asked to leave the hotel. "If you're signing up circus acts," proclaimed the manager, "you'll have to meet somewhere else."

But the work for which Niehans was eventually to become famous (or infamous, depending on whom you listen to) was foreshadowed by another incident around the same time, when a sixty-year-old peasant woman lay dying in a Central European hospital. She had been operated upon for removal of a diseased thyroid gland, but in the process, some of her parathyroids were accidentally removed as well. She was undergoing periodic convulsions, which would surely have resulted in death, when her distraught surgeon called on the young Niehans. It was hoped that he could somehow implant new parathyroid glands in the dying patient, but Niehans recognized that there wasn't sufficient time for surgery of that sort. Instead, he simply injected mashed up parathyroid glands which he had quickly obtained from a local slaughterhouse. Niehans had expected that at best the gland material would tide the patient over for a short time until it was used up. But miraculously, the patient recovered and needed no further treatment. Niehans concluded that her remaining parathyroids had somehow been stimulated by the steer extract to function sufficiently on their own. To be sure, the woman eventually died—thirty years later, at the age of ninety. In the meantime, a new technique was born: cellular therapy. And Paul Niehans became a new apostle of rejuvenation. Or rather, to some of his patients, a new Messiah.

The basic idea of cellular therapy is actually quite simple, and seductively so. If a particular organ or system of organs seems to be malfunctioning, the cellular therapist treats it by injecting extracts from that organ, derived from another animal, usually a lamb. If the problem is caused by overfunction of an organ, then treatment is by injecting extract from an antagonistic organ. The logic is straightforward, easily grasped, and, for most nonscientists, compelling—largely because most nonscientists do not realize that foreign tissue is very unlikely to "take" in the human body.

Niehans' first step with any patient was to determine which organs are malfunctioning. He insisted that this determination can only be achieved via a complex procedure known as the "Abderhalden test," which up until recently could only be correctly performed by its originator, Emil Abderhalden, and then later by his widow. By analyzing the patient's urine, this test—generally considered worthless by conventional medical authorities—supposedly pinpoints the exact problem and indicates the appropriate cell therapeutic cure.

Niehans claimed that to be maximally effective, the injected cells must be prepared within seconds—minutes at most—after they have been removed from the donor animal. Accordingly, his clinic maintains a large flock of pregnant ewes for quick service to its customers. There is good reason for this speed, since in addition to their claimed therapeutic efficacy, fresh cells are safer than older ones: unless they are treated with preservative, fresh cells break down within minutes, liberating potentially toxic substances. Furthermore, a dangerous shock reaction can sometimes occur within the patient's body, simply because of the presence of foreign cells. To some extent, this likelihood is reduced by injecting cells from sheep *embryos*, rather than adult sheep. Embryonic tissue tends to have fewer antigens and thus is less apt to generate an immune response in the recipient. (In addition, the well-publicized use of "cells scraped from the still warm flesh of unborn lambs" probably enhances both the mysterious image of the process as well as its credibility as a rejuvenator.)

Despite the precautions, people have died of infection and shock following cell therapy treatment. However, Niehans always claimed that he never lost a patient in this way, and in fairness to him, it should be recognized that his techniques have been copied by many practitioners in Europe, not all of whom are as scrupulous as he. Cellular therapy involves several injections on successive days. Of these, the first is rarely dangerous, since the patient's body has not yet built up antibodies to the newly introduced antigens. However, by the second injection the patient is more likely to suffer a shock reaction—in fact, it is somewhat puzzling why this reaction is not more common. Part of the answer may lie in Niehans' careful monitoring of his patients during treatment, as well as his selective acceptance of would-be candidates. Basically, they must be (1) healthy and (2) rich.

Although little known in North America, Niehans remains renowned in Europe, and variants of his treatments are practiced widely. Niehans himself treated such notable geriatric cases as Bernard Baruch, Gloria Swanson, Somerset Maugham (who was so impressed with the results that he bankrolled treatments for his private secretary as well), and Konrad Adenauer. Of his many famous clients, however, perhaps the most delicate situation was posed by an aged Indian rajah, and the most publicized, Pope Pius XII. The rajah, it seems, had lost his lust for life and no longer fancied either his harem or the torturing of his political prisoners. Niehans was fetched from Switzerland and administered cellular therapy. Effective response to the treatment is supposed to take several weeks or even months, and so Niehans sought to return home after the procedure was completed. He was told, however, that he must remain until the efficacy of the cure was evaluated; if it failed, he would be killed, "like the last doctor." Fortunately for Niehans (and his subsequent patients), the old roué resumed his earlier pursuits and Niehans was permitted to resume his.

The case of Pope Pius is only somewhat less dramatic. In 1954, the seventy-seven-year-old pontiff was at death's door, spitting blood, vomiting, unable to eat, drink, or sleep, sinking fast. After extensive efforts by Vatican physicians, Niehans was called. (This in itself was embarrassing for the pope's doctors, since it was seen by many as admission that Catholic physicians were inferior to Niehans, a Protestant. More than that, however, it actually reflected the high regard for Niehans as an individual.) But Protestant or not, and "scientifically valid" or not, the fact remains that Niehans cured the pope—or rather, after his treatment, Pius XII recovered.

To this day, we do not know the nature of the pope's illness; nor do we know precisely how Niehans treated him. It is forbidden to kill anything within the walls of the Vatican, so it seems unlikely that live sheep embryo cells were used. Niehans had been developing an alternative to live cells: "lyophilized" cells, that were essentially freeze-dried, and had been developed with the aid of a former Nestle Company engineer from Niehans' hometown. Perhaps these instant cells cured the pope, or perhaps it was our old friend placebo once again.

Cellular therapy, as Niehans practiced it, certainly lends itself to a powerful mind-over-matter phenomenon. The patient must have three days of bedrest, both before and after the treatments, plus one month of abstention from alcohol, tobacco, and strenuous exertion, and also must follow a carefully prescribed plan of balanced nutrition. Finally, the great cost of cellular therapy and its potential for unleashing cognitive dissonance may strongly predispose patients to expect only positive results, to ignore any indication of failure, and indeed to modify their bodies, unconsciously, so as to make the treatments beneficial.

At present, the claims of cellular therapists seem excessive. But incredibly, they have not even been seriously evaluated by the medical establishment. Following Niehans' rather arrogant and aristocratic lead, cellular therapists have remained outside the traditional scientific community, holding separate meetings and publishing their results in their own books and journal. All this separateness is certainly regrettable, since cellular therapy may yet have something to offer, and in some respects, its tenets are not that far outside of accepted medical practice. For example, bone marrow injections are now standard procedure for helping persons to recover from radiation overdose, which tends to kill bone marrow cells in the victims. Perhaps in the future, cloning will permit cell donation from one's identical clone, thereby sidestepping the present use of unborn lambs. More remarkable yet, maybe someday would-be rejuvenationists and establishment physicians will respect and communicate with one another.

❦

Finally, once more on the verge of medical respectability, we come to Dr. Anna Aslan. She is a Romanian physician whose work has earned Romania a reputation as one of the world's rejuvenation centers, while also earning a substantial income from the world's aged and wealthy, many of whom make regular pilgrimages to her state-supported clinic. Her secret substance: good old novocaine, the same chemical commonly injected by dentists to produce numbness before drilling a cavity or extracting a tooth.

Her rejuvenating chemical is known as "procaine," simply the

49

British term for novocaine. Because novocaine is quickly broken down once injected into the body, Aslan injects her novocaine in a mixture with other simple chemicals that serve to prevent its rapid decomposition. The final product, novocaine plus buffering agents, is called "Gerovital H_3."

Unlike cellular therapy, in which a small number of injections is claimed to last for a long time, Gerovital treatments require constant repetitions. Aslan prescribes three shots per week for a four-week period, then a delay of ten to twelve weeks, followed by a repeat performance. The results, she claims, have been very impressive: white hair turning dark, memory returning, arthritis relieved, and so on. It is rumored that Nikita Khrushchev was once a patient of Aslan. The German physician Fritz Wiedemann claims that after injecting a sixty-eight-year-old woman with Gerovital, she even sprouted a new set of wisdom teeth! Aslan's other notable patients have included Charles de Gaulle, Ho Chi Minh, Marlene Dietrich, and John F. Kennedy.

Unlike Niehans, Aslan has willingly subjected her findings to the scrutiny of medical science, attending meetings and inviting efforts by other researchers to confirm or refute her findings. Thus far, Western scientists have not rushed to conduct the necessary research, perhaps in part because of the bad press surrounding most wonder drug rejuvenationists (remember Brown-Séquard, the alchemists, and so on). In addition, Aslan's own work is deficient, by most Western scientific standards. For one thing, her studies have no "controls." That is, when persons are injected with Gerovital, no attempts have been made to inject a comparable number of other patients with an inert substance, such as salt water. Doing so would clarify whether Gerovital itself produces any effect, as opposed to the experience of being in Dr. Aslan's clinic, receiving a great deal of positive attention, and benefiting from a powerful placebo response. Only by such studies would most scientists be persuaded that the reported improvements in Gerovital-injected patients are due to the Gerovital and not to placebo, the climate of Romania, or perhaps Dr. Aslan's perfume.

As it happens, Anna Aslan is a perfect stimulus for mind over body effects: she is warm, caring, and charismatic. So it is at least possible that some of her reported successes have very little to do with the substances that she *in*jects, and a great deal to do with the expectations that she *pro*jects. Furthermore, a really good experiment of this sort would have to be "double blind"—both the patients and the people working directly with them should not know which patients received the Gerovital and which the placebo. In this way, the condition of different patients could not be influenced by different treatment from the staff, who might tend unconsciously to favor or have higher expectations of those patients receiving the "real" drug.

Several years ago, Dr. Aslan came to the United States, where she presented a paper on her research at a gerontologists' conference held in Miami. At the same conference, papers were given by Tom Yau, from the Ohio Mental Health and Mental Retardation Research center in Cleveland, and by J. Earle Officer, a biologist from the University of Southern California. Both papers provided provocative and rather unexpected support for Aslan's work. The focus was on chemicals known as MAO-inhibitors. It seems that the chemical MAO (monoamine oxidase) increases steadily in aged people. High MAO levels are associated with the debilitating psychiatric condition known as depression, and substances that inhibit MAO can be helpful in treating depression. Significantly, Yau presented convincing data that Aslan's Gerovital works as a MAO-inhibitor, at least in mice. Officer showed that Gerovital reduced aging in mouse cells, grown in "tissue culture" in his laboratory.

These findings are exciting for several reasons. For one, physicians have been reluctant to prescribe MAO-inhibitors for their depressed patients, especially if those patients are elderly, because most such chemicals have the undesirable side effect of elevating the blood pressure. Elderly people often suffer from high blood pressure as it is. Gerovital, it now appears, is a very mild MAO-inhibitor, without the unwanted blood pressure effect. Furthermore, perhaps part of Aslan's success as a rejuvenator is due to curing any mild depression that her patients may have been suffering. Most importantly, however, the real hope of Gerovital—slim as it may be—lies in the promise that modern medical scientists and practitioners of the ancient tradition of rejuvenation may finally be starting to listen, and profit, from one another. From Gilgamesh to alchemy, to the ill-fated erector set and the controversial efforts of Paul Niehans and Anna Aslan, we have come a long way.

What if we ever arrive?

4

What If?

What if the rejuvenators are successful someday? What if they figure out some way to extend the human life-span? Then what?

The question is not as crazy as it might seem. Admittedly, the maximum human life-span has not yet been changed—in modern times, we simply have fewer people dying early, not an increase in the maximum age we can achieve. But, as we shall see, research is actively under way, and many promising leads are being pursued.

Shortly before he died in 1937, Lord Ernest Rutherford, the discoverer of the neutron and one of the fathers of modern nuclear physics, stated categorically that we would never harness nuclear energy for power. For better or worse, we are now doing just that. Will anyone categorically state that we will never conquer old age? "The last enemy that shall be destroyed is death"— 1 Corinthians 15:26.

Thinking about the future can be interesting. How radical would be the changes ushered in by the defeat of old age and death? Clearly, the effects would vary with the terms of the victory. Even a small increase in average longevity would cause some dramatic changes, just as the reduction in early mortality is already stretching society's ability to support its increasing numbers of elderly. And if longevity is ever greatly increased, the consequences could be almost unimaginable.

In considering these changes, we ought to distinguish between a world in which our vigorous years are extended and one in which we are simply able to keep people alive as "basket cases" for prolonged or indefinite periods. The ancient Romans even recognized the problem. According to their mythology, the goddess Aurora fell in love with a mortal named Tithonus. Gods live forever, of course, but mortals don't, so the long-term future of their relationship looked bleak. Accordingly, Aurora begged Jupiter to grant eternal life to Tithonus, so that their love affair would last forever. Her wish was granted. Regrettably, however, Aurora in her ardor forgot to request that her lover also receive eternal youth along with his eternal life. So, Tithonus grew older and older, more and more feeble, until finally he begged to be released from life and allowed to die, whereupon Aurora turned him into a grasshopper.

Modern gerontologists are aware of Tithonus' dilemma. Science would be doing us no favor if it increased the quantity of our lives without seeing to their quality at the same time.

Consider a simple, practical issue: the social security system in the United States. Benefits to retired workers are not paid out of a personal fund established by each individual when he or she is young, working and paying social security taxes. Rather, money contributed by workers today goes directly toward paying others who are simultaneously drawing their social security benefits. When today's young worker grows old, his or her social security payments will be met by other workers, now unborn or too young to work, who will be paying into the system by that time. The record number of older persons presently drawing social security benefits is already causing anxiety in Washington, D.C. If we are granted increased longevity, à la Tithonus, then the duration of our retired life could increase, without necessarily increasing the duration of our productive life. The result, quite simply, would be that the number of productive workers would be too small to support the large population of retirees who refuse to die, but insist on receiving their benefits until they do.

This problem may be manageable, however. We simply must insist that we not share the fate of Tithonus. We must have years *with* life—that is, lively years—not just years *of* life. If the biological gerontologists can someday grant us 200 or even 500 years of competence and well-being, then presumably we can continue to work for perhaps the first 175 or 475 years of our lives, then retire cheerfully to tap the bulging coffers of social security. In fact, with an average longevity of 500 years, it should be possible to retire at the youthful age of 350, and the social security system would still be doing quite nicely.

But new problems arise: How many of us would agree that as our part of the deal, increased longevity would be purchased at the cost of working that much longer? For many persons (although certainly not all), retirement is something to look forward to, a welcome and well-earned slowing down after a lifetime of hard and productive work. If fifty years with the same employer seems worthy of a gold medal, what about seventy-five years? Three hundred and seventy-five?

Boredom could be immense. This might be countered, however, by "lateral mobility"—individuals retraining themselves after a suitable time in one career and then moving to a new one. Imagine spending thirty years in an automobile assembly line, then becoming a farmer for the next thirty, then entering medical school for another stint as a brain surgeon, to be followed by a career as a mailman, then a logger, and then an accountant!

Alternatively, people might cling tenaciously to their present positions, especially those at the top. This seems likely: the college president may well be unenthusiastic about changing positions with the janitor; or the millionaire board chairman with his or her chauffeur. What then? Working one's way to the top is tedious enough when most persons retire around sixty-five.

There may not be much room at the top if the aged top-dwellers just keep on living. What if they hung on until 350? Would we see an increase in murders? And how about inheritance? Imagine the consternation of being next-of-kin to rich aunt Tilly who lives to be 489!

Lifetime guarantees and commitments would certainly take on new meaning. Take marriage, for instance. It is one thing to commit oneself to another person for fifty years, maybe even more. But what about 350? Would we agree to love, honor, and obey a spouse, if a thousand years were at stake? (Actually, this question may be purely academic, since rising divorce rates show that even these days two adults often do not remain committed to each other for their entire adult lives.)

What about overpopulation? Our numbers are like water in a bathtub: They increase because of births (water coming in from the faucet) and at the same time they are reduced by deaths (water going out the drain). The balance between births and deaths, therefore, determines the population level. If more water comes in than goes out, the level rises; vice versa, and the level drops. If people live longer, then the drain is partly closed and the water level will rise.* This problem, too, is manageable, but only if greatly increased longevity is accompanied by strict population controls. There may be no theoretical reason why our life-span can't be pushed to 20,000 years, if we ultimately uncover and harness the immortality secret of cancer cells. Even with this mind-boggling change, the population effects need not be catastrophic, so long as each individual is responsible for no more than one offspring during his or her lifetime. The population would grow for a time, as fewer people die, but then level out, as fewer births take place.

It seems likely, then, that dramatic improvements in life-span would have to be combined with dramatic restrictions on reproduction. Along with this would also come greatly reduced contact with young people. If we lived to be, on average, five hundred years old, and had only two children, then the proportion of our lives spent with children would plummet. At present our lives are divided approximately into thirds: for the first third we are young, and largely dependent on others; for the middle third we produce children, who are dependent on us; for the final third we are more or less on our own—with perhaps some continued responsibility for children during the beginning of that stage, as well as some dependence on them toward the end. But if we lived to be five hundred, say, then we would spend only about one twentieth of our lives rearing children. This is likely to have its costs as well as benefits.

Certainly "adult education" would become more important, while the time, energy, and resources devoted to elementary schools would become proportionately much smaller than today. For many of us, however, spending several centuries getting educated would seem no less tedious than three hundred years of bingo or shuffleboard.

With several hundred years to learn, develop, mull things over, and accumulate vast stores of experience, would we become far-seeing, benevolent, patient, and understanding? Would we gain wisdom to go along with our knowledge? Possibly, but remem-

---

* Ecologist Paul Ehrlich has pointed out that the world bathtub is already overflowing. Consider the following situation: you go into the bathroom and see the tub overflowing. What do you do? You could scurry about with bricks and mortar, trying to raise the level of the walls (that is, concentrate on growing more food), or simply turn down the faucet (reduce the number of births).

ber Jonathan Swift and his mythical Struldbruggs: might we become petty, vain, self-involved, and narrow as we slide along in a five-hundred-year rut?

With death and debility less likely to be breathing down our necks, would we be more inclined to "take the long view" of things? For example, judging from the way we use them, most of us have only mild reservations about pillaging the world's resources. If we had to live in this same world two or five centuries hence, would we blithely continue using up its nonrenewable resources (such as oil), at the same unconscionable rate? We seem to have very few qualms about stealing from future generations. Would we feel any different if we knew we were stealing from ourselves and would have to live with the consequences?

In Andrew Marvell's glorious poem of seduction, "To His Coy Mistress," the first lines are, "Had we but world enough, and time, / This coyness, lady, were no crime." He goes on to point out that since time is fleeting and life short, the young lady may as well let him caress her; after all, once she is in her grave, only worms will do so. I do not know whether Marvell's coy mistress was convinced by his argument. Would she have been more resisting if there were 350 years of physical beauty still ahead of her? Marvell claims that if he had the time,

> An hundred years should go to praise
> Thine eyes, and on thy forehead gaze;
> Two hundred to adore each breast,
> But thirty thousand to the rest;

If we all had the time, would we live more leisurely? Would we spend a whole month in foreplay?

Presumably, we would be liberated to begin projects that are beyond our current reach. At present we know a lot about the genetics of fruit flies—they breed every few weeks—and about colon bacteria which breed every few hours or less. If we became Methuselahs, would we attack the genetics of elephants, or blue whales? On the other hand, just as the shortness of human life has deterred certain projects, hasn't it also spurred others? Isn't there a certain feeling of urgency that comes from the knowledge that time is running out? Andrew Marvell, more than three hundred years ago, felt the rush of time. His poem concludes with the lines:

Now therefore, while the youthful hue
Sits on thy skin like morning dew,
And while thy willing soul transpires
At every pore with instant fires,
Now let us sport us while we may;
And now, like am'rous birds of prey,
Rather at once our time devour,
Than languish in his slow-chapped power.
Let us roll all our strength, and all
Our sweetness, up into one ball;
And tear our pleasures with rough strife
Through the iron gates of life.
Thus, though we cannot make our sun
Stand still, yet we will make him run.

What if we could make our sun stand still? Would we still yearn to tear our pleasures from life? Would we make our time run, or rather languish in a dolorous haze of sloth and self-satisfaction?

When a young person risks his life, he is endangering the fifty or so years he might otherwise have left. What if, instead, he could have anticipated an additional 450? Would life become more precious and therefore courage more rare? Nathan Hale's sole regret, he claimed, was that he had but one life to give for his country. Would he have felt so generous if in giving that life he was forgoing 250 years on this earth? How about 10,000 years? At present, the law makes no distinction between murder of a young child and of an old person. Depriving someone of life is still a capital crime. But what if the crime deprived someone of three times, or ten times, the life that we now know? Would murder become even more heinous? Would diseases and accidents hold all the more terror, since they would deprive us of hundreds of years, instead of today's mere decades?

It is generally easier to prevent a biological process than to reverse it after it is well under way. This will probably apply to aging as well. It is likely that advances in postponing aging will be most effective when administered to those who are not yet old. But imagine the resentment of those whose aging is already too far advanced, and whose youthful counterparts receive treatments that increase *their* life-spans.

Furthermore, I have been assuming that anti-aging breakthroughs would be readily available to everyone, like aspirin or other over-the-counter home remedies. But what if they turn out to involve an elaborate and costly procedure, perhaps like renal dialysis for kidney failure? If it cost $25,000 per year to extend a life, then clearly the service wouldn't be available to everyone. On what basis, then, should the gift of longevity be doled out? Those who can afford it? Those whose lives are judged to be more valuable? But whose life is more valuable? The scientist? The politician? The composer? The skilled carpenter? The undistinguished, perfectly average citizen whose cosmic contribution is limited, but who abides by the law and does his part? The writer of books on aging? The reader of such books?

These musings have but scratched the surface. It seems likely that the first advances to occur will be short extensions of life, perhaps an added five or ten years. Even those effects will be enormous. After that, the sky may be the limit. It also remains to be seen whether life extension will necessarily involve extension of a particular part of our life cycle. For example, even if we continue to reach maturity within the current thirty years or so, it might then be possible for us to live several hundred years before we reach infirm old age. Or maybe it would take one hundred years to reach adolescence, with our lives proportionately drawn out. Will we want such a life? For example, if we had the choice, would we choose to stall our biological clock at a particular age? And would we all agree, or would society become a heterogeneous mixture of different people, each aging according to a radically different schedule? Peter Pan, anyone? Perhaps some would like to spend ten years, or maybe a hundred, with the sexual prowess of age eighteen, but only if along with it would come the knowledge and maturity achieved by age forty.

There may be some interesting biological problems as well. To take just one, brain cells and certain muscle cells don't reproduce. We are born with ten billion neurons, but we lose about 100,000 each day. Since our normal life-span rarely exceeds one hundred years, this is no problem, because we are apparently provided with many more brain cells than we need, and perhaps more than we ever use. After several hundred years, however, our brains would have slipped away. One solution would be to prevent the brain cells from dying. It might be easier yet, however, to induce them somehow to begin dividing, like most other self-respecting cells. This would have the interesting result, for each of us, of making a new "I" periodically, as enough of our brain cells turn over. As we shed old memories and turn over

58

new blank pages, we would then experience a continuous re-birthing. On the other hand, this might all be self-defeating, since any appeal of longevity must derive in large part from continuity of experience and consciousness. What if we could start afresh every three score years and ten? If it was truly afresh, would it be any different from dying? As things are now, our kidneys and corneas may live on after us, in another's body. Although the thought may be satisfying, it is hardly the consummation of Gilgamesh's dream.

Finally, major changes in longevity may carry some real surprises. Aldous Huxley's novel *After Many a Summer Dies the Swan* tells the story of a wealthy nobleman who discovers the secret of extending life. Huxley was much taken with the biological theory of human neoteny, which holds that in many of our physical traits we resemble fetal apes. At one dramatic point, we encounter the Fifth Earl of Gonister, now several hundred years old, covered with coarse hair and urinating on the floor. He has lived longer than any other person—so long, in fact, that he has become the first human being to "grow up." He has finally become an ape.

Such a fate, although good fiction, is probably not good science. To understand the science of aging and the prospects for rejuvenation or extension of our life-span à la Tithonus, our next stop is biology.

5

The Biology of Aging, Part I

Genes, Errors, and Growth

Just as we breathe in and out without giving much thought to the process, we age, also without thinking about it very much. Or, when we do think about our own aging, it is generally to plan ahead (perhaps for retirement) or maybe to note a new gray hair, to order stronger eyeglasses, and so on. We don't usually think about the *process* of aging, or, for that matter, of breathing. But at least we know a great deal about the mechanism of breathing, both how we do it and why. By contrast, aging is very much a mystery: we know little about how and virtually nothing of why.

All this seems to be changing, however. Gingerly, biologists are beginning to approach the subject, despite the bad image fostered by the many quack rejuvenators. In fact, even now the study of biological gerontology is still vaguely disreputable. Nonetheless, we are beginning to ask what aging is all about, although the answers seem to lie in the often tedious research of laboratory science rather than the glamorous surgery or magical potions of earlier times. But it is still an extraordinary and exciting quest. And the stakes are high. Albert Rosenfeld, science editor of *Saturday Review*, likened these modern-day rejuvenationists to Captain Ahab, in search of the greatest, whitest whale of them all: old age. Will they eventually destroy their quarry? Or, like Ahab, will they be destroyed first? Certainly, their voyage of discovery has already turned up many new leads. In this chapter we shall review some of the most promising.

Before we start, however, let's pause to consider the whole field of aging research. Scientific progress typically seems to occur via organized marches in the same general direction, in which the discoveries of previous workers allow those in the front ranks to progress yet farther. For example, Newton once commented, "If I appear to have seen far, it is because I stood on the shoulders of giants." Periodically, there may be a general change of direction, what historian of science Thomas Kuhn called a "paradigm shift," as when the Newtonian universe was replaced by the relativistic one of Einstein. Underlying unity, nonetheless, is typically the order of the day. This is not the case, however, when it comes to research on the causes of aging.

Aging research, exciting as it is, resembles a kaleidoscopic jumble. Everyone seems to be running this way and that, rather than taking part in an organized assault. Almost every researcher has a particular theory of aging, and to some extent each may be right. Perhaps there is a single key that underlies the whole process of aging, so that once it begins turning, all the remaining tumblers will quickly fall into place. Or perhaps the aging process itself is multidimensional, proceeding along several different avenues at the same time. In any event, we will have to consider the different theories one at a time, although fully recognizing in advance that many of them may be closely intertwined. The foolishness of adhering to one and only one theory of aging is reminiscent of the story of the blind men and the elephant, related by the nineteenth-century American poet John Saxe. It begins:

> It was six men from Industan, to learning much inclined,
> who went to see the elephant (though all of them were blind),
> that each by observation might satisfy his mind . . .

Of course, each one felt a different part: the one touching the tail thought it was a snake; the one who felt the legs thought they were tree trunks; and so on. At the end, they

> disputed loud and long, each in his opinion stiff and strong,
> though each was partly in the right, and all of them were wrong.

Saxe drew a moral from the story, warning us not to emulate these blind men, and "rail on in utter ignorance of what each other mean, / and prate about an elephant not one of them has seen." Aging researchers have begun groping for the elephant.

However, as we shall now see, they have been going about it in rather different ways.

❧

For most of us, "biomedical research" conjures up images of programs directed toward the cure of major diseases: cancer, heart disease, diabetes, schizophrenia, and so forth. Aging doesn't seem to belong in the same ballpark. After all, aging isn't a *disease*, is it? What could be more *natural* than growing old? But similarly, isn't cancer "natural"? What could be more "natural" than a typhoid bacterium? Or a polio virus? In fact, the very large number of aged persons alive today is itself "unnatural," a result of technological advances in medicine, public health, and nutrition.

One of the leaders in basic research on aging is cellular biologist Leonard Hayflick. He points out that the current situation in aging studies is similar to that faced by the National Foundation for Infantile Paralysis during the 1940s and early 1950s. That organization could have chosen to devote itself to making life easier for afflicted children. Had that happened, we probably would today be blessed with the world's most lavish, comfortable, and fully automated iron lungs for tens of thousands of children, all stricken with polio. Happily, the decision was otherwise—resources were spent for the basic research needed to tackle the disease itself, rather than just treating its symptoms. Hence, we now have the Salk and Sabin vaccines, and a virtually polio-free world.

Is it reasonable to expect an old-age-free world? Is it even desirable? Opinions differ on both these questions. Nonetheless, it seems increasingly clear that despite the meager funds directed toward it, research on the basic causes of aging has been making progress, although it seems doubtful that we will ever take inoculations against growing old, as our children routinely do against polio.

To many people, it may seem that we are already well on the way. The average life-span has increased dramatically from prehistoric times until the present, and this suggests that human beings are living longer now than ever before. Don't be misled, however. The *average* human life-span has in fact been increased, due to the elimination of many of the childhood killers such as diphtheria, smallpox, and whooping cough, as well as better sanitation and nutrition. But these impressive feats have not added anything to the *maximum* life-span attainable by members of our species. Removing the causes of human death has been like peeling an onion—more layers are simply revealed underneath. If we shed them all, including arteriosclerosis, cancer, and influenza, will there be a kernel of healthy longevity inside? Or alternatively, will we find nothing left?

At present, in the United States, nearly everyone lives to be seventy, but very few make it to one hundred. Medicine and public health have made it possible for nearly all of us to live to a ripe old age, but we all ripen nonetheless, and when ripe enough, we still fall off the vine just as we always used to. And at just about the same age.

To take an example, an American who was sixty-five years old in 1900 could expect to live, on average, another thirteen years. In 1974, someone the same age could look forward to fifteen and one-half years, an increase of merely two and one-half years, despite seventy-four years of dazzling medical advances! Even with the complete elimination of cancer, the average life-span would rise by only two years. If cardiovascular diseases were also eliminated, we would add a whopping seventeen years more. But even in this bio-medical Shangri-la, the human life-span would probably not have been pushed forward; simply more people would be reaching that limit, as they have been throughout history. The end might remind us of Cinderella's coach, with nearly everyone turning into a very dead pumpkin at, say, 110 years of age.

The question emerges: Can we actually postpone aging, not just prevent premature death?

First, we must ask about aging itself. What is it? It is time's arrow, the seemingly one-way flow of events in which our lives are played out. In a sense, it is not really different from growth and development, except that these processes are usually thought to enhance the organism, whereas aging ultimately diminishes it. The second law of thermodynamics tells us that most things are irreversible—we cannot swim in the same river twice. But time *itself* does not act on things; rather, things happen in the course of time. Three score and ten revolutions of the earth around the sun is a *measure* of time, not a cause of anything. And yet, time somehow takes the measure of all things, including all people. In this chapter and the next, we shall take a look at what scientists have found about the nitty-gritty of aging, and what makes our personal clocks tick the way they do.

୬ୡ

Our genes are really very good to us, and hard-working, too. They accomplish the incredibly difficult task of building each of us a body, starting from scratch—or rather, a single fertilized egg. These genes seem both competent and well-intentioned. Why, then, do they let us down when it comes to the much less demanding job of simply maintaining that body?

There are several possible answers. Perhaps aging and death are the results of evolution, since if individuals didn't eventually die, the world would quickly become overpopulated and there would be no room for species to evolve. The old and aged must make way for the new and young, or else evolution cannot occur. This argument may sound plausible, but it is almost certainly incorrect. Evolution does not operate for the good of species, but rather by the reproductive success of individuals and their genes. If individuals would be more successful in projecting copies of their genes into the future just by living longer, then it seems very likely that they would, in fact, live longer.

By the same token, overpopulation is a great danger to the earth and all life, but this hasn't stopped each individual of every species, except possibly our own, from reproducing as much as he or she can.

Late last century, biologist August Weismann proposed the hopeful view that aging and death are specifically evolved characteristics, products of evolution, rather than the unavoidable results of being alive and occupying a body. Different species, as we shall see, have different life-spans—strong evidence for the hand of genetic preprogramming, whatever the underlying cause.

It is also likely, however, that evolution has played a more subtle role as architect of aging. In its quiet, unassuming way, it may have produced a biological time-bomb within our bodies. Thus, whereas most genes are beneficial, some just by chance are not. These hurtful genes—mutations—might predispose us to weakness, inefficiency in use of body chemicals, inability to repair damage, and so on. During our long evolutionary history, those unwanted mutations that had their effect early in the life of an individual were likely to contribute to an early death, often before the affected individual was able to reproduce. This is important, since by incapacitating the body in which they resided, before that body was able to pass on copies of themselves into the next generation, these early-acting genes tended to remove themselves from the population. The result is likely to have been a population from which early-acting harmful genes have largely been selected out, leaving their late-acting colleagues. In other words, the biological disadvantages of old age may occur partly because deleterious genes that operate in old age persist in the population longer than other such genes which make themselves known earlier in life.

An argument similar to this was advanced in the 1950s by Nobel Prize–winning biologist Sir Peter Medawar. He proposed that instead of actually being eliminated from the population, genes which acted to the disadvantage of their bodies early in life would tend to be suppressed by other genes. It is well known that certain genes function to modify the action of other genes. Therefore, Medawar suggested that evolution has favored an accumulation of such "restrainer" genes which hold the deleterious ones in check. We would expect that the strength of this inhibition would be greatest when the individual is young, weakest when he or she is old. So, the longer we live, the more likely that any self-destructive genes we possess will be unleashed against ourselves. The ravages of time may therefore be the ravages of our own genes, previously suppressed but toward the end of our lives given free reign.

There are many possible ways in which genes could turn against the body and lead to its downfall. The simplest, perhaps, is just to stop doing whatever it is that they normally do. All living things are exquisitely complex, well-integrated units, with a host of crucial, interworking parts. Genes normally carry the instructions for making enzymes and other proteins. If at some point they simply stop performing their task, the whole fragile living system could collapse, like a house of cards.

In addition, a more specific self-destruct mechanism has already been proposed. Within our cells there are small structures known as lysosomes. These contain powerful chemicals capable of destroying ("lysing") the cell.* It has been observed that lysosome activity increases in the heart cells of aging rats. It is at least possible that at a certain point, these lysosomes begin to

* The well-known household disinfectant "Lysol" derives its name from the same word.

rupture, releasing their "lytic" enzymes, to the ultimate destruction of the cell and, eventually, the entire body. (To evaluate this, drugs are now being tested that stabilize the lysosomes, and which seem to increase the life-span of laboratory rats.) The role of lysosomes in aging remains controversial, however. Whether they are a genetic self-destruct mechanism or not—and there are numerous other candidates—the fact remains that our own genes can do us in, and there are some convincing arguments from evolutionary theory that the older we get, the more likely they are to do just that.

What, if anything, can we do about it? In his book *The Selfish Gene*, British zoologist Richard Dawkins points out that if the Medawar theory is correct, then our "restrainer" genes must have some way of knowing when they should let up and allow our self-destroying genes to begin their unpleasant acts. In other words, somehow our bodies must inform our genes when they have gotten old enough to initiate this last phase of the life cycle. Maybe this message is conveyed by the accumulation of certain chemical substances which build up over time. (In fact, as we shall see later, there is such an "aging substance," although its function is almost completely unknown.) On the other hand, maybe the key is the using up of some substance as time goes by. Whatever it may be, perhaps we can avert some of the gene-induced deterioration we call aging by fooling our genes into believing that they are actually inhabiting a younger body. How to accomplish this trick? Nobody knows. This does not mean that everyone over sixty-five should begin wearing long hair, faded blue jeans, and love beads, eat Big Mac's and Rice Krispies, and maybe start watching Saturday morning cartoons. But there may in fact be a profound biological wisdom to the old saw that "you're as young as you feel," or even "as young as you look," or act—especially if your genes are watching.

The Medawar theory is not the only explanation that lays aging at the doorstep of evolution. It is possible that genes ultimately cause our eventual deterioration with age, but in a less direct way than is implied by the self-destruct theory. To use a space-age analogy, the body is like an interplanetary satellite, sent on a particular mission: the Mariner spacecraft is designed to photograph Mars; the body is designed to live its life, and in the process reproduce itself. In order to achieve their purpose, spacecraft are equipped with a preprogrammed set of capabilities and controls. So are bodies. Within certain limits, spacecraft can even adjust to unexpected situations. So can bodies. And most spacecraft are sent on one-way trips. So are bodies.

Consider the recent Jupiter "fly-by" probe: it was exquisitely engineered to perform a very difficult technical feat—leave our atmosphere and get close enough to Jupiter to take clear photographs. After that, however, it had no further programming. After dutifully performing as it had been designed, the Jupiter spacecraft continued hurtling through space without any particular direction or instruction. It simply was not designed to do anything more, and whatever befalls it from now on, it is on its own. En route to its target, malfunctions in the spacecraft would have been corrected; if the trajectory had begun to deviate from its goal, then strenuous efforts would have been made to set it back on course again. But, having completed its mission, the spacecraft has run out of program. Nobody in "Mission Control" cares what happens to it anymore, and even if someone did, it is now too far gone—literally—to be controllable.

Our bodies may be like these "fly-by" satellites. We are designed for a particular mission: a life in which our genes are successfully reproduced. And just like a satellite, we are beautifully engineered, self-correcting, and meticulously constructed to accomplish this goal. But as with the satellite, the time may come when we simply run out of program. When things go wrong with young bodies, healing processes are usually quick and efficient: like the "young" spacecraft, we are kept carefully on course. But older bodies heal much more slowly and less efficiently. Things go wrong and remain uncorrected. Chronic disabilities accumulate, such as arthritis, arteriosclerosis, cancer, emphysema, senile dementia—and "mission control" either doesn't care, or can't do anything about it.

Why this callous disregard? Just as the purpose of the spacecraft was to photograph Jupiter, the evolutionary "purpose" of a human body is to reproduce the genes within it. Once a certain age is reached, no matter whether reproduction has actually occurred or not, our bodies may simply begin to shut down. Just as the sprinter stops trying after reaching the finish line, our bodies may "stop trying" after living long enough. And just as a sprinter's momentum may carry him or her some distance beyond the actual finish line, our bodies' biological momentum may keep us going a long way beyond the usual end of reproduction, especially since we can call on modern medicine to give us a push now and then.

Even if these analogies are accurate, there is a crucial difference between the aging human being and the sprinter or spacecraft which has completed its mission. The sprinter *wants* to slow down, and the spacecraft doesn't care if it goes on unrepaired and unguided. But most of us do care a great deal what happens to our bodies as we get older. Unfortunately, however, evolution is not necessarily concerned with making us happy, either in youth or old age.

Earlier, I raised the question of why our genes fail us in the relatively simple job of maintaining our bodies, after completing the much more difficult task of building us in the first place. The answer may be straightforward, although not necessarily palatable: our genes are not really concerned with us (our bodies) at all, but rather with themselves. They help keep our bodies going when we are young, since by doing so they help ultimately to make successful copies of themselves in the next generation. This much is evolution. And they cease caring for our bodies, once these bodies cease caring for them—in other words, once we have passed the age of reproduction and can no longer help our genes along their evolutionary way. This also is evolution.

In fact, human beings are somewhat unusual among living things in that we have any life-span at all after reproducing. Most living things in nature do not survive very long after passing on their genes. Interestingly, those animals that do have a substantial postreproductive life-span tend to be species which are highly intelligent and live in groups. Such creatures often rely heavily on one another, for defense against would-be predators, for finding food, recognizing good routes for migration, and generally getting by in a hostile world. Chimpanzees, gorillas, and possibly baboons seem to survive into old age, after their bodies have ceased reproducing. The same appears to be true of elephants, certain whales, and *Homo sapiens*. In animals such as these, bodies can assist their genes in more ways than simply by inserting them into the coming generation. As repositories of valuable know-how, aged chimps, gorillas, elephants, whales, and people may well be very useful in promoting the survival of their own genes, by now incorporated into the bodies of younger individuals. This may be the evolutionary reason why younger animals follow the lead of aged baboons with worn-down canines, and why women don't drop dead at menopause.

It may be an important fact that small birds and mammals usually die before becoming old. The potential life-span of a sparrow or a mouse, unlike that of a human being, is almost never attained among those animals living freely in nature. Rather, they meet death prematurely, from starvation, accident, disease, or in the jaws of a predator. Therefore, since advanced aging hardly ever occurs in such cases, it seems unlikely to be an evolved trait.

Nonetheless as the "fly-by" theory suggests, from the gene's perspective there is still a limit to the body's usefulness and hence a limit to the postreproductive life-span of each species. An old person may then be largely an evolutionary oversight, a spacecraft without controls, a sprinter whose course is run. Ironically, it is even possible that the strictly biologic rationale for a postreproductive life-span among humans is quickly disappearing, since old people are no longer the prime repositories of gene-perpetuating information. That function is now being supplanted by books, microfilm, and computer tapes. Among certain nontechnological people, the elderly still retain this crucial role, and as we shall see in chapters 11 and 12, this contributes greatly to their status and welfare. In modernized societies, by contrast, things have changed—and accordingly, so have the structure of these societies and the respect accorded old age. Fortunately, however, our genes don't seem to have noticed . . . yet.

On the other hand, we have begun noticing our genes. Or rather, the role of genes in aging is becoming undeniable. For example, an eighteen-year-old dog is very, very old, whereas an eighteen-year-old human is likely to be just entering college. Genetic factors are more clear, however, when comparing individuals of the same species. For example, among laboratory mice of the strain known as AKR/J, the average life-span is only about 276 days. By contrast, a mouse whose parents were both of the lineage LP/J will live on the average 800 days, nearly three times as long as its short-lived counterpart.

For human beings, perhaps the best advice for anyone wishing to live for a long time is to choose long-lived parents! Witness the findings of Alexander Graham Bell, who, in addition to inventing the telephone, was an amateur genealogist. In 1918 he examined the descendants of one William Hyde, who had lived several centuries before. All told, Bell reviewed the age at death of 2,200 men and 1,800 women, all traceable to the prolific Mr. Hyde. Bell classified the parents of each individual as to their age at death: under sixty, sixty to eighty, and over eighty, looking for possible correlations between the parents' age at death and that of their children. The results were striking: individuals whose parents both lived past eighty generally lived more than twenty years longer than those whose parents both died before sixty. When the parents' survival was intermediate, so was their children's. Interestingly, neither the father's nor the mother's longevity seemed to be more important in influencing the longevity of the offspring.

Obviously, genes are not operating alone here. A household in which both parents die young is more likely to be one with poor nutrition and hygiene, perhaps less education and less access to medical care. So it is not at all surprising that children of such families also die young. For our purposes, however, the important point is that there is some correlation between the longevity of parents and their children, even when socioeconomic differences are accounted for. No one claims that genes determine longevity; simply that they influence it.

For example, a comparison of identical and fraternal twins is quite revealing. (Identical twins have developed from the same fertilized egg; hence, they are genetically identical. Fraternal twins, by contrast, were born simultaneously but developed from different eggs and sperm, and hence are no more genetically related than any other full siblings.) Among identical twins, men were found to die within about four years of each other, and women, within two years. Fraternal twins, on the other hand, died on the average nine years apart (men) and seven years apart (women).

Despite this convincing evidence, it is probably misleading to speak of genes "for" longevity. There probably are no such things. Rather, there may be simply a relative absence of genes which result in premature death. Thus, even the early-dying mice described earlier did not show signs of senescence before their untimely death; 90 percent of them died of leukemia, not "old age." Among human beings, the longevity of your parents has virtually no effect on your likely longevity once you have passed about sixty years. By this age, "bad" genes have had a chance to reveal themselves, and furthermore, as time goes by, genetic differences among individuals seem to be more and more overwhelmed by the accumulated effects of a long lifetime of experiences.

Like so many other topics in aging, the final story of genes, evolution, and why we grow old remains to be written. Samuel Butler once pointed out that a chicken is only an egg's way of making more eggs. Modern biologists have improved only slightly on this, substituting "gene" for "egg." Our bodies are merely fragile skin-covered structures that temporarily house our potentially immortal genes. The longer this house is in good repair, the longer we live. In one way or another, we get older, although our genes do not. Surprisingly, though, *how* we age, and even *why* we age, depend heavily on what sort of bargain we strike between our bodies and our genes.

❧

One of Murphy's Laws has it that if anything can go wrong, it will. We should add, however, that this is true only if we wait long enough. This is the inverse of the famous analogy involving monkeys and typewriters: if enough monkeys were allowed to type on enough typewriters for enough time, they would eventually produce all the world's literature. Of course, in the process, they would also produce a hell of a lot of nonsense. It's all very well to wait for a baboon to write *Hamlet*, but if our health and survival depend on a more or less error-free manuscript, we had better rely on a skilled typist; otherwise our well-being is threatened. Each new mistake will compound our problems. This is the conceptual basis for one of the major theories of aging: error theory.

Leo Szilard was a great nuclear physicist who was also deeply troubled over the dangers of nuclear war and wrote the popular *Voice of the Dolphins*. In addition, in 1959 Szilard proposed that aging may be due to the accumulated effects of cosmic rays striking the nuclei of cells. These "unlucky hits" would injure the cells. Furthermore, the longer the cells existed and were potential targets, the larger the number of cells affected. Like an error-free manuscript in the hands of a baboon, each cell is at risk of being injured. The longer the exposure, the greater the risk. Eventually, when too many words have been mutilated by random errors, the manuscript becomes illegible. Similarly, the living organism deteriorates. It becomes old.

We all receive a certain level of normal background radiation. In Szilard's view, this alone may explain the gradual breakdown in body efficiency that we call aging. Exposure to additional radiation may hasten the process, but here the evidence is inconclusive. As it happens, human beings are more sensitive to radiation damage than are mice, for example, although we still live longer than mice. In fact, the shorter an animal's life-span, the less sensitive it is to radiation. One-celled animals known as paramecia are hardly affected at all (that is, their longevity is not significantly reduced by exposure to excess radiation). Fruit flies are more affected than paramecia, but less than goldfish, which in turn are more resistant than mice. It remains to be seen, of course, whether radiation "hits" are similar to normal "hits" that occur during aging. In fact, it is at least possible that such hits are responsible for what we identify as aging itself.

The Nobel Prize–winning Australian immunologist Macfarlane Burnet has called biologists' attention to a rare disease, xeroderma pigmentosum. This genetically caused illness produces a peculiar skin condition in which the sufferer is extraordinarily sensitive to ultraviolet radiation, normally present in sunlight. Persons with this disease develop skin mutations, severe and pathological freckling, and a very high frequency of skin cancers, from even a very brief exposure to the sun. As a result, persons suffering from xeroderma pigmentosum must remain indoors if at all possible. When exposure to sunlight is unavoidable, they must carefully wrap every square inch of their body to protect themselves from its lethal effects.

This rare disease is caused by a genetic defect that prevents repair of DNA, the genetic material within the nucleus of a cell. Apparently, our DNA is often damaged, particularly by radiation of different sorts, simply as we go about our daily lives. Normally, such damage is not severe; in fact, it is not even noticed, since minor breaks in our DNA are typically repaired almost as soon as they occur. Hence, the importance of xeroderma pigmentosum, since it is only when a defect prevents the normal DNA repair process that we can clearly see how important its normal functioning actually is. Significantly, a body's capacity to repair DNA does seem to correlate with life-span, at least in seven different species in which it has been evaluated. Furthermore, cells from long-lived organisms (such as human beings) perform more DNA repair after being exposed to ultraviolet radiation than do cells from short-lived animals (such as fruit flies). This suggests that long-lived animals have been selected, through evolution, for a well-developed repair capability. The longer the life-span, the greater the exposure to radiation and potentially "unlucky hits." Hence, the greater the need to repair any errors.

According to this version of the error theory, an old person is very much like a leaky battleship. He has sustained many hits from errant cosmic rays, ultraviolet rays, and radioactive particles. His repair capacity has been strained to its limit. Everyone is bailing. Eventually, however, he becomes just too riddled with leaks to remain afloat.

Despite its logic, the theory described above has its problems. In particular, the rate of errors induced by such unlucky hits (that is, mutations) seems to be too low to account for aging. Furthermore, in normal people, the DNA repair process is really very efficient and does not seem to decline with age. Finally, mutations of this sort affect primarily the rapidly dividing cells of the body—skin and the lining of the digestive system—whereas aging effects are most pronounced in the body's nondividing cells: muscle, nerve, and to a lesser extent the inner structure of the adult kidney.

A more likely possibility was first suggested in 1963 by Leslie Orgel. He proposed that errors may well be profoundly involved in aging, but that instead of residing in the DNA, perhaps the errors accumulate in the RNA, the complex messenger molecules that convey the DNA code to the rest of the cell. After all, unlike DNA, which is actually quite stable by comparison, RNA lasts only about eight or nine days. Errors in these messenger molecules would cause incorrect information to be transferred from the DNA to the cell's basic protein-building machinery. Furthermore, RNA carries the specification for the particular proteins known as enzymes, which in turn act as templates and stimulants for the production of most of a cell's chemicals. Therefore, errors in the RNA message would produce erroneous enzymes which could quickly foul up a cell. According to Orgel's theory, "error catastrophes" of this sort could develop quickly, and permanently incapacitate a cell. Becoming older, then, means to become more ramshackle, carrying an ever greater load of mistakes, like the ancient mariner with an unseen biochemical albatross which grows heavier all the time.

It may seem unfair that we must pay for the submolecular mistakes of our cells. But, in doing so, we are no different from the rest of life, and even the nonliving universe as well. One of the world's great truths is that time brings disorder to all things—this, of course, is known to physicists as the second law of thermodynamics. Even stars get old; our own sun has a life-span of about 10 billion years, which means that it has "only" 5½ billion left to go before it has used up its hydrogen fuel. On the other hand, we not only have a shorter life-span than stars, we also are much more fussy about our internal structure. We cannot tolerate many errors if we are to continue functioning. And regrettably, errors may be as unavoidable as the passage of time itself.

✖

Oliver Wendell Holmes once wrote: "We must be born again, atom by atom, from hour to hour, or perish all at once beyond repair." The world is a dangerous place. Just by living in it, we subject ourselves to biological abuses and insults. Over time, these accumulate and may cause the physical deterioration that we identify as aging. In capsule form, this is the "wear and tear" theory of aging.*

On the surface, it is plausible. If we examine the statistics of human survival, we find a pattern similar to the survival of television sets, typewriters, or dishwashers. After a brief period of relatively high-risk infant mortality, young ones do well and are abundant, but the older they get, the more they break down until eventually they die and wind up in a junkyard—or a graveyard. Things simply wear out as they get older. Moreover, the longer they exist (the longer we live), the greater the likelihood that a serious accident may occur. Existence may be hazardous to our health.

Even oxygen, it turns out, is toxic. In high doses it can be lethal and even in low normal doses it combines steadily with

* Holmes also wrote "The Deacon's Masterpiece, or, The Wonderful 'One-Hoss Shay,' " a marvelous poem about a carriage constructed out of only the most perfect components. It ran "one hundred years to the day, and then of a sudden" it turned to dust. Since it had no weakness, no part gave out first, but rather it fell apart all together "just as bubbles do when they burst."

fatty acids within our bodies, denaturing our proteins and rendering them nonfunctional. If oxygen, so necessary to life, is also ultimately destructive of it, how easy it is to imagine the destructive components of just about everything else! Maybe living simply wears us out, each of us becoming living museums of all our past accidents and abuses. As our bodies contain less and less that is still intact, we seem to get older and older. In fact, we *are* older and older, and the longer we live the more ills befall us. Eventually, there is too little left unharmed to function properly. We have become old.

Morris Rockstein, of the University of Miami Medical School, has found that males of the common housefly live an average of seventeen days. From day one, their wings become more and more tattered and torn; this is easily noticeable by day six. By seventeen days, almost no males can fly. Furthermore, the wing muscles gradually lose power even before the wings become frayed. Do male flies simply batter themselves to death? Perhaps: if the wings are removed, muscle degeneration is delayed, but not prevented. An interesting finding, however, is that female houseflies live significantly longer than males—an average of twenty-nine days compared to the males' seventeen. Some hearty muscid matrons (about one in one hundred) even live to fifty-five days. It is possible that lady flies fly less than their male counterparts, but the difference hardly seems sufficient to account for the difference in the rate at which the two sexes age. Thus, female flies can often fly right up until the day they die, whereas males are typically grounded within two weeks. The moral is that wear and tear may *contribute* to the incapacitation of male flies, but it certainly isn't sufficient to explain it by itself.

As a general rule, males of most species do not live as long as females. This is true of human beings as well. In a sense, men age faster than women, although the reasons are not clear. Perhaps the extra X chromosome should be implicated in female longevity. This seems unlikely, however, since among birds and butterflies, males still tend to die earlier than females, and among these animals the females are XY, and the males XX, a reversal of the human pattern. One possible reason for the faster aging of males may be their greater aggressiveness and propensity for competition. To some extent, the biology of maleness and femaleness dictates different life strategies: sperm are small, abundant, and cheap to manufacture, whereas eggs are large, scarce, and costly. As a result, males of most species compete vigorously with other males for access to females and their eggs. The classic male style is therefore to live fast, love hard, and die young. It is true of ground squirrels, mountain sheep, and human beings. Because they are more likely to butt heads with each other and with the harsh, competitive world, males are more subject to wear and tear, and to premature aging. It will be interesting to see whether as women achieve social parity, they achieve aging parity as well.

In 1924, the great biologist and statistician Raymond Pearl published a study of human beings that was intended to evaluate the wear and tear hypothesis of aging. He had divided human occupations into five categories, ranging from "no labor" (category 1) to very heavy labor (category 5). According to the wear and tear hypothesis, the heavier the labor, the shorter the lifespan. Not surprisingly, the predicted correlation was not found. Even if it had been, the results hardly would have been conclusive, since people whose occupations involve heavy physical work are also likely to have less money, and therefore less medical care. On the other hand, hard physical labor is not just wearing. It is also exercise, which may convey benefits (especially in postponing or preventing heart disease) that override the costs of additional wear and tear. In fact, if physical effort causes more damage than benefit, then a lot of joggers are greatly deceived!

Another variant on "wear and tear" thinking concerns the phenomenon of stress. The father of stress research is Montreal's Dr. Hans Selye. He has identified three basic stages in the body's response to stress: first comes the alarm reaction, in which resources are mobilized to respond to the stressing agent. Then comes the stage of resistance. Finally, if the stress is prolonged, comes the end stage of exhaustion, which may lead to death. Selye has proposed that the three-stage stress response may correspond roughly to childhood, adulthood, and senescence. Once more, the fit is superficially appealing, but there is no good evidence that accumulated stresses lead to premature aging. For example, numerous studies with laboratory animals have exposed them to doses of tetanus toxin, mustard gas, and other dangerous substances, which result in killing many of the experimental animals. Among the survivors, however, aging is in no way speeded up, despite the enormous stress they have suffered. In fact, the weight of evidence seems to suggest that mild stresses actually prolong life. (Similarly, small amounts of poisons such as insecticides or arsenic increase the life-span of experimental animals.)

There is a lot of redundancy built into our bodies: we can function perfectly well with only one kidney, no gall bladder, and a mere fraction of our liver. Redundancy means duplication, but not necessarily wasteful duplication. We have fall-back systems if our primary ones happen to fail. This may be seen as a blow to the wear and tear theory. On the other hand, it also validates the notion, since presumably we wouldn't have such redundancy built into us, if we didn't need it. Either way we look at it, the exact role of wear, tear, and stress in aging is presently unclear.

❧

Related to the wear and tear theories are a variety of other notions, all concerned with what we might call the "rate of living."

In 1908, Dr. Max Rubner of Munich proposed that all living things have, in effect, a lifetime energy quota. Looking at horses, cows, guinea pigs, and cats, Rubner found that by the time these animals had reached the end of their lives, they had all used up about the same amount of energy, between 30 and 55 million calories per pound of body weight. In fact, it is as though animals have a certain amount of living allotted to them; they can use it up quickly or more slowly. But any way you slice it, the total amount of living remains about the same.

There is some support for this idea. For example, mountain sheep rams that compete successfully with other rams, and therefore acquire a harem of females, do not live as long as others that are less successful in both love and war. A mouse uses energy at about thirty times the human rate, and lives about one thirtieth as long as we do. In general, animals that hibernate are long-lived; one species of bat, for example, is known to live more than 22 years, an extraordinary feat for so small an animal. Similarly, animals that pass part of the hot summer months in aestivation also outlive their counterparts that are active the year around: one species of desert mouse lives about four times longer than its laboratory cousins. The tiny water fleas known as *Daphnia* actually seem to have an allotted number of heartbeats.

If they are raised in warm water, their hearts beat faster than in cold water and they die correspondingly sooner. Raised in cold water, their pulse is slower and they live longer; in fact, the total number of heartbeats experienced during a *Daphnia* lifetime stays remarkably constant.*

There is no reason to think that we are immune from this rate-of-living phenomenon. The metabolic rate of an average woman is 10 percent lower than that of an average man, and women live about 10 percent longer. The U.S. National Aeronautics and Space Administration has been interested in studying the physiology of hibernation in animals, since if manned spacecraft are to reach distant solar systems, it will require a very long trip, during which the occupants would age considerably. In fact, several lifetimes might be necessary. This could possibly be overcome if the spaceship was automated, and the occupants hibernating during the voyage. (This theme has already been played out in several science fiction movies, such as "2001, A Space Odyssey," and "Alien.")

It has even been proposed that the life-span of normal, earthbound people could possibly be extended by judicious cooling, perhaps beginning in middle age. However, experiments thus far (on animals) have not been encouraging. It is true that cooling of cold-blooded animals tends to prolong their life. Invertebrates and reptiles, for example, keep their body temperature the same as their environment. Accordingly, cooling their environment cools them as well; their hearts beat more slowly and they live longer. However, warm-blooded animals maintain a constant internal temperature regardless of their enivronment. Cooling a warm-blooded animal simply makes it expend *more* energy attempting to keep up its temperature. The result: a *shorter* life-span. In summary, there may be good reasons for turning down your household thermostat, but enhancing your longevity isn't one of them.

Nonetheless, if each species is allotted a given number of

---

*This may seem to augur poorly for America's current physical fitness craze, especially among joggers, whose avowed goal is to increase their pulse rates during exercise. On the other hand, one effect of athletic conditioning is a *slowing* of the resting heart rate, since exercise increases cardiovascular efficiency, allowing the heart to get by with less work under normal conditions. So, maybe it all balances out in the end.

heartbeats, or of energy to expend, it does seem that human beings have done very well. For example, as opposed to the 30–55 million calories per pound that Rubner calculated for many other animals, we average about 363 million. Biologist George Sacher of the Argonne National Laboratories in Illinois has pointed out that this seeming irregularity is consistent with another observation: animals with larger brains tend to live longer. More correctly, the greater the ratio of brain weight to body weight, the longer the life-span. Among domestic dogs, for example, it is a curious fact that the small breeds such as cocker spaniels, terriers, and toy poodles live commonly to fifteen or even eighteen years, whereas the very large breeds such as Great Danes, St. Bernards, or Newfoundlands are old at ten and rarely live beyond twelve. These giant breeds certainly do not have smaller brains than their miniature cousins; rather, the ratio of brain size to body size is much smaller, simply because their bodies are so very much larger. In fact, it is remotely possible that the difference in longevity between men and women could also be related to this: men have larger bodies than women, and somewhat larger brains, but their brains have not kept pace, proportionately, with their brawn.

It seems clear that growth and longevity are somehow related. Animals such as fish and many reptiles experience "indeterminate growth," which means that they continue growing as long as they live. By contrast, all mammals—including ourselves— are "determinate" growers: we grow up to a certain point, and then we stop. Interestingly, the big reptiles and fish often attain enormous ages, and it seems reasonable that perhaps something involved in the cessation of growth is also responsible for the onset of aging. Or alternatively, maybe the mechanisms responsible for growth somehow inhibit aging. In any event, it is difficult to imagine an animal or a human that shows signs of aging while it is still growing. Somehow, the two appear to inhibit each other.

Various explanations have been put forward. In 1932, G. P. Bidder suggested in the *British Medical Journal* that among determinate growers such as ourselves, some regulatory substance first stops growth and then progressively blocks other natural systems, leading to aging and eventually death. His own research dealt with flatfish, which are indeterminate growers. Bidder suggested that for animals living in air, like ourselves, gravity establishes physical limits on possible size—unlike the fishes, whose bulk is largely supported by water. Once again, a plausible theory, but so far Bidder's "growth-off, aging-on" substance has not been discovered.

For a related episode in our story, and one of the most puzzling chapters in aging research, let us turn to some skinny rats at Cornell University. During the 1930s, Clive McKay was interested in the idea that overeating was related to life-span. In itself, the proposition is undeniable; obese people, like obese animals, do not live as long as those who maintain a normal weight. They are more likely to die of heart disease, diabetes, or kidney failure. However, these are all causes of *premature* death, and have no apparent bearing on the limits of our species' possible longevity. McKay's experiments, on the other hand, suggested that calorie intake and longevity may be closely connected.

Professor McKay maintained a population of rats on a diet of very few calories. They were given adequate vitamins and minerals, just not enough calories. They had enough food to survive, but barely enough to permit any growth. As a result, by the time normal rats were dying of old age—about two and one-half years—McKay's experimentally starved rats hadn't even grown up. By eighteen months, when normal rats have been fully grown for more than a year, the starved animals were only about one-quarter normal size. In fact, they never achieved full growth, but they did achieve a very long life: nearly twice as long as the "healthy," fully fed individuals.

Thus far, McKay's rats stand out as the only clear-cut demonstration of a procedure that dramatically increases the life-span of a mammal. Ironically, we don't even know *how* it works, but there is no question about *whether* it does. It is at least possible that the key to rat longevity in this case is provided not by the restricted diet in itself, but rather, by the fact that the animals were kept in a state of persistent youth, since they never got large enough to stop growing and hence to start aging.

Is there a direct message here for us? Some people have thought so: for example, H. S. Osgood, McKay's mentor at Cornell, took to eating quantities of washed sand, and later, tiny glass balls, in an effort to satisfy his hunger while reducing his intake of calories. Nonetheless, he died at a normal age. Actually, Osgood's nonlongevity should not surprise us: McKay's rats were put on a restricted diet immediately after weaning, not after having reached full adult size. People who are grossly obese occasionally lose vast amounts of weight by starving themselves. As a result, they almost certainly live longer than they would if they had remained overweight, but there is no evidence that they actually *increase* their life-span beyond the normal, simply by eating less.

Regardless of the mechanism that makes starved rats live longer than their well-fed counterparts, it is at least possible that something similar would occur among human beings as well. Thus far, however, no one has attempted to find out, since the "experiment" would be so brutal as to be unethical. Babies would have to be systematically starved, and the payoff, if any, would not even be known for at least seventy years or so. In addition, early starvation in human beings leads to a variety of severe problems, not the least of which is impeded brain growth and resulting mental retardation. A large price to pay for possibly living a bit longer.

On the other hand, McKay's rats did receive a normal supply of other nutrients, and it is at least possible that something approaching his results could eventually be obtained with human beings, if the right balance of nutrients and calories could be discovered. Today in America, our diet may not be perfectly balanced by the discerning criteria of many nutritionists, but we undeniably are eating more than ever before—and almost certainly, better as well. We are also growing larger, and are doing so faster. The average ten-year-old boy has increased in height by one-half inch per decade. The average fourteen-year-old in 1877 weighed 87 pounds and stood 4'7"; by 1977 the norm was 117 pounds and 5'1". In 1900, fewer than one woman in twenty-five reached 5'7"—now nearly one in five is that tall or taller. These changes are the result of better nutrition, and we have every reason to be proud. Certainly, no one would argue for malnourishment or even undernourishment, and yet it would be profoundly ironic if our abundant food is actually inducing us to grow up so quickly that, in the long run, it threatens our longevity. Significantly perhaps, those well-nourished countries with the lowest infant mortality also tend to have relatively few persons surviving into extreme old age. Are we living too well?

Good and abundant food, available to all, is devoutly to be wished. And yet, we are at least entitled to look askance at the notion that a fat baby is necessarily a healthy baby. In our search for the biology of aging, therefore, we are also obliged to keep looking.

6

The Biology of Aging, Part II

What the Rabbi Could Teach the Blind Men

The following obituary once appeared in the *St. James Gazette* (England) over two hundred years ago:

> March 19, 1754, died in Glamorganshire of mere old age and a gradual decay of nature at 17 years and 2 months, Hopkins Hopkins, the little Welshman, lately shown in London. He never weighed more than 17 pounds, but for three years past no more than 12. The parents have still 6 children left, all of whom in no way differ from other children except one girl of 12 years of age, who weighs 18 pounds and bears upon her all the marks of old age, and in all respects resembles her brother at that age.

This appears to be the first written account of a very rare and extraordinary disease: progeria (literally "early age"). There have been less than a hundred well-described cases of progeria; it apparently is caused by a recessive gene, which means that seemingly normal people may be carriers for the disease. However, it only shows itself when two carriers produce children, and even then the odds are only one in four that any one of their offspring will show the disease. When these very unusual conditions are met, however, the result is dramatic and tragic.

In November 1981, Mickey Hays, a nine-year-old from Hallsville, Texas, went to Disneyland to meet another little boy, eight-year-old Fransie Geringer, from South Africa. Both these children were a bit over three feet tall, weighing about forty pounds. They looked like wizened old men, although they thought like children—young minds encased in prematurely old bodies.

Sufferers of progeria cease growing when just a few years old.

By seven or eight years of age, they already look like little old people: balding, wrinkled, losing teeth, and generally revealing the "decay of nature" first described in the *St. James Gazette.* Progeria patients rarely live beyond twenty years, and by the time they die, they have often been suffering from hardening of the arteries, diabetes, kidney failure, bone weakness—the panoply of ills which most people normally avoid until their sixth, seventh, or eighth decade. A related illness, Werner's syndrome, is twice as common as progeria, but nonetheless still very rare. It resembles progeria, but is somewhat less extreme: Werner's sufferers reach full height at about age thirteen (showing no "growth spurt"); their hair grays at twenty years; cataracts commonly arrive by twenty-five; all the usual concomitants of old age are present by thirty to forty years; and the average age at death is forty-seven.

What can we learn from these two diseases? Perhaps very little, since they are so rare. Nonetheless, sufferers from progeria and Werner's syndrome show a remarkable parallel to "normal" human aging. Therefore, it is tempting to view them as speeded up models of the aging process. It is debatable whether this approach will prove very useful, however, especially since we cannot ethically experiment on Werner's or progeria patients (most of whom incidentally, appear to have normal intellectual functioning). One conclusion seems inescapable, though: like conductors in a great symphony gone awry, genes can orchestrate the speed of human aging. This leads us to one of the most important and productive areas in biological aging research: the theory of "preprogrammed aging."

It is one thing to suggest that we age because of accumulated wear and tear, because we have somehow lived or grown too fast, because we have simply accumulated too many mutations or errors, or because we run out of genetic program or even are sabotaged by Fifth Column genes that act more strongly as we get older. A rather different theoretical and philosophical perspective, however, comes from the notion that there is a direct, preprogrammed limit to our lives—a magic, invisible line which we cannot cross, dictated somewhere, somehow, within ourselves.

Actually, it is well known to biologists that much cell death is preprogrammed and entirely normal. During our own embryologic development, for example, our hands at one point resemble flippers. Then the cells between our digits eventually stop growing and die, leaving us with space between our fingers. Similarly for our rudimentary, primitive "tail" and also for our thymus gland (of which we shall hear more later in this chapter). And it is also known that certain cells—such as those making up our nerves and voluntary muscles—don't reproduce themselves once development is complete. But it had long been thought that other cells that do continue to divide were potentially immortal.

The basis for this belief can be traced back to some classic and influential experiments by Alexis Carrel. Carrel, a French physician, received a Nobel Prize in 1912 for his pioneering work on the surgical transplantation of blood vessels. (In fact, the entire field of vascular surgery owes its existence to Carrel's early efforts.) In 1912, he also joined the staff of the Rockefeller Institute for Medical Research, and during the same year, he began growing heart cells taken from embryonic chickens in his laboratory. This technique, known as tissue culture, involves taking living tissue, predigesting it with the enzyme trypsin (usually taken from hog pancreas), and then growing the free-living cells more or less as one would keep bacteria, on agar plates or in test tubes.

Carrel died in 1944, having first returned to Europe and an unfortunate flirtation with Nazism and the collaborationist French government. His line of chick cells outlived him, however, and were finally terminated back at Rockefeller University in 1946. In his later life, Carrel had claimed that these cells were potentially immortal, and most of the scientific world believed him. That is, until the early 1960s, when studies under the direction of Stanford University microbiologist Leonard Hayflick were published.

Hayflick had attempted to repeat Carrel's demonstration of the "immortal" chick cells. But, unlike his predecessor, Hayflick was especially careful that the chick embryo cells kept in his laboratory received only nutrients and nothing else during their lengthy period of artificial incubation. The result? After doubling themselves about twenty-five times, Hayflick's chick cells stopped dividing and died. Immortality, it seems, was beyond their reach.

Carrel's scientific integrity has never seriously been in doubt. There is no reason to think that he lied when he claimed that isolated cells can live forever. Rather, it seems more likely that when adding serum to nourish his cell cultures, he accidentally, but regularly, added a very small number of fresh cells to the existing ones. So, rather than maintaining an immortal line of cells, Carrel had almost certainly been adding fresh, new ones when he thought he was merely feeding the descendants of his original stock.

Hayflick went on to explore a whole new domain: the average life-span of isolated cells from different species. He found a fair amount of variation from one species to the next, but significantly, not much variation from individual to individual within the same species. (This suggests strongly that the different life-spans of different species reflect at least in part the different genetic preprogramming of aging in those species.) Cells from small, short-lived species such as mice survived in the laboratory for about fifteen or so doublings, before simply running out of steam and dying. But how about human cells?

Cells taken from embryonic human lung tissue survived under laboratory conditions for about fifty doublings. Under normal conditions, that was as far as they would go; after playing out that allotted number of divisions, the cells would simply die. Interestingly, human cells derived from individuals under twenty years would divide about thirty times, whereas those taken from individuals over thirty years would only divide about twenty times. The pattern seemed clear: the longer the cells had already lived, the fewer doublings they had left. Even more striking, cells taken from the skin of a nine-year-old boy suffering from progeria divided only twice before reaching the end of their line.

Early in his research, Hayflick and his colleagues felt that perhaps the death of their experimental cell lines after fifty doublings was due to some form of laboratory error, such as unclean glassware or contamination by viruses. But try as they might, they could not get cells to survive longer than their allotted number of doublings. One simple but elegant experiment provided convincing evidence that each cell does not exceed its fixed number of doublings. This involved culturing a mixture of cells taken from a male donor and from a female. This has the advantage of permitting the experimenter to tell individuals from the two strains apart, since male and female cells have different chromosomes. However, both strains could be grown in the same environment, thereby making sure that differences in their glassware homes didn't account for any differences in their longevity. Best of all, the male and female strains could be chosen so that they differed in number of divisions they had already attained—that is, they were of different ages when the experiment started.

Working with cell biologist W. Wright, Hayflick took "old" male cells that had already undergone forty population doublings and combined them in the same laboratory dish with "young" female cells that had only divided ten times. After allowing time for thirty additional doublings, the researchers then examined the cells. To no one's surprise, they found only female cells. The male cells had dropped out after completing their fifty, leaving their female counterparts in sole possession of the Petrie dish.

The giant Galapagos tortoises of the Galapagos Islands typically outlive human beings (see chapter 7). Cells taken from these animals divided about eighty times, as opposed to the maximum of fifty observed for human embryonic cells. Yet, the pattern is not invariable. For example, although human beings occasionally live beyond one hundred years and have cells that are capable of about fifty doublings, cats rarely live beyond twenty-five years, and yet their cells have ninety doublings available to them. Or, take another case: Cells from the lining of a mouse's tongue can divide between 150 and 560 times. So, the number of cell divisions possible in a laboratory does not necessarily tell the whole story about the number of years available to the living creature from which the cells are taken.

Fifty doublings (for humans) has been called the "Hayflick limit." Our cells can't normally exceed this magic number. Actually, it seems very unlikely that many of our body cells even come close during a lifetime; starting with just one cell, fifty doublings would produce about a liter of living tissue. Given that ratio, imagine the creature that would be produced if each cell in a multimillion cell embryo were to divide fifty times! We would become larger than the largest whales. (Of course, in reality many of our cells do not divide fifty times, and dead cells are constantly being removed from our bodies.)

Even before Hayflick's work, it was known that under certain conditions cells really could keep doubling indefinitely, or at least beyond anyone's ability to count. Paul Ehrlich, discoverer of the "magic bullet" against syphilis, had also isolated a strain of cells from mouse tumors in 1907, and these have been maintained ever since, despite strenuous guarding against contaminating them with new ones. Similarly, cells taken from the cervix (between the vagina and the uterus) of one Helen Lane in 1951 are still maintained in laboratories throughout the country. Known as HeLa cells, they regularly cause tumors when injected into laboratory animals. In fact, many similar cell lines are known, all of which exceed the Hayflick limit. In all these cases, however, the cells are definitely not normal—they often have clear-cut chromosomal mutations and are known as "transformed" cells, not easily distinguished from cancer. Actually, it is not surprising that the only cells known to be free from the usual constraints on their own reproduction are cancer or cancer-like. After all, cancer occurs when cells somehow begin reproducing out of control, thereby threatening the life of the patient.

By treating otherwise normal cells with a cancer-causing monkey virus, these cells can be made immortal. The ironic notion therefore arises that perhaps one way of increasing longevity, or even achieving immortality, would be to produce radical, cancer-like transformation in normal cells within the body of a would-be Methuselah. Intellectually appealing, maybe. But it would be quite a feat to persuade people to follow this perilous route. In fact, at this point, it is even harder—indeed, impossible—to persuade the cells in question that after being transformed, they should work with the body, rather than against it. We simply don't know enough about the control processes operating between cells to seriously contemplate life extension via cell transformation in the foreseeable future.

Despite the suggestive correlations of doubling number with life-span, the fact remains that we all die before our cells reach the Hayflick limit. At the instant we die, regardless of our age at the time, most of our cells are still alive and doing just fine. Minutes, even hours after the patient is legally dead, valiant cells are still carrying on, defending their posts against the advancing night. Death, then, is a failure of certain crucial organ systems in the body—heart and circulation, brain and central control, kidneys and elimination of toxic substances. It is not necessarily a failure of all the body's cells. Similarly, it is an open question whether aging occurs because our cells somehow get old.

Many recent experiments have shown that old cells, transplanted to new hosts, can outlive their donor. For example,

P. L. Krohn has serially transplanted sections of mouse skin from one mouse to another. Then, the same transplanted tissue was again grafted to another host, and so on. A mouse typically dies at two and one-half to three years, and yet Krohn's skin grafts were still going strong five years later. At this point, long after the donor had died, the experiment had to be discontinued, simply because scar tissue had formed around the perimeter after each graft, and eventually the area of transplanted tissue had gotten too small to be transferred any further. Similar studies have been conducted with breast tissue of mice as well. In each case, the findings are consistent: cells can live longer than the body from which they came, although they appear unable to live forever. Presumably, they eventually come up against the preprogrammed Hayflick limit for their species.

It seems that the age of the donor also matters: cells taken from older animals do not survive as long when transplanted as do cells taken from younger animals, although in either case most cells seem capable of surviving longer than is strictly necessary to serve the donor's body. The age of the recipient also seems to matter: cells transferred to young recipients survive longer than cells of the same age transferred to older recipients. So, apparently, the environment experienced by an animal's cells influences their longevity, with younger animals providing a more congenial place to live, grow, and reproduce.

The debility of age, it seems clear, is not due to a body-wide preprogramming of all our cells. But although the exact mechanism is unknown, it seems hard to believe that the preprogrammed life-span of cells is not somehow related to the consistent life-span of each species, ours included.

Hayflick has also shown that human cells, grown in his laboratory, somehow "remember" how many divisions they have experienced, and hence how many they have left. Thus, if cells are deep-frozen for as long as thirteen years after completing, say, forty divisions, and then thawed out, they proceed to run through their remaining ten, and then doggedly insist on dying. What causes the Hayflick limit? No one knows. Perhaps the answer lies in accumulated DNA errors, the gradual buildup of some harmful chemical, or, conversely, maybe the diluting of some important substance, such that new cells are not provisioned adequately.

It seems likely, however, that the monitoring mechanism for

cell life-span resides in the nucleus rather than the cell body. Cells will extrude their nucleus when exposed to a chemical, cytochalasin B. Preliminary experiments suggest that old nuclei, inserted into young cells, result in hybrid cells that divide like an intact old cell. Similarly, young nuclei, inserted into old cells, behave like young cells. In the laboratory, at least, cells apparently get "tired" because of changes in the nucleus, not in the rest of the cell. Consider the would-be saint, whose spirit may be willing but whose flesh is weak: it seems that our cells behave in precisely the opposite way. The cell bodies are willing to keep on dividing past the point that the aged nucleus will allow.

The novelist Thomas Wolfe was obsessed by time, and in his autobiographic novel, *The Web and the Rock,* he wrote about the curious sense in which we mark time even while it marks us: "Time. You hang time up in great bells in a tower, you keep time ticking in a delicate pulse upon your wrist, you imprison time within the small, coiled wafer of a watch, and each man has his own, a separate time." By some means we have yet to grasp, but which nonetheless grasps us with a terrible, inevitable power, our cells also have their own, their separate times.

❧

In the first century A.D. the Roman poet Gaius Manilius remarked, "As soon as we are born we begin to die." Like the weatherman who announces "partly cloudy" when "partly sunny" would be just as accurate, perhaps Gaius was just a pessimist: he could equally have pointed out that as soon as we are born we begin to live. Of course, the effect would have been much less dramatic, and nineteen centuries later we wouldn't be remarking on his prescience.

Hayflick's research has made it clear that our cells *can* age, although it remains an open question whether they actually *do.* The body, of which they are a part, clearly does. Furthermore, blood serum taken from older chicks has been shown to slow the growth rate and reduce the life-span of cells derived from a younger animal. More precisely, cells given serum from a six-week-old donor multiplied themselves about twenty times; from a three-year-old donor, eight times; from a nine-year-old donor, only twice. It seems there really is something in "young blood."

Although this may be the real-life stuff that horror movies are made of, it may eventually be the stuff of major scientific breakthroughs as well. But not yet.

For now, in fact, we are still wondering what makes old cells old, a necessary first step before we can even contemplate asking how we can make them young again, or (more realistically) slow down the rate at which they get old. Hayflick has conducted some interesting experiments designed to probe the innards of old cells, hoping to find out how they may be different from young cells. He used viruses, those tiny living particles that invade cells and reproduce, using the cell's chemical resources as supplies for their own growth. Accordingly, viruses can be used as probes, to evaluate the characteristics of their hosts. Introducing viruses into both old and young cells, Hayflick found no difference in the abilities of viruses to replicate themselves. In fact, they merrily went about making brand-new baby viruses even within cells that were themselves no longer able to replicate.

When viruses invade a cell and reproduce within it, they hijack their host's chemicals and use them to make more viruses. The fact that viruses are able to flourish within otherwise overage and nondividing cells would suggest that these cells have retained the necessary chemicals to make new cells as well. Perhaps the reason they have stopped dividing, then, is not a shortage of necessary raw materials, but rather a change in their central instructions. In other words, maybe cells stop dividing, not because they have to stop, but because somehow they "want to." On the other hand, just because a cell's innards contain the necessary materials for viruses to make more viruses doesn't necessarily mean that the cell could also make more cells, if only it could be persuaded to do so.

Actually, most cells do change with age in a predictable way. As they get older, there is an increase in a substance known as lipofuscin. This so-called aging pigment consists of oblong granules, yellow to brown in color, which accumulate over time. It seems to be a form of cellular garbage, which is produced more quickly than it is collected. Interestingly, lipofuscin deposits build up in a predictable way for each animal species investigated, but not at the same rate from one species to the next. Thus, certain nematodes (roundworms) live twenty-eight days, mice about three years, and human beings rarely over one hundred years; yet cells from twenty-eight-day-old nematodes have about as much lipofuscin as do cells from three-year-old mice, or human centenarians.

This correlation may seem to suggest a straightforward mechanism for cellular aging—during the process of living, perhaps chemical garbage builds up until eventually the cell simply chokes on its own waste products. (Shades of Metchnikoff and his "auto-intoxication.") Indeed, in some cases, lipofuscin deposits occupy fully one-quarter of the volume available to an aged cell. Figure out some way to delay or prevent the buildup of lipofuscin, the argument would go, and you delay or prevent aging. Lipofuscin is produced from lipid-protein complexes— large, compound molecules that are abundant within all cells. Over time, these molecules oxidize. That is, they lose electrons, combine, and become lipofuscin. Vitamin E, by contrast, is an anti-oxidant, which means that it acts to prevent oxidation. Accordingly, the possibility exists that vitamin E, taken judiciously, could delay or prevent the buildup of lipofuscin within aging cells. Other chemicals are also being tested as anti-lipofuscin substances. For example, the drugs isoprinosine and centrophenoxine tend to break up existing deposits of lipofuscin. Using these drugs would be analogous to cleaning up the neighborhood by getting rid of the uncollected garbage, whereas vitamin E would operate by preventing the making of garbage in the first place.

Active research is currently under way to evaluate the effects of these treatments. However, it is difficult to get very enthusiastic about the immediate prospects, because of this simple fact: there is currently no clear evidence that lipofuscin is actually detrimental. It may simply be a harmless by-product of living, something that healthy organisms can easily "work around," just as people can work around a progressive accumulation of space-demanding, useless, but harmless antiques in a small apartment. Nonetheless, the search for anti-lipofuscin agents still continues.

⚕

There are essentially three classes of cells within our bodies. One group, such as those lining the intestine, continue dividing throughout our life. Others don't divide at all; take for example red blood cells, nerve or heart muscle cells. Still others, such as kidney and liver cells, are normally inactive but can begin dividing if need be. The exact reasons are unclear, but it now seems increasingly apparent that the older the cells in this third category, the deeper they go into an inactive state. And when the need arises for them to begin dividing, it becomes more and more difficult for them to wake up and start doing so. Fewer cells respond to the body's call and those that do, take longer getting started.

If we take a slice of tissue from the brain, say, or the heart, and examine it under the microscope, we will not find any cells in the act of dividing (the process known as mitosis). There is no increase in the number of brain or heart cells in our bodies as we get old, and any that are lost cannot be replaced. On the other hand, slices taken from the intestine will reveal a rather high number of dividing cells, and this number does not change substantially with the age of the person. Finally, slices from the kidney or liver reveal dividing cells all right, but fewer and fewer as the individual grows older. Older cells have a lower "mitotic index"; that is, a smaller percentage of cells caught *in flagrante,* in the act of dividing, when examined microscopically.

An advertisement for milk used to chortle, "there's a new you coming every day, every day." For much of our body, this is true, but for other parts, that "new you" arrives quicker for the young than for the old.

Cells that are dividing go through a predictable cycle. First they manufacture copies of their DNA. Then there is a pause. Then they divide. Then another pause. Then they copy their DNA once again, and so on. It has been suggested that what we describe as aging is the result of cells going from a cycling to a noncycling state. This, in turn, could result from a block at one of the pauses in the usual dividing cycle. In old cell cultures, only about 1 percent of the cells may be cycling, whereas in young ones, up to 50 percent. With aging, cells somehow lose the ability to go from the noncycling to the cycling state.

Let's look at this somewhat differently: instead of growing sleepier as they age, perhaps cells become too specialized in their work to be able to enter the division cycle. To some extent, as a cell becomes increasingly specialized to perform in a particular way, it loses flexibility and eventually it can no longer even support itself. A fertilized egg is, in fact, a cell. But it is not highly specialized and differentiated. It divides. Then its two daughter

93

cells also divide. And so on—this process continues very rapidly in the growing embryo until a new living thing made up of many millions of cells is produced. But, of course, a living human being is not a homogeneous thing, composed throughout of the same clay, the same undifferentiated cells. Rather, out of a small number of undifferentiated, rapidly dividing cells, we become a large number of cells, most of which are highly specialized to perform particular functions. We have bone cells, red blood cells, muscle, nerve, gland, and so on. This specialization is necessary for cells to function efficiently: a nerve cell must be long and skinny to conduct impulses from one part of the body to another, bone cells must be able to produce a skeleton, etc. But there is also a cost. Red blood cells gradually fill with mercury, lose their nucleus, and die. A sperm cell is so specifically designed to swim quickly and fertilize an egg that it is essentially nothing but a gene-packed nucleus with a tail; it lacks the cytoplasm of "normal" cells, and consequently sperm age rapidly and die after just a few days.

Among the termites and ants, some species have individuals that are so specialized as soldiers that they can barely look after themselves. In particular, nearly half their body is taken up with enormous, crunching jaws which doubtless strike terror into the hearts of enemies of their colony. But these doughty warriors are so overburdened with the garb of war that they cannot even feed themselves—bits of food must be placed in their mouths by other colony members. Parts of our body may be like this, reaping both the benefits and the liabilities of specialization.

When a cell divides, it becomes two new cells. Hayflick's research has shown that these daughter cells are not strictly new, since they carry with them a "memory" of how many more times they can divide. However, in some cases it is clear that the biological clock is reset with each cell division. Otherwise, how could there still be amoebas, for example? Presumably, amoebas have been around for millions of years. They have divided trillions of times and are still going strong. Each amoeba is, in a sense, millions of years old, or else we must consider that they are somehow born anew at each division. Are amoebas specialized or not? Old or not? At some point it becomes semantics rather than science.

As mentioned earlier, certain cells, such as those making up our nerves and muscles, do not divide. Hence, we might expect them to provide some insights into the aging of cells. At least they ought to be more helpful in our investigation than amoebas, which somehow arise, Phoenix-like, out of the ashes of their last mitosis. But interestingly, the guts of long-lived, nondividing cells, such as neurons and muscle, do not generally show reduced capacities with age. Furthermore, although there are fewer dividing cells in older individuals, there are not necessarily fewer total cells. To some extent, at least, cells seem to die when their body dies. (Recall that most body cells are carried off to the undertaker before they have even come close to approaching their potential Hayflick limit.) This suggests that aging might be due, at least in part, to things going on in the body, but not necessarily in the body's cells. We turn now to some possibilities.

❧

Johan Bjorksten is not exactly a household name, but eventually, it might be. He is a Finnish-born research chemist who has proposed one of the few theories of aging to have met with nearly universal acceptance. Not only that, but his theory also suggests some possible remedies for the aging process.

While working for a camera film company, Bjorksten was struck by the similarity between the "tanning" that happens as film ages and some of the changes that occur in the aging human body. In fact, many nonliving substances age in a similar way. Leather, rubber, paint, plastics, and paper, as well as photographic film—all tend to become tougher, more rigid, brittle, crystalline, and less elastic during the passage of time. These changes are caused largely by an increase in the number of cross-linkages occurring at the level of molecules. Complex molecules often have long strands that are somewhat flexible in their shape. Over time, chemical reactions occur which link these strands together, making the molecules rigid and less able to do their normal work. Bjorksten draws an analogy with employees at an assembly line: if each worker becomes handcuffed to another, eventually all work will grind to a halt.

To understand the cross-linkage theory, it is important to recognize that much of the human body is actually not composed of cells. About 25 percent of us consists of connective tissue, skeleton, and extracellular proteins, especially a substance called collagen. This collagen changes predictably with age, becoming more brittle and less flexible as its molecules form cross-linkages with adjacent molecules. Certain enzymes, called collagenases, digest connective tissue. The ease with which this process occurs is a good measure of the rigidity and amount of cross-linkage of the connective tissue: tough, rigid, linked tissue is harder to digest. Robert Kohn and C. R. Hamlin, working at Cleveland's Case Western Reserve University, examined diaphragm tissue taken from people killed in automobile accidents. Their finding? The older the person, the more indigestible his or her connective tissue. The linking of our connective tissue is a secret ticking of our own internal clocks.

Another type of connective tissue, in addition to collagen, is elastin, prominent in the walls of our arteries. Effective pumping of our blood is not the sole province of the heart. Rather, with each beat, healthy arteries expand, then rebound from the stretch, thereby adding additional force to the blood flow. Elastin is largely responsible for this accessory pumping, and significantly, elastin in young arteries is wavy and continuous, whereas elastin from old arteries is typically frayed, broken, and split. Cross-linkages seem the likely culprit.

Remember lipofuscin, the "aging pigment," and how it increases with age in different species, always peaking among the oldest individuals? Something similar happens with connective tissue cross-linkages as well. For example, the connective tissue of a two-and-one-half-year-old rat is more similar to that of a seventy-five-year-old man than to that of a two-and-one-half-year-old child. Maybe we're also back to something like the rate-of-living hypothesis again.

To some extent, collagen is programmed to link itself together: this is how it functions to produce the extracellular matrix that holds the body in place. A plausible aging scenario, then, calls for collagen to fill the bill admirably as a substance that uses cross-linkages to achieve needed rigidity and firmness. As we get older, however, our collagen just keeps on building up cross-linkages and becoming less and less flexible. Like the Sorcerer's Apprentice, we find ourselves at the mercy of our too-efficient molecules. Furthermore, since this is occurring in older individuals, natural selection would act slowly, if at all, to counter the process (recall Medawar's evolutionary theory). Or maybe we run out of program to control the accumulating cross-linkages.

A single factor such as increasing rigidity of collagen could then have cascading effects on the internal functioning of our bodies. Increased rigidity of tissues would retard the passage of valuable nutrients and hormones, reduce the rate at which dangerous toxins are removed, lead to hardening of the arteries, and thus high blood pressure, reduction in blood supply to the brain, interference in normal kidney function, loss of strength and flexibility of muscles, and so on—the whole chamber of aging horrors.

The many and serious effects of cross-linkages make it all the more important that we identify the factors responsible for producing them in the first place. Denham Harman, a biochemist at the University of Nebraska Medical School, has drawn attention to a group of molecules known as "free radicals." These are unattached chunks of larger molecules, with available electrons. They move about the cell, "like convention delegates, looking for someone to combine with," to use Harman's analogy. Free radicals are generated by radiation, such as the ultraviolet found in sunlight, as well as fallout or leakage from nuclear reactors. They are also produced by the breakdown of normal body chemicals. Among them, polyunsaturated fats seem especially to encourage oxidation and, hence, a free-radical effect. Millions of Americans are today switching from saturated, high-cholesterol animal fats to the unsaturated vegetable varieties hoping to ward off heart attacks. Ironically, by doing so, they may also be hastening the rate at which they age. Sometimes, it seems, you just can't win.

But the situation is more convoluted yet. Professor A. L. Tappel, nutritionist and biochemist at the University of California, Davis, points out that many substances that are high in unsaturated fats are also high in vitamin E; and vitamin E, it turns out, is an effective anti-oxidant. That is, it works to prevent the formation of free radicals and, hence, the cross-linkages of aging. Devotees of vitamin E also claim that it cures sterility, impotence, miscarriage, high blood pressure, diabetes, and diaper rash. These claims just might be valid—at least for diaper rash. In any event, the addition of vitamin E to cells maintained in laboratory culture has reportedly increased the number of doublings to as many as one hundred (compared with the Hayflick limit of fifty).

There is still continuing debate over exactly where cross-link-

97

ages actually occur. Bjorksen claims they also occur within cells, and not just in the extracellular connective tissue. But Robert Kohn, of Case Western Reserve, says no, cross-linkages are only significant between cells, not inside. He points out that we have lots of extra cells, and besides, even if we lost one third of them, we would simply become one-third smaller, not necessarily any older.

A woman, it used to be said, is as old as she looks, and a man, as old as he feels. Today we can discard that worn-out, sexist saying and replace it with a more accurate one: we are as old as our connective tissue.

❧

In looking for the underlying biologic causes of aging, it is wise to distinguish cause from effect. But it is also easier said than done. For example, it is quite possible that cross-linkages are a result of aging rather than a cause. This may also be the case with the transfer of cells from cycling to noncycling condition. Even if we broaden our perspective to include whole organ systems, the same problem arises. For example, it seems clear that changes in the circulatory system occur with aging—hardening of the arteries (atherosclerosis) and high blood pressure (hypertension) among others. It is less clear, however, to what extent these changes are a result of aging, as reflected in the accumulation of connective tissue cross-linkages, and to what extent they cause age-related changes in other systems—such as the kidneys, which are easily damaged by high blood pressure.

The unsatisfying, but probably true answer is that both interpretations are correct. Similarly, the various theories we have discussed so far are not mutually exclusive. For example, theories of preprogrammed aging do not specify the particular mechanism and therefore they can peacefully coexist with other explanations. Cross-linkages may be an incidental result of certain tissue structure, which in turn may retard the elimination of lipofuscin, and all of the above may be hastened by errors either in DNA or in RNA, and/or the rate of metabolism of cells as well as the organisms they constitute. By the time a blind man manages to feel several different parts of the elephant, he can also be expected to feel pretty confused!

Before leaving this exciting but dizzying arena, let's consider two final theories. Both are somewhat more specific than the ones described thus far, and both involve an analysis more at the level of organs than of cells and basic mechanisms. Both are impressive and, like the others, both have their adherents.

As we have seen, cells maintained in the laboratory have shown that they can live and reproduce for a much longer time than is allowed by a person's normal life-span. This has led some scientists to look for aging's master switch at higher levels—in the body rather than in the cells. In such a search, where better to look than the master gland itself, the pituitary? Located at the base of the brain, the pituitary gland produces a very large number of hormones, some of which act directly on the body, and some of which are "releasing factors" that cause other glands to release *their* hormones. Furthermore, as we search for a body-wide key to aging, glands involved with growth seem likely suspects—recall the connection between aging and the cessation of growth, as well as the rate-of-living hypothesis. As it happens, there is a body organ linked to the pituitary that seems to be a natural candidate: the thyroid.

Located in our neck, the thyroid gland responds to chemical prodding from the pituitary by producing its hormone, thyroxin, which is closely bound up with normal growth. For example, individuals with inadequate thyroid function in infancy do not grow normally—they become cretins, mentally retarded dwarves. Furthermore, the thyroid is our main rate-controlling gland: excess of thyroxin produces a "hyperthyroid," jittery, rapidly metabolizing person, while insufficient thyroid inclines a person toward lethargy and obesity. But the connection with aging (if any exists at all) is not so simple. Excess thyroid does not produce earlier growth or more rapid aging. In fact, the reverse correlation seems more likely, and has been recognized for some time: insufficient thyroid leads to graying of the hair, wrinkling of the skin, and other symptoms associated with aging. This deficiency is corrected dramatically by giving thyroxin. But thyroxin seems to hold little promise as an anti-aging drug. For one thing, it is present in seemingly adequate amounts in normal people, regardless of their age. For another, turn of the century attempts to reverse normal aging by administering additional amounts of thyroid hormone simply didn't work. Not only that, but the treatment sometimes killed the patient.

However, there remains at least one additional possibility that might rescue the thyroid from oblivion in aging research. What if bodily aging is partly caused by thyroid insufficiency, not simply because the thyroid gland is not producing thyroxin, but rather because the body becomes progressively less able to utilize it? Enter, once again, the pituitary. The pituitary gland produces a "thyroid stimulating hormone" which causes the thyroid to make thyroxin. Could the pituitary also produce another substance, later in one's life, that prevents the body from using its thyroxin? At least one biologist, Donner Denckla of Roche Laboratories, believes it does. His experiments with rats have shown that when the pituitary is removed and the animals are then given thyroxin, they are somewhat rejuvenated (at least by certain biochemical measures). Presumably, with its pituitary removed, a rat is freed of the blocking hormone, and its body is then able to use thyroxin. Hence, it is rejuvenated.

But don't rush out and have your pituitary excised. The results are only preliminary, and the interpretation controversial. After all, it seems a bad deal to gain only a few youthful-seeming liver enzymes in exchange for a pituitary gland that regulates just about everything else in our body. Nonetheless, it is one of several exciting ideas floating about in aging research these days, even though it is unsettling to think that our own brain might secrete a slow-acting death hormone that, in the long run, does us in.

In addition to the pituitary-thyroid axis, the other major body system implicated as a possible cause of aging is our immune system. Immunity is the body's response to foreign agents, usually either invading organisms, such as viruses or bacteria, or dangerous nonliving chemicals and particles. When we are young, our immune system works very effectively, especially if we are breast-fed and start life with a good dose of our mother's antibodies—chemicals that help confer immunity. But as we age, there are two changes in our immune functions, both of them disadvantageous. The protective function of our immunity declines—that is, we become less effective at both recognizing and responding to invasions of our body. Secondly, there is an increase in our "autoimmune" functioning—that is, we are more and more likely to generate an immune response to our own tissues. In a sense, we become allergic to ourselves. It is an unfortunate combination, and we get hit both ways. At the same time that we become less able to defend ourselves against our enemies, we also become more likely to mistake friends—our own body cells—for foes.

Australian biologist Macfarlane Burnet, whose research in immunology has earned him a Nobel Prize, theorizes that failure of our immune system not only makes life harder for us as we get older, but actually is responsible for many of the body's changes that we label as aging. Atherosclerosis and hypertension, for example, may be autoimmune diseases. Thus, drugs that suppress the immune response (thereby making kidney and heart transplants possible, for example), also increase the life-span of rats, presumably by preventing some of the autoimmune difficulties of elderly animals. However, suppression of the immune system should certainly not be recommended as an aging antidote, since the same individuals who reap the benefits of less autoimmune difficulties must also pay the piper of lessened immune defenses against true enemies, and hence greater susceptibility to disease threats from outside the body. Once again, it seems that we are caught between the frying pan and the fire. Weaken our immune system and we lower the risk that our body will turn against itself, hastening its own aging, but at the cost of rendering us defenseless against outside threats. Or, if we strengthen our immune system to provide protection against invading substances and diseases throughout life, we increase the chances that our hyped-up body defenses will incorrectly be turned against ourselves.

At least one puzzling question remains: Why does our immune system's protective functioning decline with age, and *why* do we increasingly misidentify our own cells as foreigners? We have partial answers, but no more.

The development of our immune system is closely allied to the fate of another gland, the thymus (to be distinguished from the thyroid). Normal children possess a well-developed thymus gland in the upper part of their chest. It typically disappears early in life, around adolescence. Those unfortunate children who lack a thymus also lack immune protection, and are doomed to life in protective spacesuits, which ward off the disease organisms against which their bodies are defenseless. In the rest of us, the thymus gland shrinks and eventually disappears after it has served its immunity-generating function. But the suspicion persists that maybe the swan song of our thymus is also the sunset of our youth and the onset of our aging.

Immunologist Burnet has developed the notion that with age, mutations accumulate in our lymphocytes, the cells that produce antibodies. Accordingly, the antibodies that they produce are likely to be errant—inadequate as disease-fighters, and also perhaps more likely to mistake friend for foe, and hence turn against ourselves. Roy Walford, of the UCLA Medical School, has proposed a somewhat different twist. He points out that as mutations accumulate in the body's cells, our still-healthy lymphocytes may be moved to produce antibodies that once again are misguided, in that they prove dangerous to normal, otherwise healthy cells as well as foreign invaders.

It is interesting that immune theories are also consistent with one of the early, prominent notions of cell aging: the mutation theory of nuclear physicist Leo Szilard. Furthermore, they may also prove compatible with the cross-linkage theory, since the changes induced by cross-linkages could certainly be involved in initiating autoimmunity, if stiffened and cross-linked connective tissue is considered "foreign" by the body's overwary and overstressed defense system. The hasty retreat of our thymus gland may well reflect preprogrammed aging at the cell level, and/or the functioning of our pituitary once again—either by producing a thymus-ridding hormone, or alternatively, by withdrawing some necessary thymus-maintaining hormone.

For some time, Eastern philosophers have emphasized that truth is rarely found in either/or, right/wrong, black/white alternatives. Nonetheless, North Americans have a special fondness for the two-fisted, good guy versus bad guy approach to life. Either you're with us or you're against us, either this is correct or that. Accordingly, the welter of nonexclusive explanations for why we age may prove frustrating. But that's the way life is, and why should aging be any different?

We have just completed a brief expedition into biological gerontology, the field that inquires into the basic processes responsible for aging.* Later chapters will examine aspects of psycho-

---

*Gerontology is the science of aging. As such, it is a broad field, embracing parts of biology, psychology, sociology, history, economics, and other disciplines. Don't confuse it with geriatrics, however, which is a strictly medical specialty that concentrates on elderly persons. Geriatrics is the other side of pediatrics.

102

logical and social gerontology—what happens to our minds and to our place in society as we get older. For now, we must conclude this part of our voyage recognizing that things are always more complicated and less clear-cut than we might wish them. There is an old story about a rabbi who was expected to decide between two alternatives—it applies to theories of aging, as well as to many other things in life: A woman in his congregation complained bitterly to the rabbi about her husband, and the rabbi responded by consoling and supporting her. Shortly afterward, the woman's husband arrived and complained similarly, and convincingly, about his wife. The rabbi also agreed with him. When the man left, the rabbi's wife, who had overheard both conversations, accused him of being dishonest: "They can't *both* be right!" she exclaimed. "You know," answered the rabbi, "You're right too."

7

Of Tortoises and Trees

We are not alone. Other things also age—even nonliving things. Stars pass through a predictable sequence, changing in size, color, and energy output as they use up their store of materials. Mountains also age: the sharp pointy ones, such as America's Rockies, Cascades, and Sierras, are generally young. As mountains age, they become lower, gentler, and more rounded, as they are rubbed and worn by the persistent action of wind and rain. The mountains of eastern North America—the Appalachians, Alleghenies, Adirondacks, and Canada's Laurentians—are old and mature compared with their dizzying western counterparts and the vigorous young ranges of the Andes, Alps, and Himalayas. Just like some people, mountains change over time, becoming more mellow.

Compared to stars or mountains, we never really get very old. But compared to most living things, we actually do quite well. We seem to live longer than any other mammal. Whales rarely exceed fifty years, and the same is true for hippos and rhinos. Horses, cattle, and lions are ancient by forty years, and rarely even reach that age. Cats don't make it beyond thirty, and dogs rarely past twenty. Our one serious competitor among the mammals might be the elephants. They have a twenty-two-month gestation period, as compared to our nine; their final molars do not erupt until about fifty years, whereas human wisdom teeth commonly appear around age twenty. For the elephant, both the gestation period and age at molar eruption are about two and one-half times that of human beings. Does this suggest that they also live two and one-half times as long? Perhaps. An elephant's tusks grow at about three-fourths to one pound per year, and some 250 pounders have been reported! This would indicate three hundred years or so of growing.

On the other hand, few scientists have had the patience (or

longevity) to keep careful records of the growth rates of elephant tusks. Perhaps they grow more rapidly once a certain size has been reached. Furthermore, just as people often delight in lying about their own age (claiming to be either older or younger, depending on the situation), they frequently exaggerate the ages of their animals as well. For example, Princess Alice, the girlfriend of P. T. Barnum's Jumbo, was born in 1784, in captivity; therefore her exact age is known. She reportedly died in 1941, which would have made her 157 years old at the time. Unfortunately, however, she was an African elephant at birth, but an Indian elephant when she died. Either she changed species at some point during her long and eventful life, or, more likely, Mr. Barnum changed elephants. After all, he knew there was a sucker born every minute.

Longevity records are often and easily faked. Several centuries ago, Francis Bacon observed that "touching the length or shortness of life in Beasts, the knowledge which may be had is slender, the observations negligent, the Tradition fabulous." Sadly, things haven't changed very much since Bacon's time.

For example, the giant tortoises of the Galapagos Islands in Ecuador, and those found on Aldabra Island, off the coast of East Africa, undoubtedly live for a very long time. One Aldabra tortoise, captured in 1766 and brought to the island of Mauritius, died after a serious fall in 1918. It seems to have lived an honest 152 years in captivity, and furthermore, since it was already an adult of unknown age when caught, we can only make a minimum estimate. On the other hand, we should always beware the Barnum switcheroo: A Galapagos tortoise named Tui Malila, "the King of Tonga," was supposedly brought from its native island to the island of Tonga (in the Pacific) by Captain Cook, in 1767. Still alive in 1953, it was proudly displayed to the visiting Queen Elizabeth and Prince Philip, and was claimed to be over 186 years old. It appeared venerable enough, with a shell that had been badly scorched in a fire during the previous century. However, disillusion set in when the King of Tonga was examined by Dr. James Oliver, curator of reptiles for the New York Zoological Society: the ancient King turned out to be an Aldabra tortoise from the Indian Ocean, and not a Galapagos tortoise, as it had started out.

Among birds, eagles can live to eighty years, and parrots and certain vultures can even push one hundred, if kept under ideal captive conditions. The absolute animal record (one-celled creatures not included) probably goes to the large, slow-growing fishes that continue growing as long as they live. Of these, Russian sturgeons of caviar fame may reign supreme. A 1,500-pound sturgeon is likely to have survived for two hundred years, and behemoths over 3,000 pounds have been reported.

Most small birds and mammals have rather short life-spans, even if kept under ideal conditions in captivity. Old age sets in typically after two or three years. But even this is an optimistic estimate. Nature is usually not kind to small animals and, in fact, most little birds and mammals never even get a chance to age. Mortality is so high that they nearly always die before revealing any signs of growing old. A heavy toll is exacted by the rigors of finding a safe place to live, withstanding the elements, avoiding diseases, competing with each other, and getting enough food while not becoming food for someone else. Since most small animals live on the knife edge of survival, it takes very little in the way of physical weakness to induce an "early" death.

Of course, species with high and early death rates also have high birth rates, and vice versa. Large animals, such as horses, cows, elephants, hippos, whales, and human beings, can look forward to a much longer life-span, and not surprisingly they reproduce much more slowly. Even so, there are remarkably few documented cases of prolonged old age in animals other than our own species. It may even be that extreme old age is a fairly recent phenomenon for *Homo sapiens* as well, owing largely to our discovery of all those things that have made living easier (and more likely): warm clothing, storage and preservation of food, agriculture, medicine, hygiene, and so forth. If we were still living "in nature," perhaps our lives would also be short, and old age a stranger. Given our novel circumstances, maybe we degenerate with age because our body becomes confused, not being designed to deal with the longevity so recently thrust upon it.

For the undoubted old age champions, however, we must look to the plants rather than the animals. It has been said that lotus seeds, thousands of years old, have sprouted and produced healthy plants. Something like this might be possible, but has yet to be documented. On the other hand, 237-year-old lotus seeds have sprouted, and that is impressive enough. An old seed, however, somehow seems different from an old creature. Still, the title of

World's Oldest Living Thing unquestionably belongs to the plants, probably to a huge, gnarled tree.

The "Tule Tree," a 130-foot giant bald cyprus near Oaxaca, Mexico, is estimated by some to be 5,600 years old. It is duly venerated by local villagers, who haul water to it during the dry season, fearing for its ability to withstand drought in its present condition. In the United States, giant sequoias and redwoods commonly exceed 1,000 years of age, and the ancient bristlecone pines of the White Mountains between Nevada and California have been proven to be older still. At least one is 4,600 years old, verified by radiocarbon dating as well as counting the annual growth rings.

Paradoxically, however, even these ancient beings are not entirely old. In fact, their living cells are actually quite young. The vast bulk of all trees, including the venerable bristlecone pines, is composed of dead cells. Once they lived, but their sole contribution now is to help provide a nonliving skeleton for the living part. That living part, a tiny fraction of the tree's total substance, is composed of cells, none of which are more than thirty years old—younger than most adult North Americans, in fact. So by all means, tip your hat to the bristlecone pine. But save a little respect for yourself.

The whole—the self—can be understood by looking at its parts: genes, cells, glands, and so forth. Clearly, changes in these parts make for changes in the whole, as with aging. But when it comes to human beings, the whole really does seem to be greater than the sum of its parts. In the next three chapters, therefore, we shall explore aging at the level of the individual: body, mind, and sex.

8

Aging and the Individual

Body

Look down on the stump of an old tree. Written in its annual rings is the progress of its life. The same is true of the antlers of elk, the teeth of elephants, and the scales of certain fishes. But we humans are a bit more private. We carry no permanent log of our aging, at least not one that is easily read.

How old are you? Your eyes may be young, but your hair gray. Or vice versa. Wrinkles are frequent, often eloquent reminders of age, but not a reliable measure. The lenses of your eyes get heavier each year, because the cells therein keep on dividing. As a result, aging often brings far-sightedness, since the lenses become less flexible. Could we measure our years, then, by the distance at which we hold the morning newspaper? When the arms grow too short, we need eyeglasses. But if you are near-sighted to begin with, aging may bring a period of acute vision, as the elderly recalcitrant lenses just balance the overeager young corneas. In any case, the status of our lenses is rather an individual affair.

What is our true age, as measured by the body, not the calendar? Is it the average for all our organs (a strong heart being canceled by a weak prostate)? Is it, instead, the weakest link in our physical armamentarium? Or could it be the limiting factor for some important activity (as the kidneys go, so goes the liver, and so on)? What relationship, if any, does all this have to the number of years that have elapsed since our birth?

We are told, over and over, that age equals weakness. The warranty is good for fifty thousand miles or five years, whichever comes first. Unfortunately, there is some wisdom—or at least accuracy—in this verdict. The seventeenth-century playwright

108

Pierre Corneille was the father of French tragedy; he saw aging as the tragedy *par excellence:* "Time delights in insulting the loveliest things." Does time wound all heals?

As Galen pointed out two thousand years ago, aging begins "at the very moment of conception." As young children, we have taste buds on the roof of our mouths, the walls of our throat, and the upper center of our tongues. All these are gone by ten years of age, leaving us with taste buds only on the edge of our tongue and, of course, a gradually diminishing sense of smell. (Could this be why young children are repelled by the highly spiced food that adults often enjoy?)

Infants have accurate hearing up to 40,000 cycles per second, and they may even wince at a dog whistle that the rest of us don't even notice. By adulthood, we cannot register sounds above 20,000 cycles per second, with the ceiling gradually closing in at the rate of about eighty high-frequency cycles per second every six months from age forty on. This process is known as "presbycusis," a progressive failure of the hearing cells in our inner ear. It seems reasonable to attribute it to the body's decline with age: once the warranty has expired, things inevitably begin falling apart. Maybe this is just the way we are made—a function of planned obsolescence—or, alternatively, one of the ills to which flesh is heir. But into this void of sad resignation come the findings of Dr. Sam Rosen, an ear specialist. He spent some time with the Mabaans of Sudan, a group of people who have not yet been reached by the beneficent roar of jack hammers, typewriters, washing machines, and airplanes. Occasionally, a lion's roar or the rumble of distant thunder assaults the Mabaans' ears, but mostly it is quiet. Dr. Rosen found that the Mabaans not only spoke softly, but they also heard extremely well, clearly making out whispers at one hundred yards. Not only was presbycusis virtually absent, but so were appendicitis, ulcers, and bronchial asthma. Furthermore, the Mabaans showed no increase in blood pressure from age ten to ninety. Noise kills hearing cells and hastens deafness. It could also make us old before our time, whatever that time may be.

It is interesting that in most Westernized countries, men lose their hearing more often than women do. Maybe male hearing cells are less robust, or maybe men are more likely to be exposed to job-related loudness. For example, airline pilots appear to become hard of hearing more quickly in their left ear than in their right, because senior-level captains sit on the left side of the cockpit, where their left ear is bombarded with engine noise. Lopsided hearing, then, is a vocational disease among pilots. Operators of heavy machines sometimes consider it unmanly to wear protective earphones; perhaps hardness of hearing will become a "macho" badge of courage in our technologic world.

In any event, and regardless of the immediate cause, old people typically lose accuracy and acuity in their senses. They become more and more isolated from their surroundings, sealed off behind a wall that grows progressively thicker. One aged person commented that growing old was like "living on an island that was steadily shrinking in size."

Once it goes far enough, aging is usually noticeable, especially in someone else. The skin loses its smoothness as subcutaneous fat sinks deeper, making the waist thicker and the face thinner, with folds of unsupported skin forming wrinkles as the body's connective tissue becomes less adroit at holding the underpinnings in place. The earlobes lengthen as elastic tissues give way, and the nose droops ever closer to the chin. The effect is often accentuated by the loss of teeth. From forty-five to eighty-five years, the circumference of a man's chest diminishes by ten centimeters and a woman's by fifteen. The bones lose calcium salts and become more brittle, resulting in "osteoporosis." If we fall when we are young, we bounce; when old, we break. Osteoporosis is responsible annually for 190,000 hip fractures, 180,000 vertebral fractures, and 90,000 broken forearms in the United States alone. Losing the battle against gravity becomes increasingly costly the older we get. Interestingly, women suffer more from this condition than do men, probably because they enter the fray with less bone mass. (Female sex hormone may inhibit the loss of bone calcium; this is currently being investigated.)

Arteriosclerosis is a general term for hardening of the arteries. *Athero*sclerosis is, technically, a form of arteriosclerosis, in which arteries lose their resilience because of changes occurring in their inner lining. A combination of fats (especially cholesterol, or so it seems), connective tissue, and calcium deposits leads to the formation of atherosclerotic "plaques" which rob arteries of their usual—and youthful—flexibility. The arteries carry blood away from the heart; hence, they must contain a liquid pumped under great pressure. As we saw earlier in discussing "elastins," the heart alone is not responsible for the force with which blood circulates; with each pump of the powerful ventricles, blood surges from the heart into the arteries, causing their walls to stretch under the force. Then, the elastic arterial walls contract, regaining their former shape and making their own contribution to the blood's movement. So, our flexible arteries store the energy of each heartbeat and pass it along, only slightly diminished, to the rest of the body. However, as our arteries lose flexibility, they contribute less and less to the blood's passage, so that the heart's efforts are dissipated more quickly. Something must make up the difference. The result is an increase in blood pressure—i.e., the heart pumps harder to keep the blood flowing. This is not only dangerous in itself, since it could damage sensitive tissues in the kidneys and elsewhere, but also results in greater strain on the heart.

In addition, accumulated atherosclerotic plaques could block a coronary artery, resulting in a "myocardial infarction"—a heart attack, or "coronary," in which part of the heart muscle dies from lack of blood. Furthermore, pieces of plaque could break off and float away downstream, or the mere presence of uneven, irritating plaques could stimulate the clotting of blood. Globs of clot or plaque (each one a "thrombus"), broken off and floating freely, may then lodge in some narrower blood vessel, causing the pain of phlebitis, if blocking an arm or leg, or a stroke, if blocking flow to the brain. Not a pretty picture.

Although hardening of the arteries is thought to be largely a problem of the aged, it—like aging itself—begins in the young. Postmortems of Korean War soldiers showed pronounced atherosclerotic arteries in eighteen- to twenty-year-olds. Is it a product of aging, and hence normal when it appears in the elderly, but a "disease" when it emerges in youth? In a recent study of 700 elderly persons, 27 were found to have no hardening of the arteries and no hypertension. Were they abnormal, while the other 673 were showing the "normal" signs of aging?

Cancer, diabetes, and pneumonia are also scourges of old age. Even in the young, diabetes produces many changes that are remarkably similar to aging—earlier onset of atherosclerosis, early stiffening of arteries, lungs, and joints. The cells of diabetics, grown in tissue culture, fail to thrive and will stop reproducing earlier than similar tissue taken from healthy subjects. Pneumonia, for its part, is not a single disease, but many. It is a generic term for any disease that involves serious interference with

111

normal lung function; there are many pneumonias, therefore, caused by bacteria (these are easiest to treat), viruses, or simply by the inhalation of some partly-chewed food. The lungs, normally light and airy, resemble a squeezable and only slightly moist sponge. When stricken with pneumonia, they become heavy and waterlogged, no longer able to exchange oxygen and carbon dioxide. Often innocuous in the young, pneumonias turn killers among the old. Unlike pneumonias, and unknown to many people, the incidence of most cancers actually declines in old age. If you have escaped cancer by age eighty or so, there is a pretty good chance that you are home free; or at least you will probably die of something else. The notable exception is cancer of the large intestine, which increases dramatically in old age, just as other cancers are declining. In fact, the increase is so precipitous, it is tempting to conclude that if we lived "forever" we would all die of colonic cancer.

Then, of course, there is the dreaded prostate: Scylla and Charybdis, two lobes guarding a narrow but very precious strait. With age, they often enlarge and harden, so that navigation is free no more. The satisfying, bladder-emptying sluice becomes a frequent but frustrating and petulant trickle. The cure is simple enough, however; exorcise Scylla and Charybdis, and the waterway is free once more.

❧

Let us turn now from disease to health. Or if not health, then at least the absence of disease. If disease is avoided, what does aging have in store for our bodies?

The timing of events is more predictable early in life than later. We know with some confidence when an infant will begin to smile, to reach for objects, cry at strangers, to walk, talk, be toilet-trained, and get teeth, both baby and adult. In each case, of course, there is variation from child to child, but the difference is typically one of months, rarely more than a year. Even adolescence is predictable, although admittedly, adolescents often are not.

We are much more stubbornly individualistic when it comes to the other side of our life. Some of us never turn gray; others are white by thirty. An octogenarian may have all his teeth; another, a full set of dentures. Satchel Paige was playing professional baseball at fifty, more than ten years after most are considered over the hill. Some people get arthritis, some don't. Unlike the Deacon's Masterpiece, Oliver Wendell Holmes' famous "One-Hoss Shay," our pieces don't fall apart at the same time, and furthermore no two of us age in the same way or at the same rate.

Certain consistent changes do occur, however, especially if we look at enough individual cases to speak in statistical generalities. Some time in their forties or early fifties, women cease ovulating and menstruating. In most cases, the last period is less eagerly awaited than the first, but it is no less likely to happen. After a disruptive time which may include "hot flashes" and perhaps some brief mood swings, things settle down again, the only real difference being that both the tampons and the contraceptives can finally be discarded. The evolutionary wisdom might be this: now that you are old enough to be a grandmother, albeit a young one, you can probably do more for the survival of your descendants by grandmothering than by mothering. Therefore, nature intervenes. (Of course, our cultural evolution has been outracing our biological evolution for quite some time. As a result, menopausal women often live separate from their adult children, and grandmothering may be the last thing grandma has in mind.)

Men don't go through anything like the abrupt physical changes of menopause, despite much claptrap about the "male menopause." However, there are many changes that are shared by both sexes.

Measured by ability to turn a crank, 60 percent less work can be done at age eighty, than at thirty-five. Strength of hand-grip declines by half during the same period. Significantly less blood is pumped in every emptying of the heart. If radioactive dye is injected into the arm of a twenty-year-old, it will be detected by a Geiger counter at the chest in about twenty seconds. The same procedure in a sixty-year-old will take about three times as long. A seventy-five-year-old breathes less than one half as much air as a twenty-year-old. Furthermore, oxygen exchange is less efficient—an eighty-year-old must breathe three times as hard to do the same amount of work as a twenty-year-old. Kidney function is also markedly reduced among the elderly.

Gerontologist Nathan Shock has pointed out that single systems don't decline as rapidly with age as do complex, integrated responses. Essentially, when it comes to the aging body, the decline of the whole is greater than the decline of its parts. Thus, for example, ability to do work drops off more rapidly than does the rate of nerve conduction, cardiac output, or the production of liver enzymes.

Although the details vary, all things break down over time, unless enough energy is put into them to maintain the high level of organization that distinguishes most objects from their relatively disorganized surroundings. Indeed, the world is made up of stuff, some of which is more organized and some less. Garbage piles are pretty unorganized; books—most books!—are quite organized, by contrast. *Within* each garbage pile, however, there is quite a bit of individually organized stuff: an orange peel, a tin can, a discarded newspaper. Most organized of all is the rat or crow who nibbles there. Living things, such as rats or crows, are very nonrandom, and one of the basic rules of nature, the second law of thermodynamics, is that nature abhors order. It is a variant of Murphy's Law: Whatever can become disordered, will. Just wait; all we need is time. Even as the rat gnaws at his meal, something else gnaws at the rat: time, inexorable time, with its insistence on disorganizing, on turning the special and nonrandom back into the not-so-special and random whence it came. Eventually, it succeeds; the rat succumbs to time and disorganization. Its entropy increases and it ceases to be an organized, living thing.

The life of every living thing is a battle against the forces of disorganization. The assaults are daily; indeed, they occur from minute to minute, second to second. Therefore, a major part of our functioning as living things is directed toward countering these forces of disorder. Much of the business of staying alive is our striving to retain our body integrity, the very special, nonrandom aggregation that is *us*. If it is too hot outside, we must cool down; if too cold, heat up. When our internal chemicals become too acid, we must release a little alkali; or vice versa. Too much carbon dioxide, not enough oxygen? Breathe in. Oops, breathe out now. Now in again. All this to keep our environment livable—our internal environment, that is. Long before any of us realized it, we were all environmentalists, keeping our bodies highly organized and as pollution-free as possible. This is accomplished by a complex, integrated series of internal thermostats, which keep our insides, like our homes, within a narrow limit of acceptability. It may get hot or cold outside, but as long as we are alive, we stay snug, warm, and pretty much unchanging inside.

As we age, unfortunately, our ability to self-regulate in this way begins to decline. Old people are especially subject to death from overheating, as well as underheating. Their bodies don't thermoregulate like they used to. The kidneys are less able to maintain the ideal salt balance, and too much or too little in the diet can have serious consequences. One candy bar too many can exceed the ability of the pancreas to produce insulin, and a normal person then suddenly can be mistaken for a diabetic. When old and young rats are stressed by forcing them to breathe air with insufficient oxygen, and their cells are then examined under an electron microscope, the young rats appear normal, whereas in the old rats, the mitochondria—the energy-producing parts of the cell—are swollen and broken. When the going gets tough, old rats have more difficulty keeping things going. The response to stress, we are told, often separates the mice from the men. Also, the young from the old.

❧

How hard and painful are the last days of an aged man! He grows weaker every day; his eyes become dim, his ears deaf; his strength fades; his heart knows peace no longer; his mouth falls silent and he speaks no word. The power of his mind lessens and today he cannot remember what yesterday was like. All his bones hurt. Those things which not long ago were done with pleasure are painful now; and taste vanishes. Old age is the worst of misfortunes that can afflict a man.

(Ptah-hotep, Egyptian philosopher and poet, 2500 B.C.)

Some things don't seem to have changed very much. If one were to write a paean to old age—which this is not—it would probably be best to confine the discussion to poetry, political power, perspective, and peace. The physical body would strike a sour note, just as it did in Ptah-hotep's day.

And yet, we are learning enough to make things better. For example, we now know that much of the reduced physical capacity that comes with aging is due to simple inactivity. In fact, being too sedentary may be a serious condition, "hypokinetic disease," likely to produce further complications. Three weeks of bed rest, for example, will have the following effect on a young, healthy man: maximum cardiac output down 26 percent; lung

115

capacity down 30 percent; oxygen consumption down 30 percent; even the amount of body tissue down 1.5 percent. Osteoporosis, the bone-weakening scourge of old age, is greatly hastened if we keep off our bones. When it comes to improvement via exercise, the elderly have as much to gain as the young; they can profit at least as much from an organized exercise plan. Of course, old people typically start from a somewhat lower level of initial performance, but they are capable of improvement with exercise that is proportionately as great as for other age groups. Such activities as walking, jogging, and swimming are better than isometrics, since it is difficult to force blood through contracted immobile muscles, whereas complete movements facilitate blood flow and improve nearly all measurable aspects of body condition.

An otherwise healthy young man can have an aged body, and vice versa, depending especially upon exercise, smoking, and obesity. Physical fitness researcher Thomas Cureton studied one hundred men aged twenty-five to thirty-five. He found that twenty-five-year-olds who were 50 percent overweight had the heart, lung, strength, and exercise capacities of a fifty-year-old. Does it work the other way as well? Do old people who exercise regularly and well get to sip from the fountain of youth? Perhaps: take Noel Johnson, a retired shop supervisor who, at sixty-nine, couldn't walk one mile, had a touch of heart trouble, and, not surprisingly, felt out of shape. He entered an exercise program designed for older people and was eventually running 150 miles per month and lost forty pounds. In July 1971, he won three gold medals at the American Athletic Union's masters track meet in San Diego and was named the outstanding senior athlete. In some ways at least, Mr. Johnson grew younger.

Nonetheless, time passes, and in the long run nothing can be done about it. We can sensibly try to ease the burden, to strengthen the scaffolding on which the weight of years will be hung. But eventually, the weight becomes too great. The structure buckles and it all comes down. After age forty, even if we watch our diet, don't smoke, and get exercise, our body functions gradually diminish. Curiously, despite the gradual, almost imperceptible nature of this process, the human death rate increases very abruptly, doubling about every eight years beyond age forty. This relationship, first described by statistician Benjamin Gompertz more than a century ago, remains true despite modern medicine. It also remains unexplained. Why is the change in our longevity so much more drastic than the change in caliber of our bodies? A likely possibility is that staying alive is not entirely a gradual, continuous affair; rather, we must surmount a series of discrete hurdles: a bout with pneumonia, running to a bus without overstressing the heart, keeping warm enough or cool enough, and so on. A gradual decline in any one trait—kidney function, for instance, or cardiac output—could then provide the weak link that breaks and trips us up at the next hurdle.

In the face of all this, we have little alternative than to shore up our weaknesses as they appear or, better yet, try to anticipate them and take early corrective action. Failing this, we can heed the words of W. B. Yeats:

An aged man is but a paltry thing,
A tattered coat upon a stick, unless
Soul clap its hands and sing, and louder sing
For every tatter in its mortal dress,

One answer to the plight of aging, then, is for our souls to wax as our bodies wane. The aged Yeats yearned to be gathered "into the artifice of eternity" where he might sing forever "of what is past, or passing, or to come." But for the rest of us, it might bring some comfort to sew up a few of the tatters in our mortal dress, and let eternity take care of itself.

But caring for one's tatters cannot be accomplished alone. The elderly must receive help: from themselves, from the rest of society, from the medical profession in particular. A lesson can be learned from the 101-year-old man whose leg hurt. His doctor's response: "What do you expect at your age?" To which the old man replied, "My left leg is the same age as the right, yet *it* doesn't hurt!" The point is, elderly patients have a right to good, compassionate care, which some doctors unconsciously resist, perhaps because the infirm elderly may remind them of their own mortality, as well as possibly reduce their personal feelings of omnipotence—for very old patients are more likely to die than young ones.

The 12 July 1979 issue of the *New England Journal of Medicine* (North America's premier medical publication) reported the case of an eighty-year-old patient with a heart defect. The final recommendation was for surgery to replace a faulty aortic valve. Shortly after, a letter appeared in that same journal, from a physician who was "appalled" by the case. The letter-writer complained, "It is unthinkable that a person who has lived a good life-span and who is nearing the end of that span for fairly obvious reasons should be subjected to invasive procedures that produce nothing but further discomfort to the patient at great expense." (I would like to think that this good doctor's association with Blue Shield is purely coincidental to his worries.)

The letter was answered by the patient's doctor: ". . . there are patients in their 70's and even 80's who are vigorous and will not tolerate severe limitation by their disease, or who, as in this case, have intolerable symptoms despite full medical therapy. . . . We have seen a considerable number of superb results from valve-replacement operations in the age group in question, often followed by many years of happy and productive life. To deny surgical therapy on the basis of age alone would seem indefensible to me, for humanitarian reasons and on the basis of substantial medical experience."

୬୧

So much for our bodies, susceptible as they are to breakdown—and to repair. What about our minds, the special, hidden places where each individual privately dwells?

9

Aging and the Individual

Mind

We can look with some detachment at a new wrinkle above our eyebrows or another gray hair. We can even suffer amputation of a limb, excision of an uncooperative prostate, or surgical replacement of a faulty blood vessel—all without necessarily feeling that *we* have been changed. Wherever *we* live, it is not in our skin, our hair, or our plumbing. The "I" inside may even look on with curiosity and surprise, as though it is all happening to someone else, perhaps some uninhabited body—one that stubbornly goes its own way on occasion.

But our mind is different. As it changes, we change. In this chapter, we shall take a brief look at what happens to mind and brain as aging proceeds.

I am a very foolish, fond old man
Fourscore and upward, not an hour more or less
And, to deal plainly,
I fear I am not in my perfect mind.

(Shakespeare, *King Lear*)

We all know the ugly word: "senile." Too old, and therefore no longer mentally competent. Let an old person be quarrelsome, or show some temporary lapse in memory, and the accusation is quickly raised: aunt Bertha has grown senile. And not surprisingly, one of the greatest fears of the older person is, "Am I growing senile?" For those not yet old, the question becomes, "Will I?"

As people grow older, they are at greater risk for developing some form of psychological impairment, but the chances are low

119

that the impairment will be drastic. In fact, the term "senile" has been so misunderstood, so overused and under-useful, that it had best be abandoned.

Many psychiatrists identify two basic classes of severe psychological pathology: functional and organic. The functional pathologies include those disorders for which no clear underlying biological cause can be identified; organic pathologies, by contrast, have an identifiable cause, somewhere in the physiology and/or anatomy of the sufferer's brain.

A big problem is depression, which can be either functional or organic. For example, it may be caused by biochemical imbalance, that is, organically. When this is the case, it can often be corrected by appropriate chemicals, such as the tri-cyclic drugs, or possibly another group known as MAO inhibitors. The person suffering from presumed depression is in good company: King Saul, George Washington, Napoleon, Edgar Allan Poe, Abraham Lincoln, Dostoevsky, and Winston Churchill were all fellow sufferers. Depression commonly results in feelings of profound hopelessness and helplessness, a sense of being alone and isolated, with no hope for the future, no interest in the present, weight loss, fatigue, and sleeplessness. Although people of any age can suffer from depression, it is especially common among the elderly, and when it is not organic, it is functional.

Some depression makes sense. In fact, it is entirely possible that the high incidence of depression among the elderly does not say anything about the biologic effects of age *per se,* but rather about the reality of being old: quite simply, old age can be frustrating and demoralizing. The old person often experiences a decline in his physical powers, a decline in his social role, a loss of loved ones, and in addition a further likelihood of biochemical problems. For these reasons, old people are particularly susceptible to depression. The accumulation of depressing experiences can certainly make anyone unhappy, and may possibly predispose the elderly to clinical depression as well. Even if it has no organic side, depression—at least a mild case of it—may thus be an understandable response by anyone, regardless of age, to the problems encountered by the elderly.

Aristotle recognized this when he wrote of the aged, "They lack confidence in the future, partly through experience—for most things go wrong or anyhow turn out worse than one expects." In the preface to his memoirs, the aged Chateaubriand wrote: "At the end of life there comes a bitter age: nothing gives pleasure because one is worthy of nothing; of use to no one, a burden to all, one has but to take a single step to reach one's last resting place. What is the point of dreaming on a deserted shore? What charming shapes could the future possibly have to show?"

At sixty-nine years of age, Hans Christian Andersen wrote, "If I go into the garden and walk among the roses, what have they (and even the snails on their stalks) to say to me that they have not already said? . . . Under the old oak tree in the woods I remember that long ago it told me the last of all its dreams. So no new impression comes to me; and it is sad." Can the present be ruined by a past too strongly remembered? Simone de Beauvoir: "If things seem already to have been swallowed by the past and to have no freshness any more, it is not because we drag too great a wealth of memories with us; it is because our vision is no longer given life by fresh projects." A problem of old age, then, may not be too much past, but rather, not enough future, and often a joyless present. The result can be depression. It is a difficult thing to argue with; under those circumstances, even the "most normal" person might well be depressed.

Suicide attempts are frequent. In many cases they are cries for help, but especially among the old, there is little help forthcoming. Successful suicides (as distinct from attempts) are three times the national average for persons over sixty-five. In 1970, there were 23,480 recorded suicides in the United States; of these, 7,399 were persons over sixty-five years.

Paranoia is second only to depression among functional mental illnesses of the elderly (but note that it can also be organic). Among young people and adults, paranoia typically indicates a severe disturbance, such as schizophrenia. The delusion that "someone is out to get me" is typically grandiose and powerful: God is in hot pursuit, special beams from Jupiter are being directed at the sufferer, the Soviet Politburo is sending messages directly into his brain. By contrast, functional paranoia among the elderly is typically more immediate, less crazy, and frequently rather appropriate. It is especially common among those with sensory deficits. For example, someone with bad vision may have misplaced his wallet and be unable to find it; he then accuses others of thievery. Untrue perhaps, but not unreasonable. If his food tastes different (because some taste buds are lost with

121

age), he may accuse others of trying to poison him. If less mail is arriving than in the past, the mailman may be accused of conspiring against him, whereas in truth he may simply be writing less and also many of his old friends may have died. Psychiatrist Eric Pfeiffer of Duke University recounts the tale of one elderly woman who complained reproachfully that her neighbors were sneaking into her house and stuffing lint into the filter of her clothes dryer. This kind of paranoia, fortunately, usually responds well to appropriate intervention: eyeglasses, hearing aids, and, perhaps most important, a friendly, caring, and secure environment.

Finally, we come to hypochondriasis, that is, being a hypochondriac. Bodies do become frail with age, and more things go wrong. To some extent, greater involvement with one's body is therefore appropriate. However, this can easily become exaggerated, especially when there is a different underlying problem; namely, a need for attention that is not satisfied by society, friends, and family. We pay our doctors to pay attention to us. They can at least be counted on for that, and not surprisingly, those in need of caring attention sometimes complain loudly and long of their infirmities, real or imagined.

Even the healthy and loved old person is often led to imagine that he or she has one particular disease: insomnia. This is especially true in North America, where it seems that every third television ad urges us to take one sleeping pill or another. Insomnia can be a symptom of severe depression. But, the fact is, we also need less sleep as we get older, and that's exactly what most of us should get. For young adults, deep sleep comprises about 11 percent of total sleeping time; for the aged, 1.4 percent. On average, it takes eight to twelve minutes for a younger person to fall asleep, as compared to twenty minutes for the elderly. Instead of using drugs to close this gap, older people are better off when they recognize and adjust to the natural changes in their own chemistry (so long as they are healthy), rather than trying to force their bodies artificially to perform in ways that are uncomfortable and unnecessary.

Let's turn now to the organic mental illnesses of old age. These can be further subdivided into two categories: acute and chronic. Acute problems arise quickly, and if treated properly, they may disappear just as quickly. Chronic mental illness has a much less hopeful outcome. It typically begins gradually and builds up progressively, with little chance of a cure, at least not at present. Because of this difference, it is very important that organic mental illnesses be diagnosed correctly and promptly. All too often, acute organic problems have been casually described as chronic "senility," with the result that a curable illness is left untreated.

Older people are more fragile, especially beyond the seventh decade. As a result, almost any physical illness can have wide ramifications, often causing mental disorganization, inability to care for oneself, loss of memory, and so forth. Emphysema, malnutrition, hypothyroidism, pneumonia, arteriosclerosis, even vitamin deficiency can affect very old people in ways that look exactly like "senility." Many cases of so-called senility have even been cured by penicillin—given to treat a urinary tract infection! A forty-year-old may be diagnosed as suffering from congestive heart failure, whereas the same problem in his father may be missed entirely, with his mental confusion attributed to senility rather than the identical straightforward medical problem which also causes insufficient oxygen supply to the brain. The point is that in most cases such acute organic disabilities can be treated, and the real tragedy lies in not doing so. The main hurdle is a willingness to consider people as *people* regardless of their age: people subject to illness, rather than creatures teetering on the edge of a garbage can conveniently labeled "senility."

Finally, we come to the chronic organic brain diseases of age, lurking like bad dreams, beyond all hope. Two of them, Pick's disease and Alzheimer's, are so-called "presenile dementias," in that they usually make their effects known by the fifth or sixth decade of life. The third, "classic senile dementia," begins later, generally not before the seventh or eighth decade. The symptoms are similar for all three dementias: loss of memory, even to the point of being unable to recall one's own name; dramatic personality change, often with heightened irritability; speech distortions and—especially in Alzheimer's—unsteadiness of gait. All three illnesses involve a drastic loss of cells in the sufferer's brain.* This brain atrophy is concentrated in certain brain areas in the case of Pick's disease, but is more general and widespread

---

* This can also result from numerous, small injuries to the cerebral blood vessels—essentially mini-strokes, or "multi-infarcts" as the physicians call them. In addition, dementia may also result from certain rare diseases that are more often encountered in old age: Parkinson's disease, Creutzfeld-Jakob disease, Huntington's chorea, and the like.

in the other two. Alzheimer's and senile dementia also differ from Pick's in that the afflicted brain contains large numbers of tangled and pigmented nerve fibers, in addition to the actual loss of cells. Some researchers have also suggested that all three dementias are simply different forms of the same disease. In this view, senile dementia, for example, would be Alzheimer's that begins about two decades later.

Alzheimer's is about twenty times more common than Pick's and both probably have a strong genetic component. For example, a recent Swedish study showed that first degree relatives of Alzheimer's patients are 4.3 times more likely to develop the disease than are members of the population chosen at random. The suggestion has also been raised that Alzheimer's (and perhaps all three) may be caused by a virus—probably one of the new groups of "slow viruses" that have recently been recognized. In addition, at least one study has shown that Alzheimer's patients have seven times the normal aluminum concentration in their brain tissue. Admittedly, this abnormality could be either cause or effect, and it has also been hotly disputed by other researchers. Until the final verdict is in, however, it might behoove us to read the labels of our favorite antacids more carefully: aluminum hydroxide is a popular ingredient (it is also found in Drāno).

The outlook for anyone suffering from one of the irreversible, chronic dementias is currently dismal. Indeed, there is little in our discussion so far to make one's heart sing. On the other hand, as attention is increasingly focused on aging and its problems, it seems reasonable to expect that real progress will be made. In the meantime, there are two important lessons to be drawn from this discussion of aging and mental illness. First, many cases of severe psychiatric symptoms among the elderly are not in fact caused by any of the three chronic organic dementias. In most cases, these problems, whether situational or acutely organic, can be treated, if only they are identified as such, and treatment is attempted. So, lesson number one is: Don't give up on someone who seems demented, just because he or she is also old. Lesson number two is also one of hope. The chronic organic dementias affect about one million elderly. That's an appallingly large number. However, it is worth bearing in mind that we are still speaking of fewer than one aged individual in every twenty-five. In other words, chronic organic dementia is a *disease* condition, and not in any way the necessary result of *normal* aging. It is very serious, but also uncommon, and not necessarily a part of your future or of mine. We do not automatically "become senile" when we reach a certain age. Some of us may develop dementia in our later years, just as some of us may develop leukemia in youth. Both are illnesses and both should inspire treatment and, at this point in our knowledge, dread as well. But we certainly should not take either one lying down.

※

And so, from hour to hour we ripe and ripe,
And then, from hour to hour we rot and rot;
And thereby hangs a tale.

(Shakespeare, *As You Like It*)

The brain: about three pounds of very soft white cheese, wavy like a cauliflower; criss-crossed by electrical circuits that beggar the wildest imaginings of a Bell Telephone engineer; a juicy gland whose chemical drippings we are just beginning to identify, never mind to understand; home to all our thoughts, memories, passions, and fears. In all the world there can be no wider gap than this: from the physical reality of cells, chemicals, and electric circuits to the vibrant, personal experience of consciousness; from the structure, heavy and real, capable of being projected on a screen, tickled with an electrode, or sliced with a scalpel, to the living emotion, experienced by us all and yet more intensely private than anything else, the very sensation of being alive. And yet, it is all there, somehow, the one in the other, the mind in the brain.

Aging is not always kind to the brain, although it is less vicious than many of us might fear. For one thing, nerve cells cannot divide and make more of themselves. An alcoholic may have a severely damaged liver, but if he stops drinking, in time the cirrhosis will largely go away as new, healthy liver cells are produced from the wreckage of the old. But, sadly, the brain doesn't work that way. Dead or worn-out nerve cells are simply not replaced; every one we lose leaves us that much poorer as the show goes on. Why such stubbornness? Why is it that we can replace skin if cut or abraded, liver if sagging under the metabolic weight of alcohol, even kidney cells, those masters of fine-tuned aquatic discrimination, but not nerve cells, where *we* ultimately reside?

125

Perhaps it is just one of God's little dirty tricks. More likely, however, this profound sterility of our neurons is the cost we pay for an equally profound benefit: in order to do what we expect of them, our brain cells apparently require precise, complex, and more-or-less permanent connections. The stability of our memories, thoughts, and personality may very well require a comparable stability of nerve cells. The Greek Titan, Atlas, holds up the world; once in place, he cannot shift the load to someone else, without juggling it dangerously—and even then, the newcomer would probably never get as good a grip. So, Atlas is stuck and so are we. Perhaps we ought to congratulate our brain for holding everything together so faithfully, rather than complain that it doesn't do an even better job.

We lose nerve cells every day, about 100,000 in twenty-four hours, roughly .8 percent of our total per year from age thirty. Actually, the rate of cell loss is greatest in the young, increasing logarithmically up to about age twenty. Then our brain cells die at a fairly constant rate after that. Because of this steady loss of cells, the brain of a ninety-year-old is about the same size as that of a three-year-old child. But do not despair—these gruesome facts do not relegate us all to a shrunken-brained second childhood. The brain of a thirty-year-old weighs on average 3.03 pounds. That of a ninety-year-old (and of a three-year-old child), 2.72 pounds. Either we have a great deal of redundancy built into our brains, in which case we can spare those neurons that are not pulling their load now, or the remaining cells can pitch in for those that drop by the wayside.

Story has it that shortly after his inauguration in 1933, Franklin Delano Roosevelt paid a visit on Oliver Wendell Holmes, retired from the Supreme Court, and ninety-two years old at the time. He found Holmes in his study, reading Plato. Roosevelt: "May I ask why you're reading Plato, Mr. Justice?" Holmes: "Certainly, Mr. President. To improve my mind."

✺

Two thousand years before, Cicero wrote, "The old man keeps all his mental powers so long as he gives up neither using them nor adding to them."

In some ways, however, older brains are less plastic. Damage to specific parts of the cerebral cortex may cause loss of speech in young persons, but this disability is often only temporary as other neurons, in different regions, restore the child's capacity to speak. Identical damage, but in an older adult, is more likely to be irreversible. So, perhaps as we lose neurons, our loss is in flexibility rather than ability *per se*—hardening of the categories.

The possibility remains, however, that the progressive depletion of brain cells, imperceptible from day to day, nonetheless has long-term effects, especially if eventually we fall below some threshold for normal functioning.

Arteriosclerosis presents another problem. As blood flow becomes increasingly obstructed, the transfer of nutrients and oxygen to the brain may be impeded. Oxygen is especially important for normal brain function. Aside from the more dramatic consequences of oxygen deprivation (including death), very little is known about the possible effects of chronic, low-intensity deprivation in the aging brain. Some studies have even reported substantial improvement in patients with Alzheimer's and senile dementia, after these patients are treated with high pressure oxygen in a hyperbaric chamber. This device, similar to those used for decompressing scuba divers, presumably provides the oxygen for which out-of-breath brains have been gasping. Cerebral blood flow in healthy old people is not lower than in twenty-year-olds. But with increasingly occluded arteries (perhaps because of too much cholesterol and not enough exercise), many old people are less than healthy. And their very sensitive brains may be the first to show it.

Sensitive machines can also reveal what's going on within someone's skull. For instance, consider these findings from electroencephalogram (EEG) studies. There are at least four identified EEG rhythms: 1 to 3 cycles per second occur during sleep; 4 to 7 cycles per second occur while daydreaming or in a state of drowsiness; 8 to 13 cycles per second (known as alpha waves) indicate a relaxed but generally alert state; and a rate of above 13 shows vigorous mental effort. For young adults, the dominant brain wave rhythm is from 10.2 to 10.5 cycles per second. For those aged sixty to sixty-five, the dominant rhythm drops to around 9. Even in very healthy old people, the rhythms are slower than among the young. Since this represents a step toward the quieter rhythms of rest and sleep, does it also indicate a slowing down of the brain in the normal course of aging? Quite possibly.

There is an alternative, however; namely, that in older persons the same amount of mental alertness can be achieved at a lower measurable level of brain activity.

To some extent, there is a general slowing with age. This is probably most notable—and measureable—as an increase in "reaction time," the pregnant pause between stimulus and response. Willie Mays, at forty, just couldn't run the bases the way he could at thirty. He had "lost a step," as they put it; it wasn't so much that he had lost actual speed, but rather it took him a little longer to start running once he told himself to do so. Similarly, something had slowed in the precise little muscular adjustments that enable a young master, but not an old one, to swing a wooden bat so as to make solid contact with a ball traveling upward of ninety-eight miles per hour.

Psychologist Walter Wurwillo suggested that perhaps the relative reduction in alpha brain wave activity in older people contributes to their slowed reaction time. Using bio-feedback techniques, graduate student Diana Woodruff showed that old people can learn to produce fast brain waves, and furthermore that when they do so, their reaction times decrease (that is, they are able to respond to a stimulus more quickly). Maybe sometime in the future, we shall have people walking around with pocket-sized EEG monitors, keeping their brain waves up to snuff.

❧

What about aging and intelligence (or, to use the professional jargon, "cognitive function")? Do we get dumber as we get older?

There is no clear answer, and in fact a fair amount of controversy among the specialists. It is clear that older people score worse on most types of intelligence tests. But it isn't clear why. On the one hand, some experts claim that among healthy subjects no change whatsoever occurs simply because they get older. In this view, it is not age itself that causes any measured drop in cognition, but rather certain disease states, such as hypertension or arteriosclerosis. On the other side are those who point to a wide panoply of body changes with age, and the equally impressive and consistent pattern of poorer test scores among older subjects. It seems reasonable, as in most cases of this sort, that the truth lies somewhere in between.

A useful distinction, made by psychologists, differentiates between two kinds of intelligence, crystallized and fluid. Fluid intelligence reflects the capacities and abilities of the person; it is best developed in younger individuals. Crystallized intelligence derives from one's experience in a particular culture and relies more heavily on accumulated knowledge and wisdom. Not surprisingly, crystallized intelligence tends to increase with age, while its fluid counterpart decreases. This distinction may help us to understand why old people nearly always score lower in IQ tests than do young people. A twenty-five-year-old and a seventy-five-year-old could show a 40-point difference on the most commonly used IQ test, and yet their IQ's would be reported as the same. In other words, a built-in assumption is that a 40-point drop in IQ is normal from age twenty-five to seventy-five.

There are many different ways of interpreting this situation:

1. IQ is a composite statistic, measured by responses to a variety of different questions. There is no assurance that all questions are getting at the same thing. IQ tests may well be oriented toward the skills of the young; after all, these tests were designed primarily to aid in educational planning, vocational guidance, and the like. If, for example, the tests emphasize fluid over crystallized IQ the results would appear to indicate an overall decline with age, whereas in truth perhaps older people have *different* mental abilities, not necessarily fewer or worse.

2. Maybe people really do get duller as they get older, whether because of the loss of brain cells, progressive arteriosclerosis, or some as yet unidentified electrochemical changes in neuronal anatomy or physiology.

3. The environments of old people are often less conducive to learning, mental awareness, and agility. Just as young people might well be as subject to depression as old people if they had to live in older bodies, young people who were forced to experience nursing homes, inactivity, and boredom might well score lower on IQ tests also. Leonardo da Vinci recognized the same problem almost five hundred years ago: "Iron rusts from disuse, stagnant water loses its purity and in cold weather becomes frozen; even so does inaction sap the vigors of the mind."

4. There is a well-known "terminal drop" in intelligence scores immediately before death. Given that other systems are failing by this time, why shouldn't the brain do the same? When old people are tested for IQ scores, some of them are liable to be

close to death, although neither they nor the test-givers will know it at the time.

5. Just because old people score lower than young people, this doesn't necessarily mean that their age is responsible. Perhaps we don't get less smart with age, just more obsolete. IQ tests typically sample a cross-section of people at any given time. Thus, for example, tests given in 1980 might be administered to eighty-year-olds, sixty-year-olds, forty-year-olds, and twenty-year-olds. The older ones would probably do somewhat worse than the younger. But we would also find that the older groups had fewer years of education; no one would propose that people progressively lose years of schooling as they get older, and yet the comparable proposal is regularly made—that people lose IQ. In a sense, each generation is "smarter" than the preceding. Not that their capabilities are any better, but rather they have grown up being exposed early to things that older people had to learn over time, often with the added difficulty of unlearning previous material. The crucial point here is to distinguish age differences from age changes. In fact, the very few studies that have actually followed a large group of people from youth to old age do not show the age-related decreases in IQ that are revealed when we examine a cross section of the population at any one time.

6. Research has shown that old people and young people respond differently to test conditions, often to the detriment of the former. Thus, older subjects don't like trial and error, and tend to avoid that strategy, even if it would lead to a higher score. They are better at solving problems that involve deliberation and thinking things through, but are more likely to get flustered—and make mistakes—if rushed. It is not clear what all this means, or why it happens, but in any event it seems foolish to call these differences, "differences in intelligence"; and yet, they lead to lower IQ scores and, unless we are careful, the conclusion that the aged are less intelligent. And here's one more thing: certain tests involve memorization of nonsense syllables. Once again, older people were found to do worse than younger. But the elderly are also more likely to balk at the whole procedure, considering that lists of "mab, gug, lit, zul, and neg" are silly and not worth their time. If words are substituted for nonsense syllables, older subjects do much better (although still somewhat worse than younger ones).

7. Finally, what does it mean if old/young differences are "sta-

tistically significant"? This phrase is simply another way of saying that the distinctions are reliable and real; with a large enough
sample, almost any difference is "significant" to the statisticians. Let us ignore the preceding arguments, and grant, for the
moment, that age-related differences in cognitive function are
real and "significant." Even if a thirty-five-year-old can recall
forty nonsense syllables during a three-minute period, whereas
the average sixty-five-year-old can only recall thirty-eight—so
what? The differences may be statistically significant but still
have no significance whatever in real life. It would only matter
if life somehow occurred at the threshold between these two
abilities—that is, if adequate memory function required at least
thirty-nine nonsense syllables per three minutes. Only then could
the young man function effectively whereas the old man could
not.

❧

One facet of intelligence would seem to be creativity, the ability to synthesize new structures out of old building blocks. Does
the age of the builder make any difference? What about creativity and aging? The only strong, consistent pattern seems to be
that there is no strong, consistent pattern. Different fields of human endeavor seem to peak at different ages: mathematicians
and physicists often in their twenties (perhaps reflecting the large
component of fluid intelligence in these areas); writers, forty to
forty-five; composers, painters, sculptors, and musicians often
much later in life. For some well-known figures, however, creativity appears to have declined with age. Jean Sibelius lived to
be ninety-two, but composed nothing significant after sixty.
Charles Ives died at eighty, but stopped creating at fifty. By forty-
three, Ben Jonson had written all of his notable plays. Einstein's great contributions were made before he was thirty; by
contrast, the rest of his long life could be considered a creative
failure.* The early genius of Einstein, Mozart, Keats, Shelley,
Rimbaud, Raphael, Baudelaire, Descartes, and Gauss was revealed in their twenties or thirties. There is an urgency to their

---

* Perhaps this was because he tackled an impossible problem, the development
of a unified field theory, encompassing both relativity and quantum mechanics.
Of equal importance, however, is that in his later work, Einstein also did not
display the fresh mind, the intellectual iconoclasm that made his initial advances possible.

creations, as though just wrenched white-hot from a furnace. By contrast, creativity after the age of forty seems more studied and balanced.

There are many impressive examples of profound creativity in old age. When Edgar Degas (1834–1917) began losing his sight, he turned from paints to pastels. When he could no longer distinguish shades, he turned to charcoals. Later, nearly blind, he took up making small wax sculptures, which were then cast in bronze. Claude Monet (1840–1926) was working on a major project—a series of paintings of water lilies—when he had cataract surgery at age eighty-three. He continued to do nineteen such panels, as priceless gifts to France (each is seventeen to nineteen feet long). Anna Mary Robertson, better known as Grandma Moses (1860–1961), started painting at seventy-six, when arthritis made her unable to hold embroidery needles! She held her first show at age eighty. Titian was said to have painted "Christ Crowned with Thorns" at ninety-five and the "Battle of Lepanto" at ninety-eight.

Sophocles was nearly one hundred when he wrote *Oedipus at Colonus*, and Mary Baker Eddy founded and began publishing the *Christian Science Monitor* at eighty-seven. Verdi composed *Falstaff* at eighty; and Picasso, while in his eighties, clasped a female friend at an exhibition in his honor and exclaimed, "We don't get older, we just get riper." To these names could be added Michelangelo, Tintoretto, Cervantes, Goethe, Goya, Alexander von Humboldt, Hugo, Tolstoy, Freud, Shaw, Pauling, Bertrand Russell, and Winston Churchill—all of them people whose great creativity continued into equally great age. When it comes to the workings of the mind, perhaps we must agree with Longfellow that "nothing is too late, / Till the heart shall cease to palpitate."

❧

What about memory? Jonathan Swift had this to say about his own failing memory, in his "Verses on the Death of Dr. Swift":

He cannot call his Friends to Mind;
Forgets the Place where last he din'd;
Plyes you with Stories, o'er and o'er,
He told them fifty Times before.
How does he fancy we can sit,

To hear his out-of-fashion'd wit?
But he takes up with younger Fokes,
Who for his Wine will bear his Jokes:

The bouncy, jouncy rhythm and rhyme makes it all seem like a good joke. Others, however, have felt less sanguine. The usually irrepressible Bernard Berenson wrote, "Now I am seventy-five, strange things happen to me: so much of what seemed part of my intellectual furniture only yesterday has disappeared, fading and gone before I realized it! . . . Great sections of memory crumble and vanish in forgetfulness." François Mauriac: "A very old man's memories are like ants whose ant-hill has been destroyed. One's eyes cannot follow any single one of them for long." And Emmanuel Berl, in his novel *Sylvia:* "My past escapes me. I tug at one end, I tug at the other, and all that stays in my hand is a rotten scrap of fraying cloth."

A rotten scrap of fraying cloth. Ants milling about a destroyed anthill. The crumbling and vanishing of all that once was solid in one's past. Is that the way it happens? For some people, the answer seems to be yes. For others, however, no. The story is told of the honeymooners at the dude ranch who visited an old Indian who, they were told, had the world's finest memory and welcomed anyone who wished to test him. At a loss for what to ask, the young couple inquired what he had had for breakfast the previous day. The answer: "Eggs." Fifty years later, the couple celebrated their golden anniversary by returning to the same ranch. They were delighted to learn that the Indian was still alive, and with reputation intact. Approaching the old man, they said, "How!" His reply: "Scrambled." But that, of course, is just a story.

The reality is more somber. In one of Sir Arthur Conan Doyle's stories, Sherlock Holmes astonished Watson by revealing that despite his enormous knowledge of poisons, murder weapons, languages, and so forth, Holmes was unaware that the earth went around the sun, rather than vice versa. You see, my dear Watson, it is elementary: the brain is like an attic; it can be cluttered with only so much stuff. After a while there is no more room. So, anything new that is learned must be at the expense of something else that is forgotten. By extension, the Sherlock Holmes principle suggests that memory declines with age because of the crush and press of so much accumulated attic furniture. Add more and something already there is accidentally pushed out the window. Just a theory—and mind you, one with absolutely no scientific support.

Perhaps the loss of brain cells during aging is somehow responsible, with memories perishing along with the cells. One cell, one bit of memory? Or maybe two for one.

Whatever the reason, memory does seem to falter with age. Just as with the other self-fulfilling prophecies of aging, however, we often *expect* losses of this sort and are all-too-quick to see them as faltering of the intellect, either in ourselves or others. As a result, sometimes the elderly person is denied the benefit of the doubt that we would almost certainly extend to anyone younger. As Samuel Johnson put it, "There is a wicked inclination in most people to suppose an old man decayed in his intellect. If a young or middle-aged man, when leaving a company, does not recollect where he laid his hat, it is nothing; but, if the same inattention is discovered in an old man, people will shrug their shoulders and say, 'his memory is going.' "

Even though very old people do, in fact, tend to have some loss of memory, the pattern is not invariant. Memory expert David Roth celebrated his ninety-seventh birthday by reciting Thomas Gray's "Elegy Written in a Country Churchyard" (all 128 lines), could compute the day of the week for any date between the years 1752 and 3000, and, just for good measure, threw in the telephone numbers of each of the members of his Rotary Club chapter (all six hundred of them).

Conventional wisdom has it that as we grow older, memory for recent events tends to falter, whereas events that occurred long ago, during early childhood, remain clear and strong, "just like yesterday." There may be a profound evolutionary wisdom in this. It is rare in nature for animals to survive much beyond their reproductive period (remember the "fly-by" theory discussed in chapter 5?). Once they have done their part to project copies of their genes into the next generation, living things have served their natural function. Only a small minority of animals, like human beings, have a long postreproductive life-span. Significantly, these are invariably cases in which the old are able to contribute to the success of their offspring even after the latter have grown up. Thus, the evolutionary rationale for old age probably involves wisdom, experience, and the ability of the old to provide something of value not otherwise available to the young. Memory of yesterday's breakfast is unlikely to be of this sort—you need not be eighty years old to provide that information. But what happened seventy-five years ago, during the great drought, flood, famine, plague, war, or depression—now, that is something else.

Ironically, however, a recent study shows that the early memories of old people may not be nearly as accurate as we often believe. One problem in testing this proposition has been the absence of reliable ways of verifying a memory claim, especially among old people who describe personal events that occurred to them many decades ago. The study in question involved fifty-year-old high school yearbooks, and showed that old people actually did worse in recalling the names of their classmates than did more recent graduates. Nonetheless, perhaps the remarkable thing is that old memories do remain very strong at all. Fifty years is a long time to preserve the neurons bearing the name of the freckle-faced boy in the third row.

Perhaps old memories are rehearsed many times between the distant past and the present. If so, rather than dredge something up from fifty years ago, we simply remember it from the last time we thought about it. Or alternatively, maybe our earlier memories only *seem* more clear, compared to recent ones. Perhaps they actually are no more accurate, and the whole notion of accurate childhood memories in old people is just a myth.

But the idea is so widespread that it is difficult to discount. And if psychological tests from research laboratories fail to confirm the conventional wisdom, then perhaps it is just as reasonable to doubt the tests as the wisdom. In fact, these tests are almost always artificial, using measures such as word lists or nonsense syllables, far removed from reality. It is generally agreed that memory has three stages: storage, retention, and retrieval. Elderly subjects seem to have no difficulty in remembering the most recent words or syllables in a long list; however, they do score below younger subjects in remembering items from the beginning and middle of the lists. It is not clear whether the loss occurs because the information is: (1) incorrectly filed away in the brain; (2) inadequately retained in storage (that is, maybe some memories decay more rapidly in older brains); or (3) less available to be retrieved when wanted.

Regardless of their accuracy, and of the mechanisms that may be employed to store and retrieve them, the fact remains that memories are universally important to old people.

Aging: An Exploration

Youth longs and manhood strives but age remembers,
Sits by the raked-up ashes of the past
Spreads its thin hands above the whitening embers,
That warm its creeping lifeblood till the last.

(Oliver Wendell Holmes)

Maybe that's it. Maybe memories become important to the elderly because they are warming and pleasant. They come from a time when the rememberer may have felt more vital, vibrant, and alive. If our present lot is dreary, then it should be no surprise that we prefer to live in the past—it is a better place to be.

There is a curious sense in which an aging body makes us strangers to ourselves. Somewhere in our hearts, each of us remains convinced that he or she is still a little boy or girl, and will always remain so. To summon up memories of the past is to act as our own personal medium, constantly assuring ourselves of the fixed, unchanging reality of our ghostly selves, now consigned to another world, but yet passionately believed in, and just waiting the call to life. By telling stories of the child or young person within us, we make a living reality of that past, proving that despite the degradations of age, an unchanging *I* lives on inside.

And yet, these memories are not always pleasant. Often, they disappoint:

> . . . The past is not a powerful landscape lying there behind me, a country in which I can stroll wherever I please, and which will gradually show me all the secret hills and dales. As I was moving forward, so it was crumbling. Most of the wreckage that can still be seen is colourless, distorted, frozen; its meaning escapes me. . . . We lived it in the present, a present rich in the future towards which it was hurrying; and all that is left is a skeleton. . . . There are streets . . . where I can walk about recognizing the houses, the stones; but I shall never find my plans again, my hopes and fears— I shall not find myself. And if, when I am there, I call to mind some scene that happened long ago, it is fixed against the background like a butterfly pinned in a glass case: the characters no longer move in any direction.
>
> (Simone de Beauvoir)

For a long time, the tendency of the aged to reminisce has been considered pathologic, sick. More recently, however, American psychiatrist Robert Butler—then director of the National Institute on Aging—proposed a different interpretation.

136

The memories of an old person, according to Butler, may be an important road to health. It is a valuable life review, a taking-stock of one's time as a person, and an attempt to synthesize it into a meaningful package. The hoped-for result of a successful life review is a feeling that one's house is in order, and with it a degree of wisdom, integration, and serenity. There may also be an immediate and practical benefit from reminiscing in old age. By reminding one's younger listeners of what one was and what one did, the old person reminds today's adults that although he may now be weak, once he was strong and vigorous, just as they are now. Once, he was the loved, feared, and nurturing parent, just as they are now. And finally, not only are the listeners reminded of their filial duties, but also of the fact that there, but for the grace of Time, go they.

On the other hand, an intensive life review can be dangerous as well. Butler points out that "hidden themes of great vintage may emerge and change the quality of a life-long relationship; revelations of the past may forge a new intimacy, render a deceit honest; they may sever peculiar bonds and free tongues; or again, they may sculpture terrifying hatreds out of fluid, fitful antagonisms." The life review of an aged person may be disquieting, especially because of conflict between earlier goals and the sometimes pitiful reality of actual accomplishments. Furthermore, there is always the possible burden of unresolved guilt. Somerset Maugham wrote, "What makes old age hard to bear is not a failing of one's faculties, mental and physical, but the burden of one's memories." Reminisce, then, but at your own risk. Your memories may not be orderly and tidy; certain themes may recur again and again, with the nauseating persistence of a fevered dream. Others may bring joy and peace. Our memories are of our lives, and they are no neater than life itself.

It is a unique opportunity and privilege, to seek in a lengthy past for the meaning of one's present. T. S. Eliot, for one, maintained that old men ought to be explorers:

We shall not cease from exploration
And the end of all our exploring
Will be to arrive where we started
And know the place for the first time.

(*Four Quartets*)

137

No one would accuse Shakespeare of being a professional psychologist; heaven forbid, he knew much too much about human nature for that! Speaking more as the inspired poet, he gave us a framework for looking at the course of our lives, in the famous "seven ages of man" sequence. We hear it from the mouth of melancholy Jacques, the itinerant philosopher in *As You Like It:*

> All the world's a stage,
> And all the men and women merely players:
> They have their exits and their entrances;
> And one man in his time plays many parts,
> His acts being seven ages. At first the infant,
> Mewling and puking in the nurse's arms.
> And then the whining school-boy, with his satchel
> And shining morning face, creeping like snail
> Unwillingly to school. And then the lover,
> Sighing like furnace, with a woeful ballad
> Made to his mistress' eyebrow. Then a soldier,
> Full of strange oaths, and bearded like the pard,
> Jealous in honour, sudden and quick in quarrel,
> Seeking the bubble reputation
> Even in the cannon's mouth. And then the justice,
> In fair round belly with good capon lined
> With eyes severe, and beard of formal cut,
> Full of wise saws and modern instances;
> And so he plays his part. The sixth age shifts
> Into the lean and slippered pantaloon,
> With spectacles on nose and pouch on side,
> His youthful hose well saved a world too wide
> For his shrunk shank; and his big manly voice,
> Turning again toward childish treble, pipes
> And whistles in his sound. Last scene of all,
> That ends this strange eventful history,
> Is second childishness and mere oblivion,
> Sans teeth, sans eyes, sans taste, sans everything.

Not a very cheery picture. And yet, if we compare Shakespeare's seven ages with more recent attempts at categorization, we find that the great bard showed unusual respect for the complexities of old age. Take, for example, Erik Erikson's well-known model of human development, based on the "eight stages of man." A comparison is instructive. Erikson's eight stages are as follows: (1) oral-sensory, (2) muscular-anal, (3) locomotor-genital, (4) latency, (5) puberty and adolescence, (6) young adulthood, (7) adulthood, and (8) maturity. Whereas Shakespeare's Jacques allotted only two or three stages to youth, Erikson gave it five of his eight. From conception to death, the human being is one, a continuum. For our own convenience, we may elect to chop him up in various ways. In doing so, we can never have absolute confidence that we are truly cutting nature at its joints. We can, however, be confident that by examining these divisions, we can learn something about what time periods in life are *considered* significant by those conducting the surgery.

Not surprisingly, then, "developmental psychology" is almost entirely taken up with "child psychology," as reflected in thinking that divides youth into many different stages, each one supposedly distinct from the others. By contrast, old age gets a rather short stick, since not much of interest is supposed to happen then. In classical Freudian theory, early experiences are also emphasized, with the adult personality presumably formed early in life. Even with recent increased attention to "life-span psychology," old age gets barely a mention. Gail Sheehy's very successful *Passages* does not even go beyond late middle age. And Erikson's stages are basically a modernization of the Freudian notion that "the child is father to the man."

Maybe Yeats was right and life is "a long preparation for something that never happens." But for better or ill, old age does eventually happen, and then, according to Erikson, our life careers come to a great terminal forking: one path leads to "despair," and the other to "integrity." The former is self-explanatory. Integrity, on the other hand, means accepting one's life as one has lived it—like the aged doctor in Ingmar Bergman's film *Wild Strawberries*, or the hero in Tolstoy's *The Death of Ivan Ilyich*. Although such "integrity" may seem static and dull, it need not be. T. S. Eliot expressed the feeling of transcendence in his *Four Quartets*:

We must be still and still moving
Into another intensity
For a further union, a deeper communion
Through the dark cold and the empty desolation,
The wave cry, the wind cry, the vast waters
Of the petrel and the porpoise. In the end is my beginning.

❧

Perhaps the ultimate wisdom is shown by those who grow old well. Among playwrights, it is said that anyone can compose a decent first act; it takes competence, but even an uninspired worker can create a passable second act; but a good final act requires a master's touch. Is living like that?

Psychologist David Gutmann of the University of Michigan hopes that someday we might understand the "species psychology of aging." It is arguable whether there are right or wrong ways to grow old, although certainly some people are happier than others in their old age. Maybe this has something to do with one's personal style of aging. Furthermore, maybe people will generally be happier if their style is in harmony with whatever their underlying biology happens to suggest. What patterns, what suggestions, could those be?

Searching for universal patterns in human aging, Gutmann has investigated several different cultures, looking for common themes in the final act of life's play. He may have found two—one for men and another for women. Among both the lowland and highland Maya, both the traditional and Westernized Navajo, and the Moslem Druze of Israel and the Golan Heights, Gutmann has found evidence that men, as they age, tend to shift their view of the world from an active, interventionist stance to one that is more accepting and passive. In other words, old men tend to become more like women—at least, young women.

Gutmann's research tool is the Thematic Apperception Test, a series of simple drawings presented to individuals, who are asked to make up a story that is portrayed in the drawing. It is something like a Rohrschach inkblot test, except that the TAT drawings are not formless smudges of ink; rather, they are recognizable scenes, such as a young man with his hand on the shoulder of an old woman, or an old man eating food while a young child looks on. The point is that these TAT pictures are nonetheless ambiguous. They can be interpreted in very different ways, and the story that is told provides insight into the mental set of the person doing the telling.

Young men and old men differ in their response to these tests, and in consistent ways: young men see the aggressive, take-charge aspects of each situation, whereas old men see the identical scene in a more passive light. For example, one TAT scene depicts a young man holding onto a rope, which he is either climbing or descending. Young men typically interpret this as the climber demonstrating his strength, often in a competition, or pulling himself up so that he will have a better vantage point to search for food or find a shortcut for his animal herds. By contrast, old men see something very different in the same picture: the figure is fleeing from some enemy, an animal, or fire; or alternatively, he is helpless, hanging onto the rope, and not actively *climbing* it. For another example, the "sexual conflict card" shows a young man reaching toward a young woman, who is turning away from him. Young men see this as representing a sexually or physically aggressive male whose behavior is troublesome for the quiet, nurturing, and loving female. By contrast, old men see the same scene as the young man reaching for the motherly aid which the woman offers, or as a peaceful Platonic relationship.

The subconscious impulses of old and young thus seem to be different, and the TAT enables us to observe those differences. A similar pattern is revealed by looking at actual behavior. For example, as Fijian men grow old, they become more domesticated, spending more time with their family than with other men. They also devote more time to gardening. Old Hopi men routinely do "women's work," such as shelling corn. Among the Masai of precolonial East Africa, young unmarried men became members of the Moran, a fierce group of warriors who preyed upon the herds and wives of neighboring people. They, in turn, were kept in line by the elders, who used powerful curses, rather than physical force, to prevent any excesses. A similar pattern was found among the African Kikuyu and the American Comanches: young men were expected to use their own energies, whereas old men borrowed their more passive authority from the gods.

Elders are generally seen as appropriate intermediaries with the gods, partly because, being closer to death, they are already closer to the supernatural. In addition, messengers to the gods must themselves be nonabrasive and nonthreatening. Most of the world's peoples recognize that with age, we become more passive and hence more acceptable to the gods. Ironically, the same traits that make the elderly weak in body make them spiritually strong in most primitive societies.

The consensus from East Asia is similar: youth strives for success and achievement, whereas elders are expected to seek inner peace and to be serene. Margaret Mead has described how young Chinese are expected to strive for achievement and status, whereas the old are supposed to be relaxed, to meditate and be "noble." The elderly should also abstain from sex and from eating meat. The Burmese recognize four life stages:

1. Until puberty, one is to respect one's parents and other elders, and to learn from them.

2. During the "virgin" stage, one searches for a spouse.

3. As an adult, one should "give, show, and teach"—that is, provide for one's children. After they have married, then at last one can move on to the last stage.

4. Now, one devotes oneself to religion, meditation, and other saintly and passive pursuits. (Incidentally, the Burmese are agreed that this last stage is by far the best.)

Among the Hindus, the prescribed "asrama," or life cycle, is similar, culminating in "Sangasa," the stage when all worldly drives are renounced and one becomes a possible candidate for "Nirvana."

Interestingly, an opposite trend obtains for women. Even as men are becoming more passive and meditative with age, women are typically liberated from their passive role and become more active—that is, more "masculine." An old Hindu woman may become a "malikin," one who controls family affairs. Among the warrior American Indian tribes such as the Comanche, old women were called "manly-hearted women." In Latin America, old "chicanas" typically become more dominant with age. The domineering role of elderly women in North American black society is proverbial. On psychological tests, older Japanese women are consistently more extroverted than old men, and more so than young women as well. (Young women, however, tend to be less extroverted than young men.) In Burma, the elderly widow becomes the unquestioned head of the household; the same holds true in Bali, where such women occupy the "patriarchal" role. A traditional saying among Moroccans is that at birth a boy is surrounded by a hundred devils, and a girl by a hundred angels. Each year, a devil is exchanged for an angel, and vice versa. So, by the age one hundred . . .

It is interesting to speculate that this increasingly aggressive approach to life by old women has in turn led to the near-universal notion of the old woman as witch. She must walk a fine line, the old lady—society can either support her gradual personality shift, possibly even elevating her from wife to malikin, as with some Hindus, or it could condemn her as a witch.

Since the activities of young men are typically devoted to the outside workplace, whereas the energies of young women are typically concentrated at home, women may gradually develop a competence in domestic affairs that is both impressive and potentially threatening, by the time they grow old. Men, by contrast, fall back into the domestic sphere only in their later years; being less experienced in this arena, they tend to be less domineering.

Several questions remain, among them the cause of this male-female shift in aggressiveness and activity. Gutmann favors a rather psychoanalytic interpretation, pointing to the fact that during child-rearing, women are necessarily nurturing, and men active and "instrumental." When their reproductive stage has been completed, both men and women are free to experience the previously repressed side of their personalities.

So, perhaps androgyny (literally, "man-woman") is the life cycle for males and "gynandry" ("woman-man") for females. In that case, maybe the "dirty old man" is so threatening because he fails to conform to the stereotype of what manliness—at least, elderly manliness—is supposedly all about.

Ironically, those who survive into extreme old age often do not show the passivity that seems to characterize most old men in most societies. Rather, survivors tend to be those who remain active, vigorous, and involved. Similarly, M. Liebermann, studying a Jewish old people's home in Chicago, reported in 1975 that "grouchiness" may be a survival asset. It is interesting in this respect that Communists and Zionists survived better than did others in Nazi concentration camps; among American survivors of Japanese POW camps, it was reported that if a sick inmate could be made angry, rather than lethargic, he was more likely to recover. Perhaps longevity is enhanced if anger can be externalized, instead of being turned inwards. So, even if there is a "species psychology of aging," we may be better off if we go against the grain—at least, men may live longer if they resist the apparent male tendency to be passive and withdrawn in old age.

It is frustrating to generalize about the behavior of old people, largely because as we get older, we get more different from each other. Generalizations about infancy seem to be more accurate than those concerning toddlerhood. Adolescence, with all its overheated confusion, is nonetheless more consistent than early

143

adulthood. And when we get to old age, individuality is rampant. This is certainly logical: a longer life gives more opportunity for our idiosyncratic personal experiences to separate Me from Thee. Just as physicists speak of our expanding universe, rushing away from the primordial Big Bang that started it all, perhaps our minds and behavior are continuing that pattern, expanding and differentiating merrily as we go.

Our exploration of the aging mind has exposed some widespread myths. Next, we shall turn to one of the most prevalent and potentially destructive of these: the myth of the desexed elderly.

10

Aging and the Individual

Sex

Pick a pope, any pope. All right now, is he young or old? Now-
adays, we generally think of popes as old men, as indeed they
are; but once upon a time, young men got the call. This changed
with the counterreformation following the Council of Trent, and
popes have subsequently been chosen almost exclusively from
the ranks of the aged. The Catholic church seems to have had
two reasons for shifting to older leaders; for one, an old man was
seen as less likely to make drastic breaks with established tradition (they didn't count on John XXIII), and for the other, earlier
popes had had an embarrassing number of young "nephews"
running about the Vatican. It was hoped that old men would feel
content to live a life of celibacy.

Regardless of how the elderly feel about it, the *young* seem to
find sex unbecoming—for the old, that is. Hell hath no fury like
the young, confronted with the sexuality of the old. Yeats wrote,
"You think it horrible that lust and rage / Should dance attention upon my old age. . . ." He was not alone. One of the only
negative references to old age in the Bible is the episode of Susannah and the elders, from the Apocrypha. These old men see
the young and winsome Susannah bathing in her garden. Overcome by her beauty and their own lust, they proposition her.
When Susannah virtuously refuses, they seek revenge by falsely
claiming to have seen her committing adultery. (Fortunately,
Daniel comes to Susannah's rescue. He gallantly proves her in-
nocence by questioning each of the disreputable lechers sepa-
rately, thereby revealing inconsistencies in their stories.)

Interestingly, while sex in old men is often seen as reprehen-
sible, frightening, and wicked, any sign of sexuality in old women

is traditionally regarded as merely laughable. In Aristophanes' comedy *Women in Parliament*, the women seize political power. To assure equal sexual satisfaction for old women as well as young, every young man who desires a particular young woman is first required to bed an old woman. Furthermore, old women are given the right to seize upon any man of their choice and demand their sexual rights. In William Congreve's *The Way of the World*, old Lady Wishfort is a laughingstock because of her amorous longings for a young man: "Female frailty! We must all come to it, if we live to be old and feel the craving of a false appetite when the true is decayed."

Why does youth view sex in the old as a false appetite? It is anybody's guess, but there are several possibilities, none of them mutually exclusive. For one, sex drive does diminish with age, although not as drastically as a youthful society would have us believe. Perhaps, then, we simply take a reality and then exaggerate it. But why exaggerate it? Why not understate it? Or even, God forbid, be honest about it? Sex among animals is entirely for reproduction, and certainly sex is also how we reproduce. As people get older, they lose their ability to reproduce—women much more dramatically than men. Maybe we generalize from one loss to the other. But old people don't lose their sexuality. Indeed, with age, sex moves from procreation to recreation, but that does not make it any less real.

All people have some form of incest taboo, a prohibition against sexual relations between close relatives: brothers and sisters, and, most especially, parents and offspring. Perhaps the sexuality of our parents makes us uncomfortable by extension of this universal taboo. Even if Freud was right and deep down inside we all want to kill our fathers and marry our mothers (or vice versa, depending on our gender), even the thought of the act may also be attended with a good deal of primal, subconscious horror. We are very complex creatures, after all. By desexing the older generation, we fantasize them as incapable of incestuous behavior, and in so doing perhaps we protect ourselves against what we want but must not have.

Finally, by stereotyping the aged as unsexed, we lessen their threat as our sexual competitors. In a kind of self-fulfilling prophecy, if old people can be persuaded that they are unsexed, then in fact they will be. The result is less competition for young people, whose sexuality was never in doubt. This also helps explain why there is more antagonism toward the sexuality of old men than that of old women: successful old men can effectively monopolize (and even impregnate) young women. Accordingly, they are a threat to younger men, whereas old women threaten neither lad nor lass.

It seems that we do not even want to know the truth: in Kinsey's famous study of the sexual behavior of 14,084 people, only 106 were above sixty years of age, and only 18 above seventy years. In itself, this speaks eloquently.

If the image of sex among the aged is somehow disagreeable, many persons, young and old alike, take comfort in the supposedly greater balance and cerebral reliability of the desexed old person. Seneca wrote that "the soul, no longer having any great commerce with the body, burgeons and comes into full flower." And earlier, Sophocles had this to say about sex and love: "It was with the utmost relief that I escaped from it—it was as though I had escaped from slavery under a ferocious master."

On the other hand, the escape may be something of a Pyrrhic victory. One of the French luminaries of the seventeenth century was Charles de Marguetel de Saint-Denis de Saint-Evremond, courtier, wit, and literateur, who at fifty-four set up a salon in London with a beautiful young woman, specializing in lovemaking, gambling, and witty conversation. He also wrote essays, dialogues, and poems, and in his old age (he died at ninety-three) finally had this to report: "I have lost all inclination to vice without knowing whether I owe this change to the weakness of an outworn body or the moderation of a mind that has grown wiser than it was before. At my age it is hard to tell whether the passions one no longer feels are extinguished or overcome."

Extinguished or overcome? If it must be one or the other, most of us would doubtless opt for the latter; at least it preserves the illusion of control. Nobel prize–winning playwright André Gide once sought to overcome lust, only to recognize that without it, his life would be empty:

There was a time when I was cruelly tormented, indeed obsessed by desire, and I prayed "Oh, let the moment come when my subjugated flesh will allow me to give myself entirely to . . . But to what? To art? To pure thought? To God?" How ignorant I was! How mad! It was the same as believing that the flame would burn brighter in a lamp with no oil left. If it were abstract, my thought would go out; even today [Gide was seventy-two when he wrote this] it is

147

my carnal self that feeds the flame, and now I pray that I may retain carnal desire until I die.

When it comes to the retention of carnal desire, few luminaries exceed that paragon of American virtue, Benjamin Franklin. During his tenure as ambassador to France, he had numerous affairs. One of the best known was with a Madame Helvetius* (age sixty), while Franklin was in his mid-seventies.

Anyone who has not already done so, owes it to himself (or herself) to read through Franklin's famous letter replying to a young friend's request for advice on how to curb his sexual desires. Franklin's response is notable both for its lechery and for its unabashed sexism, and is reproduced below in full:

June 25, 1745

My Dear Friend:–

I know of no Medicine fit to diminish the violent and natural inclination you mention; and if I did, I think I should not communicate it to you. Marriage is the proper Remedy. It is the most natural State of Man, and therefore the State in which you will find solid Happiness. Your Reason against entering into it at present appears to be not well founded. The Circumstantial Advantages you have in View by postponing it, are not only uncertain, but they are small in comparison with the Thing itself, the being married and settled. It is the Man and Woman united that makes the complete human Being. Separate she wants his force of Body and Strength of Reason, he her Softness, Sensibility and acute Discernment. Together they are most likely to succeed in the World. A single Man has not nearly the Value he would have in that State of Union. He is an incomplete Animal. He resembles the odd Half of a Pair of Scissors.

If you get a prudent, healthy wife, your Industry in your Profession, with her good Economy, will be a Fortune sufficient.

But if you will not take this Counsel, and persist in thinking a Commerce with the Sex is inevitable, then I repeat my former Advice that in your Amours you should prefer old Women to young ones. This you call a Paradox, and demand my reasons. They are these:

1 Because they have more Knowledge of the world and their minds are better stored with Observations; their Conversation is more improving, and more lastingly agreeable.

---

* To her, Fontenelle (at age one hundred) once said: "Ah, my dear, if only I were ninety again!"

148

2 Because when Women cease to be handsome, they study to be good. To maintain their Influence over Man, they supply the Diminution of Beauty by an Augmentation of Utility. They learn to do a thousand Services, small and great, and are the most tender and useful of all Friends when you are sick. Thus they continue amiable. And hence there is hardly such a thing to be found as an old Woman who is not a good Woman.

3 Because there is no hazard of children, which irregularly produced may be attended with much inconvenience.

4 Because through more Experience they are more prudent and discreet in conducting an Intrigue to prevent Suspicion. The Commerce with them is therefore safer with regard to your reputation; and with regard to theirs, if the Affair should happen to be known, considerate People might be inclined to excuse an Old Woman, who would kindly take care of a young Man, form his manners by her good Councils, and prevent his ruining his Health and Fortune among mercenary Prostitutes.

5 Because in every Animal that walks upright, the Deficiency of the Fluids that fill the Muscles appears first in the highest Part. The Face first grows lank and wrinkled; then the Neck; then the Breast and Arms; the lower parts continuing to the last as plump as ever; so that covering all above with a Basket, and regarding only what is below the Girdle, it is impossible of two Women to know an old from a young one. And as in the Dark all Cats are at least equal and frequently superior; every Knack being by Practice capable of improvement.

6 Because the sin is less. The Debauching of a Virgin may be her Ruin, and make her for Life unhappy.

7 Because the Compunction is less. The having made a young Girl miserable may give you frequent and bitter Reflections; none of which can attend making an old Woman happy.

8th & lastly. They are so grateful!!!

Thus much for my Paradox. But still I advise you to marry immediately; being sincerely

Your Affectionate Friend,
Benj. Franklin

Here is a little ditty that reveals some common misconceptions about sexuality and age:

From twenty to thirty if a man lives right
It's once in the morning and once at night.
From thirty to forty if he still lives right

He skips the morning, or else the night.
From forty to fifty it's now and then.
From fifty to sixty it's God knows when.
From sixty to seventy if he's still inclined
Don't let him fool you, it's all in his mind.

The real sin here lies, not in representing sex, but rather in misrepresenting it. Just as the sexual appetites of young men are here exaggerated, those of old men are written off much too cavalierly. The fact is, for both men and women, sexual activity does lessen with age. Nonetheless, for many people it remains alive and kicking, not only in the mind, but elsewhere as well.

Sexual activity may remain substantial among couples in their sixties, seventies, eighties, and even nineties, with reports of intercourse averaging twice per week. Some inhabitants of the Soviet Caucasus have apparently fathered children while over one hundred. Sperm have been found in the ejaculate of 68.5 percent of men aged sixty to seventy, 59.5 percent of those between seventy and eighty, and 48 percent of those in the eighty to ninety category. A survey taken in 1926 found that one in twenty-five males between the ages of seventy and seventy-nine was having intercourse *every third day;* an additional one in ten was doing so at least once per week. Another survey taken in 1959 found that 34 percent of persons over seventy were still sexually active, and 40 percent of those over eighty were still enjoying intercourse about once per month. One year later, a different survey found that there was no decline in sexual activity under age seventy-five; beyond that age, 25 percent remained sexually active, with the drop-off almost wholly accounted for by illness, either of spouse or self. Finally, a 1968 study at Duke University found that 47 percent of subjects between sixty and seventy-one had frequent intercourse, as did 15 percent of those seventy-eight and over. During a five-year follow-up, 16 percent reported a decrease in activity and 14 percent reported an increase.

Impotence, when it occurs, is due almost entirely to psychological factors, not physical ones.* Particularly damaging is "performance anxiety," a vicious circle in which fear of sexual failure leads to worry, self-consciousness, and then failure—which in turn leads to further worry and therefore more failure.

---

* Drugs to reduce blood pressure are a notable exception. Even here, however, it is usually possible to reduce hypertension while still permitting sexual tension.

150

This is all compounded, of course, when the elderly are force-fed the self-fulfilling prophecy of unsexed old age.

Even sex hormones, a frequent villain in the false melodrama of "The Perils of Age," are largely innocent. A recent study by the Gerontology Research Center in Baltimore examined seventy-six elderly men and found no less testosterone circulating within them than in younger men. Admittedly, these elderly men were a sterling sample: free of disease and obesity, well educated, and not heavy drinkers. But the findings are generally encouraging nonetheless: a decline in male sex hormone is clearly not an inevitable concommitant of aging. For women, on the other hand, hormone levels do drop sharply with menopause, but these can be easily replaced if needed, and furthermore many women find enhanced sexual enjoyment *after* menopause, mainly because of relief about not risking pregnancy, as well as freedom from unpleasant contraceptive chores.

Men who enjoy vigorous sex lives in their old age tend to be in good health, of higher socio-economic class, and the same individuals who were sexually active earlier in life. In fact, perhaps the strongest single predictor of an on-going sex life when old is the pattern of one's sex life when young. Maybe sex becomes a habit and practice makes perfect. Maybe sex is a "positive addiction," like running, playing the piano, or reading. Or maybe we all differ a bit in our sexual proclivities; those for whom sex is a chore, an embarrassment, or generally less-than-rewarding are more likely to stop as they get older. And those who have reveled in the joy of sex aren't about to stop just because they have been doing it for so many years. (On the other hand, in rare cases one's sex life can actually *begin* in old age; it is a little-known fact that Havelock Ellis, the great early twentieth-century pioneer in sex research, was himself impotent until finally cured in his sixties.)

For women, by contrast to men, the most important factor determining whether sex will continue into old age is the availability of a suitable partner. Since women live an average of about seven or eight years longer than men, there are significantly more widows than widowers. At least one authority has therefore suggested that we legalize bigamy or even "trigamy" for persons over sixty-five.

Compared to his youth, an old man takes more time to become sexually aroused, and even then his penis may remain less firm and stiff. Ejaculation may be of shorter duration and decreased force, with fewer contractions and less fluid expelled. The latency period that must elapse before the next intercourse is usually extended, often as long as several days. In addition, not every intercourse will end with an ejaculation. But just as our bodies change with age, our sexuality is entitled to change as well; this does not mean that it goes away. Indeed, in some ways it may even get better: premature ejaculation is, along with impotence, the greatest male sexual problem. A young man who can have intercourse for a long time without ejaculating is considered to be a good lover. Ironically, when an old man does the same thing, he worries! In fact, since their orgasms take longer, many old men become better sexual partners as they age. Could this be what Browning really meant when he wrote, "Grow old along with me / the best is yet to be?"

For women, aging brings less vaginal lubrication. The clitoris shrinks somewhat, although sensitivity stays the same. The vagina becomes somewhat less stretchable, although still accommodating. Masters and Johnson found a reduction in breast engorgement, nipple erection, and clitoral and labial engorgement during intercourse, and also reduced sexual flush over the breasts. However, women's ability to reach orgasm was undiminished with age.

Summarizing, we find that old age brings changes in our sex life, just as it does in other respects. But these changes are not dramatic, and certainly not catastrophic. One of the uniquely human traits for *Homo sapiens* is our penchant for enjoying sex in its own right, aside from its role in reproduction. The coupling of dogs, cats, birds, and bees is woefully single-minded by contrast. The bitch in heat, the bird on her next, the queen bee laying eggs for her hive—all these are "served" by their respective males with enthusiasm, to be sure, but with ardor that is limited to the season and procreative purpose. We are different. We get more out of sex than the making of babies: we cement bonds of love and affection, and forge new ones. Or, at the very least, we engage in occasional groping efforts to find love, warmth, and mutual appreciation, and to fulfill mutual needs. Sex is part of life, and for those fortunate enough to be healthy and not alone, it can last as long as life itself.

❧

Of course, no human being can live truly alone. In our tour of aging and the individual, we have viewed body, mind, and finally sex, a progression toward more and more involvement with others. The social contest of aging simply cannot be denied, no matter how personal and private the experience of growing old may seem. It also should not be ignored. We need others, and it is in the context of others that we grow up and eventually grow old. To be sure, there are as many ways of growing old as there are individuals. However, there are also certain recognizable patterns, determined not only by how we fit into society, but also by the nature of that society. We cannot choose the society into which we are born, and most of us rarely consider how or where we would like to grow old. But, as we shall now see, it makes quite a difference.

11

Aging in Other Places

Shangri-la, in Three Parts

There are three places in the world where many people seem to attain extraordinary ages: Abkhasia in the Soviet Caucasus, Vilcabamba in southern Ecuador, and Hunzaland of Pakistan. In this chapter we shall take a brief look at the people and cultures of these supposed modern-day, real-life Shrangri-las.

Before we start, however, it should be noted that American gerontologists are often skeptical of these claims. In part, their doubts are well founded. The Hunzas are still largely illiterate, and a written language wasn't introduced into Soviet Abkhasia until 1954. Without written records it is difficult to authenticate claims of vast age. By contrast, the Ecuadorians in the region around Vilcabamba are ardent Catholics and have been for centuries. Hence, their baptismal certificates, often yellowed and frail, but still legible, can vouch for most ages as claimed. Among the Abkhasians, and presumably the Hunzas as well, there are good reasons for exaggerating one's age—in particular, the enormous respect that old people receive. In these societies, one's personal status goes up with one's years. Upon reaching a ripe old age, a person may be greatly tempted to add on a few extra years. The deception is likely to work, especially when most others are younger and therefore unable to contradict the old person's word.

Abkhasia has been the best studied case. Here, a carnival atmosphere of publicity developed during the late forties and early fifties, greatly rewarding claims of extreme longevity. Persons over one hundred years became celebrities: they were featured on magazine covers, photographed and interviewed extensively, and used by the Soviet government as propaganda for the merits of communism. This last development was absurd, since the Abkhasians are largely Moslems, not ethnic Russians, and only in the mid-twentieth century did they become incorporated into a vast nation that just happened to be communist. Soviet politics seem almost irrelevant to daily peasant life in Abkhasia. Nonetheless, it also happens that Josef Stalin was a native of Soviet Georgia—close to Abkhasia—had this may have intensified the political motivations to showcase Abkhasia as a special place with special people.

It is also true that many men of that region carry false identification papers, often forged during World War I and earlier, to help keep them out of the Tsar's hated army. A common ploy was to assume the name and identity of one's father—including, of course, his age.

On the other hand, scientists who have visited Abkhasia, Vilcabamba, and Hunzaland have invariably been impressed with the vigor of the elderly. These visitors include such notables as British geriatrician David Davies (Vilcabamba), Alexander Leaf, chief of medical services at the Massachusetts General Hospital (Hunzaland), and American anthropologist Sula Benet (Abkhasia). Furthermore, even when written verification in the form of birth records or baptismal certificates is lacking, a great deal of confidence can be gained by interviewing the subjects, checking their statements for internal consistency, and also cross-checking their stories with other elderly people. For example, an Abkhasian claiming to be 124 years old might be asked: How old were you at the time of the great cholera epidemic (in 1892)? What was your age when serfdom was abolished (1869)? How old were you when you had children and how old are they now? How many brothers and sisters did (do) you have, and how old were they (and you) when they died? If the subjects are consistent in answering these sorts of questions, and if others independently verify their stories, then it becomes reasonable to believe that they are as old as they claim. We should never suspend our critical judgment, but the evidence at present seems to be overwhelming: many people in these areas really do reach unusually old age, and often stay vigorous all the while. Accordingly, let's take a closer look. We might learn something.

❧

Sula Benet is an anthropologist at the City University of New York. She was born in Eastern Europe and is one of the very few American anthropologists to speak the difficult language of Abkhasia. She first went to Abkhasia to study the effects of modernization on a peasant community, since these pastoral people had only recently become part of the Soviet Union. Once there, however, she was struck by the large number of vigorous old people, and she returned to study them and their culture. Besides Dr. Benet, Soviet physicians have also intensively studied the Abkhasians. In 1956, for example, they found that 2,144 Abkhasians were over ninety years old—about 2.6 percent of the population. By contrast, less than .2 percent of the entire Soviet population was over ninety at the same time. Clearly, something is different about Abkhasia and its people.

In 1956, Dr. G. N. Sichiniva of the Institute of Gerontology in Kiev began a nine-year study of seventy-eight men and forty-five women, all of whom were over one hundred years of age. Nine years later, all of those surviving were still classified as "functionally healthy." They all showed clear and logical thinking, took good care of themselves, and had an active, ongoing interest in family and village affairs. Over 90 percent of them felt a need to do physical work. The following report from anthropologist Benet describes a typical Abkhasian centenarian:

> E. J. Jachava, of the village of Gumista, was seen by the doctors over a long period of time. In 1938, at the age of one hundred, he was functionally healthy, very agile and fit to work. Sixteen years later he was in the same condition. He was outgoing, good-natured, and talkative, and the only thing that annoyed him was that he could not hear well.
>
> In 1958, at the age of one hundred twenty, he was diagnosed as having arteriosclerosis. In 1961 his behavior changed and he appeared somewhat timid and untrusting. In 1962, he was much less talkative and more passive. When the doctors proposed that he should be in the hospital, he agreed. As he was bidding good-bye to his family, he asked his daughter-in-law to serve food to the guests, which he should have done at the beginning of the visit. His daughter-in-law had no authority to serve refreshments without his orders. He was already ill, and died suddenly at the age of one hundred twenty-four.

In a blood pressure study, more than 127 Abkhasians aged over one hundred years were followed for sixteen years. Contrary to the usual trend in both America and the Soviet Union, there was no significant increase in blood pressure as these people grew older. Systolic pressure remained between 110 and 140, and diastolic between 60 and 90. Only five persons had hypertension, six had cerebral arteriosclerosis, and only five had arteriosclerosis of the coronary vessels. Sula Benet also comments on the remarkable ability of Abkhasian elderly to recover from illness or stress:

> One example is Akhutsa Kunach, one hundred fourteen years old. He lived with several generations of his family in the area where he was born. Dr. Walter McKain of the University of Connecticut and Dr. Sichiniva visited him. During the previous winter, while cutting timber in the woods, he had been injured by a falling tree. Three ribs were broken. Two months later the doctors had diagnosed him as fit to work, and he resumed all his former duties. He still felt responsible for his family, and directed the proper reception of his guests.

The examples are many and impressive: Kfaf Lazuria, 139 years old and at the time the oldest woman in the world, could still thread a needle when over one hundred, and often posed for photographers with a cigarette in her mouth—she felt it gave her a suitably jaunty air. Shkhangeri Bzhania was photographed at 148 years of age; at the time he was renowned as a storyteller and local historian. Hassain Gikoz, 109, from the village of Bagmarini, read without glasses and was a sharpshooting hunter. When Shirali Mislimov died in 1973, he was believed to be 168 years old, the oldest person in the world.

Mislimov had lived in the small Abkhasian village of Barzavu, and apparently longevity was a family characteristic: one of his brothers had died at age 134 and the other—the baby—was still living at 106 when older brother Shirali died. His mother had lived to be 110 years, and his father 120. At his death, Shirali Mislimov was living with his third wife, a mere child of 107 years, whom Shirali had married fifty-eight years before, when he was 110. Up to his death, Mislimov remained mentally alert, with a full head of gray hair and a flowing gray beard. His memory had become a bit fuzzy concerning recent events, but he could recall vivid details concerning raids on his village from across the border in Iran, 150 years before! He is believed to have left his village only twice in 168 years: once to obtain his second wife, and a second time to visit the provincial capital. Throughout his life, he remained active doing farm chores around the family homestead, mending fences, feeding the animals, and sawing wood. He retained a healthy appetite and enthusiasm for life, although he was greatly saddened when his closest friend, Makmud Eivasov, died at the tender age of 153, about seven years before Mislimov himself. With his friend's death, it must have become difficult to find anyone else with whom he could reminisce about the good old days.

Aware of their unusual longevity, the Abkhasians have recently formed a dance troupe, requiring that all participants be over ninety years of age.

What is this place, who are the people, and how do they live? More specifically, why do they live so long, and so well?

There are about 100,000 native Abkhasians living in a region about one-half the size of New Jersey. It is just east of the Black Sea, with Turkey and Armenia to the south, and the Ukraine to the north and east, separated by the steep Caucasus Mountains. It is the mythic home of Medea, where Jason voyaged in search of the Golden Fleece, and upon whose mountains Prometheus was bound by an angry Zeus, in punishment for giving fire to mankind. Winters are short and mild, and summers are moderate. But Abkhasia is no garden of Eden; it is steep, thorny, and hard, and the natives say that God created their land as an afterthought. But they say it proudly and with love.

For centuries, the Abkhasians suffered from invasions: Turks attacking from the south, and Russians from the north. The people are predominantly Moslem, and are currently part of the USSR, although they retain a clear sense of ethnic identity and pride. Because the Abkhasian language is exceptionally difficult and their land is quite isolated, the Abkhasians have so far managed to avoid being swallowed up by the much larger Turkish and Russian populations. It is therefore at least possible that some of their extraordinary longevity is due to their rather distinct genetic makeup. As we mentioned earlier, in order to live long, it helps to be born to long-lived parents. This is clearly the case with the Abkhasians, and it probably contributes something to their longevity.

Abkhasians are slim, with very erect posture. They are fair-skinned, and their hair turns gray only late in life. Baldness is very rare. The men typically grow handlebar mustaches and have bushy eyebrows. They appear dignified, even stern. The women, like the men, have black eyes; they are slender and graceful, and both sexes have high cheekbones and prominent noses. Both men and women would be considered handsome and beautiful by Western standards. They generally have their own teeth, even after living one hundred years.

Not surprisingly for such long-lived people, the Abkhasians often look younger than they really are, at least to Western eyes that are used to pronounced physical deterioration by age seventy-five or so. Story has it that recently a visitor was being entertained by an Abkhasian family at a traditional hospitality feast. He raised his glass in toast to a gentleman who looked no older than seventy or seventy-five: "May you live as long as Moses" (120 years, according to legend). But the man was not pleased—he was already 119!

Menarche (the first menstruation) is late, often not until seventeen or eighteen years. Similarly, menopause comes late, and numerous reports describe women in their sixties bearing children.

As for the men, it is not uncommon for centenarians to become fathers. They typically marry late and rarely have more than two or three children.

Perhaps the Abkhasians have genetics on their side. Even so, they must also have something else. To find out what, let's briefly review the major patterns of Abkhasian life, concentrating first on their diet and work habits, and then on the much more complex question of how old people are integrated into the everyday life of Abkhasia, and the nature of that everyday life.

The most striking thing about Abkhasian diet is how little is eaten. Abkhasians consume almost one-third fewer calories than the average American, and hence they are very slim. In fact, the Abkhasian ideal is for men to be downright skinny, and they consider overweight, even in young children, a sign of illness. The major food is "abista," a cornmeal mush that is consumed almost daily. Milk and vegetables constitute 70 percent of the Abkhasian diet, which also includes generous amounts of fruit and honey. In fact, Abkhasia is noted for its flavorful honey, probably due in part to its abundant wildflowers.

Abkhasians consume very little butter and consciously avoid fat. Meat is rarely eaten, except for special ceremonial occasions, when it is cooked in a large iron kettle and carefully distributed, with particular cuts going to particular people, usually because of their age and status in the family. Abkhasians use lots of garlic, fruits, berries, and nuts, especially chestnuts. A wide range of fresh vegetables are eaten, sometimes raw, occasionally lightly cooked, and often pickled. The only thing in their diet not considered "healthful" by Soviet doctors is "adzhika," a hot sauce made of red peppers, salt, dill, garlic, and other natural spices.

Each day, Abkhasians typically drink one or two glasses of "matzoni," a cultured milk rather like buttermilk or kefir. It is also worth noting that, along with neighboring Soviet Georgia, Abkhasia is the vineyard of Russia. Grapes grow everywhere and are made into a dry red wine that is highly prized at dinner and during special feasts. Moderation is valued in all aspects of life, including eating and drinking. Not only is it *de rigeur* to eat small portions, but these must be consumed slowly, with much deliberation. Dietary etiquette requires that one eat daintily, with small nibbling bites, and that drinking be done in small sips.

Many Abkhasians now have tap water, but they use it only for washing and cleaning. They insist on spring water for cooking and drinking, and the women often carry pitchers for long distances on their shoulders. Strong liquor is seldom consumed, although a local home remedy may have helped Abkhasia survive the 1914 smallpox epidemic, when no vaccine was available in the area: "chacha," a 160-proof vodka, distilled from grape skins and mixed with crushed garlic!

Perhaps because of their long history of war and the constant need to protect themselves against Tsarist armies from the north and Turkish slave-raiders from the south, the Abkhasians have developed a military tradition. They pride themselves on being excellent horsemen, which demands agility, slenderness, and all-around athleticism.

Elderly Abkhasians eat much the same as their younger compatriots, only less. Similarly, they work, play, and ride as others do, only less. Retirement is unheard-of. Instead of the drastic change from "working" to "retired," so common in North America, Abkhasian life is a steady, dependable continuum. Older persons gradually work less as they grow older, but so long as they are physically able (which they usually are) they continue to work and to remain active. They may spend less time chopping wood and perhaps more time picking tea and looking after fruit and nut orchards. But though the hours are somewhat fewer and the tasks somewhat easier, the crucial thing is that for older Abkhasians, work goes on. Continuity is the password; continuity of their life and of their work, as long as they live. And that, as we have seen, is long indeed.

A study of twenty-one men and seven women, all over one hundred years old, found that they averaged four hours per day of farm work. And some elderly Abkhasians worked more than that. For example, Kelkilina Rhesa, 109, worked eight hours a day for forty-nine days straight one summer. And Minosyan Grigorii, 90, worked 230 days in one year—about the average for American workers during a five-day week.

It is tempting to attribute part of the extraordinary vigor and longevity of the Abkhasians to their eating and work habits. About the former there can be little doubt. They eat good stuff, low in cholesterol and low in calories. They also keep active and get lots of healthy exercise. But when it comes to work and the question of cause and effect, we have something of a chicken-and-egg problem: Which comes first? Which causes which? Do Abkhasians live long, healthy lives because they continue to work and never truly retire? Or are they able to continue working long into what we would consider old age because they happen to remain healthy and vigorous? Clearly, if a group of people are seriously crippled with arthritis, hardening of the arteries, or senile dementia when old, they are unlikely to be cured by simply requiring that everyone keep working. On the other hand, it is at least possible that some of the Abkhasians' extraordinary vigor arises *because* they keep busy and are never made to feel useless.

❧

Significantly, the Abkhasians have no word for "old people." Rather, they speak of "long-living" people. The difference is subtle but important; in the Abkhasian phrase "long-living," the emphasis is shifted to something positive. Age is seen as an accomplishment that others respect. It is a source of pride.*

The American poet Stephen Vincent Benét expressed a quintessentially modern American view of aging when he wrote:

---

*To some extent, this attitude is characteristic of the Russian people generally, despite their ethnic diversity. Thus, Khrushchev's famous phrase, "we shall bury you," repeated as dire prophecy by the American press, was not necessarily a bellicose threat. Rather it could also be translated, "we shall outlive you," emphasizing the long-standing Soviet concern with longevity.

161

A stone's a stone
And a tree's a tree,
But what was the sense
Of aging me?

It's no improvement
That *I* can see.

By contrast with Benét's complaint, the Abkhasians see age as a definite improvement, like the changes wrought by time in fine wine. Each village has a highly respected Council of Elders, which makes all the important local decisions. In this usage, "elder" refers to position, not age in itself, although the two are very closely allied. (These days, a major function of the Council of Elders is to reconcile tradition with modern Soviet political directives. So far, they have been very successful.)

An ancient Abkhasian proverb says, "Besides God, we also need the village elders." Without a doubt, the Abkhasians do need their "long-living" people, and plainly the need is mutual. Let us now look briefly at Abkhasian life and the role of the long-living people in their society.

Before the introduction of a written alphabet, Abkhasian elderly were probably even more important than they are today. Without writing, human history is limited by the memory of the oldest living persons, and for this reason alone the older persons in any society were always valued. Sometimes they were even treasured and revered. Today in Abkhasia the elderly retain a special status: they know the local medicinal herbs, they mediate disputes, and they provide authority, continuity, and models for the young. An old Abkhasian woman was asked to relate the most damning curse that she knew (and she knew many!). Her response: "Let there be no old folk in your house to give you wise counsel, and no young people to heed their advice."

Abkhasian social life is highly structured, almost rigid. And organizing it all, riding the crest of custom, are the long-living people. Yearly feasts are cooked in huge ceremonial cauldrons, kept by the family elders. Hospitality is a keystone of Abkhasian life, and welcoming meals are typically lengthy and very stylized, often lasting three or four hours. They are punctuated by extended oratorical toasts, through which everyone waits patiently, the young never interrupting. The whole affair is presided over by the oldest male, and if need be, an elder is even borrowed from somewhere else.

Aging in Other Places: Shangri-la, in Three Parts

The Abkhasian language does not seem to translate well into English. Nonetheless, the poem "Abkhasian Wedding" by Konstantin Lomia contains the following impressive (and revealing) lines:

. . . The first speech.
An honored clansman rises
like an ancient cliff.
Attention! . . .

It seems unlikely that a North American poet would ever use such an image: just imagine a "senior citizen" or "golden ager" rising like an ancient cliff. But the long-living Abkhasians are viewed precisely this way. Is it any wonder, then, that they regularly rise to the occasion . . . like ancient cliffs?

Typically, forty to fifty Abkhasians live on the same homestead, comprising three, four, or even five generations. Homesteads are often spaced one-half mile away from one another, and each may consist of several different houses. The largest house is typically reserved for guests, although, significantly, the home of the eldest parents is called "the big house," even though it may actually be the smallest. No sarcasm is intended, however: since the most long-living people live there, it is indeed considered "the big house." Food for the whole family is cooked in the same kitchen, often in the same pot. When the family has grown so large that the pot can no longer contain enough "abista" (cornmeal) for all, the eldest son, his wife, and children move out and build themselves a new house, right next to the parents (with their own cooking pot). Thus, homesteads develop as clusters around the eldest, or "biggest," house.

The most important possessions to an Abkhasian are his personal relationships with others: his family, friends, villagers, and visitors. In the rigid, authoritarian Abkhasian system, no counterculture is tolerated, and everything is carefully prescribed and regulated. There is little room for competition, excessive ambition, or any change from the traditional ways. Children may not even talk to parents if their grandparents or other senior relatives are present; in this way, the existence of older persons demands constant attention and respect.

In earlier days, if the father sat at a chair or bench, the son could not use it the rest of the day. Young people never sat when elders were present. Women could not speak to their fathers-in-law at any time, and husband and wife could not speak to each other if a stranger was present. Even today, they must not sit near one another or express any affection in public. In fact, a wife may not even pronounce her husband's name if others are around.

As anthropologist Benet describes it, Abkhasian life is overwhelmingly sexist, with the differences beginning very early in life:

> To be brought up properly meant, for a boy, to become a heroic warrior, physically strong and courageous, able to use weapons and ride skillfully. He also had to be well-mannered, a fluent orator, and knowledgeable in Abkhasian lore. The girl was taught housework, spinning, weaving, and embroidery. For her, proper behavior meant modesty, respect, and self control.

In fact, self-control and discipline are expected of all Abkhasians, male and female. Both men and women are expected to hide their emotions in public, to speak little, and to avoid all forms of overindulgence, whether eating, drinking, or sex.

The rigid, unbending Abkhasian social life may seem unappealing to modern Westerners. The Abkhasians are granted fewer personal freedoms and less opportunity for each individual to explore his or her own potential. But, if the Abkhasians aren't permitted to "find themselves," they also are unlikely ever to lose themselves in the first place. They grow up with a profound sense of their own personal identity. No one is left out. The result? A deep feeling of security, a certainty of who one is, and a complete confidence of growing old and ever more powerful within that system.

The Abkhasians seem to apply order and structure to every situation. As Dr. Benet notes:

> Women greet female visitors by slightly pressing their shoulder against the visitor's chest. If the guest is not offered these ceremonial greetings, she may turn around and leave immediately. Men and women extend greetings to one another when they are on horseback by standing in their stirrups.
>
> Seating arrangements are taken as seriously as in diplomatic circles. The place of honor at a meal is the farthest from the door, except when the table is set in the courtyard. When a meal is to be served in the courtyard, the most important seats are those closest to the house. When people eat in an open field, those of highest rank sit closest to a tree. For want of a tree, a mountain, or a river, the direction of the sun or moon will substitute. If it is pitch dark,

an Abkhasian will drive a staff into the ground and use it as a point
of reference.

A point of reference. The long-living Abkhasians provide points
of reference for those who have not yet lived as long. And in
turn, Abkhasian society provides a point of reference for the long-
lived ones among them. The behavior of individuals and groups
is uniform, unvarying, and highly predictable. So is the identity
of each person, embedded in a matrix of relatives and friends—
but relatives above all. The Abkhasians have a saying: "He who
has no relatives will embrace a fence post." And the worst pen-
alty that can be visited upon someone is to have his family name
taken away.

Not surprisingly, Abkhasians are seldom found embracing
fence posts. Each person is part of an "azhvala," a large clan of
relatives, all with the same last name. Each azhvala has its own
shrine—perhaps a sacred grove of trees, or a particular mountain.
Every azhvala is, in turn, composed of several subdivisions ("abi-
para") which are further subdivided into separate extended families, each with its own homestead. When Dr. Benet asked different Abkhasians how many relatives they had, she got such
answers as 350 and 500. How many relatives do *you* have?

Abkhasian infants are tightly swaddled and are not even held
while being nursed: the mother leans over the cradle and gives
her infant a breast. Maybe this early treatment conditions them
to accept authority (some psychoanalytically-inclined anthropologists have suggested just this). Certainly, they obey their elders
unquestioningly and do so without ever being punished physically. There are no rigorous initiations or rites of passage separating the generations, and this may help to explain why all ages
are harmoniously integrated in Abkhasian life. Yet, there is no
question that Abkhasians know the meaning of age and value it
highly, and there is also no question that the long-living people
earn the respect of their younger countrymen.

Abkhasian poet Rasul Gamzatuv summed it up and also—un-
intentionally—responded to skeptical Western gerontologists
when he wrote:

I care not for critics and their learned prose,
But for elder folk in their mountain homes.

❦

For our second Shangri-la, we must travel to the other side of the globe—to southern Ecuador and the region surrounding Vilcabamba. Here we find a remote valley, with a total population of about one thousand. In the nearby Catholic city of Lojas, the "viejos," or old ones, of the Vilcabamba region are considered to be nothing short of a miracle. To professional gerontologists, that may be somewhat exaggerated, but not much.

Vilcabamba may derive its name from the native Andean language of Quechua, in which "Vilca" means sacred and "bamba" means valley. Alternatively, it could come from the vilco tree, from which a commonly-used hallucinatory drug is extracted. In any event, there is an air of magic and mystery about the region, lying amidst the tumbled rocky ruins of ancient Inca dwellings, and it has attracted its share of odd characters. One "Dr. Lovewisdom," the "renowned international sage," lived for a time on the mountainside above the village. There, he spent his time absorbing the "magnetic sunstorms which can eliminate the toxins that cause death—the cell being immortal if it has the means of detoxifying itself."

There is even a buried treasure. Atahualpa, the last of the Inca kings, was held captive in Lima by the conquering Spaniards long ago. His people sought to ransom him, by bringing treasure to the ever-greedy conquistadores. In fact, tourists in Lima can still see the mark on a storeroom wall, indicating the height to which Inca treasure was to be piled, in order for Atahualpa to be released. Story has it that the final treasure caravan, one thousand mules strong, was late arriving. The Spaniards grew impatient and Atahualpa was killed. When the caravan leader heard of this, he supposedly buried the treasure—including the king's solid gold throne—down seven deep shafts.

Despite its romantic (and practical) appeal, the treasure seems not to be conducive to good health, or longevity. At least one Jesuit missionary is said to have gone mad seeking it. On the other hand, in the mid-eighteenth century, Sanchez Orinjana, a poor peasant, found a trove of gold ingots and small ornaments. It took 120 mules to carry the find, and Sanchez Orinjana became wealthy. He bought a great estate in the region and became a "marquis." (That leaves 880 mule loads yet to be found.)

Strange and mysterious tales seem to abound in Vilcabamba. It is filled with sacred places and an extraordinary atmosphere, steeped in tradition.

The immediate, day-to-day atmosphere is not bad either. At an elevation of 4,500 feet, yet near the equator, Vilcabamba enjoys a mild climate, with the temperature varying little from one season to the next, and between day and night. Winters tend to be rainy and summers dry. Human beings—too many human beings—have lived here for a long time, and little remains of the "natural habitat." However, bears and mountain tapir are said to inhabit the higher mountains, and armadillos are eaten when caught, along with the "tumulla," a kind of porcupine without quills. The lakes and rivers are generally polluted, except high in the mountains, and an old spring, sacred to the Incas, is used to supply water. Interestingly, gold often appears in the river water, washed down from the mountains following heavy rains.

Using the same methods of cross-checking applied to the Abkhasians, British geriatrician David Davies has produced impressive evidence that the inhabitants of Vilcabamba and environs live to be extraordinarily old, while remaining active and healthy all the while. Further proof comes from the written baptismal certificates carefully registered and filed in the local churches. In fact, this region boasted the oldest clearly authenticated person in the world, Samuel Rochas, who in 1973 was 131 years old. In most economically developed countries, only one person in ten thousand or twenty thousand ever reaches a century of life. Vilcabamba, by contrast, with a population of 819, boasted nine centenarians in 1973. Davies himself suspects that the proportion might be higher yet in the more inaccessible mountain regions.

Here is Davies' own account of his first meeting with one of Vilcabamba's "viejos," this one a mere stripling of eighty-eight:

> From a side lane we suddenly saw what looked like a moving mountain of sugar cane bearing down on us rapidly. Victor called on it to halt. The large bundle of sugar cane, on its way to the Rio Frio's sugar mill, dropped to the ground to reveal a weather-beaten old gentleman in patched clothes and a large Panama hat. He took off his hat as he bowed to us to reveal a head of almost jet black hair, with a little gray at the side. He was very lean and slim, though the smile he gave us was rather toothless. Victor told him that I was a scientist who had come to look at the old people of the valley and then asked him his age. He was eighty-eight. Victor thought this was nothing unusual and was quite blase about it. With a smile and a nod, rejecting our offers of help with the heavy load that I could hardly lift off the ground, the old man briskly put the sugar

167

cane back on his unbent shoulders and walked on in the direction of the sugar mill. He had probably cut the sugar cane that morning and traveled several kilometers immediately to avoid the sugar juice bleeding too much from the cane—he must have been up with the dawn. Although he was toothless, his face had not the sunken look often found on Europeans when they have lost all their teeth. There was something almost boyish about him as he continued down the trail with his load.

The centenarians of Ecuador are typically short, the men rarely more than five feet five inches tall. They have prominent, eagle-like noses and are usually very slim. The women have long, straight, abundant black hair and the men rarely become bald. Often the men sport great tufts of thick, coarse hair on their chests, calves, and the backs of their hands, and it even grows from their ears. Menarche is late, rarely before thirteen; and not uncommonly, women in their sixties continue to bear children. In fact, 30 percent of all births are to women aged forty-five years and more. And some men, for their part, continue fathering children after age one hundred.

Sex is hearty and active, with the men actually expected to have regular extramarital affairs. Nor is age an obstacle to sex. The Vilcabambans have no notion of a "dirty old man"; rather, active sexuality is an accepted and prideful part of being alive and healthy, at any age. (A small model of an erect penis, carved from stone, is carried by adult women between their breasts, and by men in their pockets.)

Pregnancy is valued, especially by the men, who validate their masculinity when their wives bear children. The men are also prone to smoke and drink heavily, and also take hallucinogenic drugs derived from the vilco tree. Interestingly, marriage seems particularly to oppress women in this highly sexist society, and young married women age rapidly—much more quickly than unmarried women, or men. The duties of mother, cook, house-keeper, and wife take an obvious toll of married Vilcabamban women and, not surprisingly, most female centenarians have not been married. The married ones tend to die earlier.

The muscles and joints of Vilcabambans typically remain flexible even past their hundredth year. Heart disease, high blood pressure, and cancer are virtually unknown, and no one knows why. On the other hand, influenza and internal parasites are a frequent problem—as is modern medicine, at least on occasion.

Witness the case of Miguel Carpio, age 120, who was found to have a benign liver tumor a few years ago. He walked several miles to a hospital, had the tumor surgically removed, and later walked back home. Fortunately, he survived the absolutely unnecessary surgery, but now he must use a stick when he walks.

Vilcabambans typically have terrible teeth. The front ones are often gone by age thirteen or fourteen, and the molars reduced to mere shells. Nonetheless, the gums remain healthy and tough, more than adequate for the gruel-based diet. Their eating is monotonous and austere, heavily based on corn. Meat is very rare, cholesterol levels are very low, and the children appear skinny, almost emaciated. In addition to the ever-present corn, Vilcabambans eat cassava (yucca), potatoes, beans, soy, cottage cheese made from both cow and goat's milk, some wheat, and barley. The soil is rich in calcium, and so presumably is the produce. Green vegetables (including cabbage, cauliflower, celery, and peas) are also important, as well as citrus fruits such as oranges, mangoes, pomegranates, guavas, limes, and sweet lemons. They also grow excellent coffee, which is exported. Despite this seeming diversity, however, the diet of Vilcabambans is terribly boring by North American standards, although it may well promote longevity.

The oldest people typically do not live in town, but rather on the small farms up in the mountains. Here they get better water than the townspeople, and a more healthful although less varied diet. Thus, the village diet is largely based on carbohydrates from which most of the food value has been removed: white processed flour, white sugar, and, increasingly, tinned and fatty food. Centenarians occasionally come to live in town, and when they do, they seem to deteriorate rapidly.

The typical Andean centenarian is poor, lives up in the mountains, eats very little meat, and works hard every day except Sunday when he comes to town, goes to church, and gets drunk. He walks miles every day on steep mountain trails and works hard cultivating small fields that are often too steep for safety—at least, to the non-Ecuadorian observer. The day begins early, about 5:30 A.M., with the crowing of ever-present roosters, and ends equally early, often by 7:30 P.M., with the sunset. It is a life of equilibrium and tranquility: little variance in temperature and humidity; dawn and dusk at the same times each day; and the predictable, steady ebb and flow of the human life cycle. Life in the mountains around Vilcabamba is not exciting in the Westernized sense. Indeed, nothing much seems to happen, and the old people themselves are agreed that their lives are long because they are so "tranquilo."

❧

The Hunzas, or Hunzucuts, are the third group of extremely long-lived people. Unfortunately, they are virtually unknown, both to anthropologists and to physicians, largely because their home is even more remote than either the Abkhasians' or the Vilcabambans'—and that is saying quite a lot. There appear to be roughly 40,000 Hunzas, about three-quarters of them living in Pakistani-controlled Kashmir, and the remainder in China's Sinkiang province. Several teams of Western observers have at least managed to visit the Pakistani population. It lives in steep, mountain country, just northeast of the fabled Khyber Pass, near the Soviet border.

The Hunzas are light-skinned, and are rumored to be descended from some of Alexander the Great's soldiers and their Persian lovers. Like the Vilcabambans, they tend mountain farms, are quite poor, and walk a great deal. Their diet appears to be based largely on grains, especially wheat, barley, and buckwheat, as well as legumes such as beans, chickpeas, and lentils. They also eat a great deal of cottage cheese, green vegetables such as spinach and lettuce, and roots such as carrots, turnips, potatoes, and radishes. Fruits are also abundant, and meat, once again, is very rare. Pakistani nutritionist Dr. S. Maqsood Ali studied their diet and found that the average Hunzucut consumed less than 2,000 calories per day; by contrast, the average American packs away about 3,300. Moreover, meat and dairy products constitute a mere 1.5 percent of the Hunzucut diet. Oils, for example, are more likely to come from pressed apricot pits than from animal fat.

As with the Abkhasians, the Hunzucuts lack a written language and therefore they have no conclusive documentation of their age. Prominent Harvard physician Alexander Leaf, who visited the Pakistani Hunzas in the early 1970s, reported that "I was not able to confirm exact ages in Hunza. Yet I had the definite impression of an unusual number of very vigorous old folk clambering over the steep slopes that make up this mountainous land. It was the fitness of many of the elderly rather than their extreme ages that impressed me." Clearly, if the elderly are un-usually fit, it seems likely that they will continue to live for a long time.

Reputedly the oldest living Hunza is a distinguished gentle-man named Tulah Beg, who at the age of 110 bedecks himself in elegant ceremonial garb. And 95-year-old Akbar Khan goes daily into his steep mountain pastures—averaging about 30 de-grees of slope—to bale hay for the coming winter.

As with the Abkhasians and Vilcabambans, the Hunzas re-main active throughout their long lives. And as with the Abkha-sians in particular, Hunza society pays special heed to its elders, rewarding their age by respecting their experience. Thus, the rul-ing Mir of Hunza holds court daily at 10 every morning, sur-rounded by his council of elders—twenty wise old men who sit around the throne on special cushions, listen to the various ar-guments, debate among themselves, and then contribute to the governance of their people.

Because their homeland is physically isolated, and also politi-cally sensitive, the Hunzas remain shrouded in mystery. None-theless, it seems clear that like the Abkhasians and the Vilca-bambans, they retain their vigor into advanced old age—remaining active at an age when most of their North American and European counterparts reside in nursing homes, retirement communities, or mortuaries.

❧

This chapter is concerned not with North America or even Europe, but rather with those few, faraway places in which ex-treme longevity seems remarkably common. Reading these ac-counts, however, one cannot help but wonder: What about the West? Certainly, we have our centenarians too, although fewer proportionately than Abkhasia, Vilcabamba, or Hunzaland. As a society, in fact, the old we often abhor, whereas the *very* old, we adore. Not surprisingly, therefore, people who are already old have long tended to exaggerate their ages, just like in the Shan-gri-las we have just visited.

For example, Thomas Parr, better known to the English as "Old Parr," was buried at Westminster Abbey, after he supposedly reached the age of 152. However, this is almost certainly a fake, although no less a scientist than William Harvey, discoverer of how the heart and circulatory system work, certified him to be very ancient indeed. Charlie Smith, an American black, died in 1979. This Florida resident claimed to have been brought to the United States in 1854, when he was sold at a slave auction in New Orleans at age twelve. That would place his final age at 137, a figure that many doubt, but which has been accepted by the American Medical Association, as well as the Social Security Administration. In his impulsive youth, he had retired from work as a fruit picker at 113, when his employer felt that Mr. Smith was getting too old to climb trees. Undaunted, he then opened a candy store.

Walter Williams, who called himself the "Old Rebel," died in Texas in 1959, at the reputed age of 117—he claimed to be the last surviving Confederate soldier. There are many authenticated records of persons surviving to be 110 or 111; interestingly, such people often die just after their birthdays. It is as though they strain to keep themselves alive long enough to achieve the next milestone, like a runner putting out that extra effort when the finish line is in view.

❦

What can we conclude from the information we have on the remarkably long-living Abkhasians, Vilcabambans, and Hunzas? Of course, we can—and should—be somewhat skeptical about some of their age claims. The Vilcabambans are the best documented, although the Abkhasians are the best studied, with the Hunzas being the least known overall. But even if we admit that some of their ages are exaggerated, it is evident that people in these three areas do generally live longer and remain vigorous longer than most other people. By contrast, centenarians in North America are few and far between. They are idiosyncratic cases, rather than examples of the kinds of general patterns shown in the world's three Shangri-las. Clearly, something unusual is going on in those places. But what?

It is possible that all three peoples are genetically long-living. They all live in isolated places and have not interbred greatly with other people. By chance alone their ancestors may have had genes promoting longevity—or, more likely, they lacked genes for early death. This may be a partial explanation, but it probably doesn't carry us very far. It doesn't take into account, for instance, the fact that human physical characteristics vary considerably from one Ecuadorian village to another. Such physical variation suggests genetic variation as well, and yet longevity is still found. Furthermore, in Abkhasia, other long-living peoples whose gene pool is probably quite different from the Abkhasians' also inhabit the region. Most notably, it is home to mountain-dwelling Jews, who also appear to reach fabulous old age. They are almost completely unknown to modern-day anthropologists, although it appears that they do not intermarry with their Moslem neighbors. It is hard to believe that both Moslem Abkhasians and Jewish Abkhasians just happen to be especially endowed with an abundance of longevity-permitting genes, while the rest of the world (except for southern Ecuador and Hunzaland) are sadly deficient.

Socially and environmentally, all three modern-day Shangri-las have several things in common. For one, they are all poor. In itself, however, poverty almost certainly does not promote longevity. The Vilcabambans, in fact, suffer from a very high infant and early childhood mortality, due to parasites, cholera, and other diseases. But once they reach old age, they are likely to live a long time. Poverty may enhance longevity by reducing the amount of meat and fat in the diet. Poor people can't afford the rich foods that clog our arteries and overburden our hearts. Abkhasians consume very little meat (by Western standards) and Vilcabambans and Hunzas eat even less. In fact, all three peoples consume very few calories. Not surprisingly, they also tend to be skinny—from birth—and this may be related to their remarkably low incidence of heart disease and arteriosclerosis. Recall McKay's semi-starved but long-living rats; by restricting calorie intake early in life, these people may also increase their lifespan. Of course, a deficient diet does not guarantee longevity. Rather, the key may lie in a stringent but adequate diet that contains all the necessary nutrients, but in minimum supply.

Gourmets and gourmands would not like the menus at Shangri-la. They might well echo the classic complaint of the restaurant goer: "First, the food is terrible. Second, the portions are too small!" (On the other hand, they would probably have a longer time in which to be dissatisfied.)

Beyond the lean and stringent diet, the world's three Shangri-las have other things in common. For example, all are located at moderately high elevations. Since people living at higher altitudes tend to develop a higher concentration of red blood cells, it is at least possible that medium elevations—with resulting intermediate red blood cell densities—are most conducive to longevity. Furthermore, all three peoples regularly get a good dose of healthy, vigorous exercise, generally by walking. Just as healthful eating may lie between starvation and gluttony, and optimum elevation between sea level and mountain tops, perhaps the most productive exercise lies between inactivity and daily marathon running. Several thousand years ago, Aristotle called it the "Golden Mean." More recently, economist Kenneth Boulding called it the "Goldilocks Principle": not too little, not too much, but rather, just right.

Another characteristic of all three societies is their outdoor, rural life and slow pace. All three areas seem to have been by-passed by modern technology, industrialization, and the hurried, harried, frantic rush of our times. (Actually, collective farms and mechanized agriculture have begun to affect Soviet Abkhasia, but Abkhasian society, with its firmly entrenched Councils of Elders, has been able to roll with the punches and remain fundamentally unchanged.) Perhaps being close to nature rather than asphalt is somehow life-preserving and age-defying. Maybe the rhythm of seasons and harvests, of natural ebb and flow, leads to a more healthful, natural rhythm within ourselves.

So far, most of us are likely to agree with these conclusions. It seems intuitively reasonable that eating less and leaner, getting regular exercise, and maybe even living at medium altitudes could help us live longer. And certainly, most Americans already cling to a Tom Sawyer image of the perfect life in a more peaceful, bucolic Garden of Eden. But another common thread in all three Shangri-las may be much less appealing; namely, the curious social rigidity that seems to go along with becoming a super-centenarian. Of the three peoples, the Abkhasians are best known in this respect, although the Vilcabambans and Hunzas seem likely to fall in a similar mold: the social code is rigid and inflexible, carefully prescribing everybody's relationship to everybody else, and delimiting exactly what can and cannot be done. Given our current predilection for "doing our own thing," for "letting it all hang out," and other expressions of unstructured individualism, we may be repelled by a society with a place for everyone and the requirement that everyone remain in his or her place. Having a place may well promote longevity, but having to stay exactly in that place may be intolerable and perhaps simply not worth it. To avoid hardening of the arteries, must we endure a hardening of the social categories?

Perhaps the inhabitants of an ideal Shangri-la could discover how to provide themselves with the emotional comfort and security of an unquestioned identity, while at the same time encouraging personal growth and fulfillment. It is a tall order.

Finally, we come to one of the most appealing yet problematic aspects of Abkhasian, Vilcabamban, and Hunza society: the continued, active involvement of aged persons in personal and community life. It is tempting to conclude that these people live to a great age because their society gives them something to live for. They are expected to remain active, vigorous, and involved, and accordingly they do. They receive respect and often veneration. They rightly feel proud of their age and experience, certainly not ashamed. And they just keep on living, as their society expects them to.

But once again, this poses a chicken-and-egg problem. Maybe the vigor and longevity of certain people is encouraged by the important roles given them in their society. On the other hand, maybe the vigor and longevity came first. Given that people are living into a hearty and robust old age (for whatever reason), it seems only natural that their society would make an important place for them. If, instead, people typically were becoming incompetent and decrepit by age seventy, it is hard to imagine that their society would expect much of them. And there certainly wouldn't be much room for centenarians. Observers, like ourselves, might then conclude that these people were short-lived because their society did not accommodate them. We just do not know whether healthy longevity is a *cause* of the prominent place of the aged in Abkhasian, Vilcabamban, and Hunzan society, or if it is a result of society's attitude toward its aged members. As the rabbi told his wife, both are probably correct.

12

Aging in Other Places

A Selected Anthropology of Growing Old

We have all heard the expression "muscle-bound." The typical
Mr. Universe, with overdeveloped biceps, has concentrated on
just one thing: building muscles. As a result, he has lost flexibility and range of movement. In our thinking about aging, it is
all too easy to concentrate on just one society—our own—and
thereby become "culture-bound." Accordingly, it is useful to
stretch our thinking a bit, develop some flexibility, and give some
attention to people in other places. There are many ways of
growing old.

There are two particular benefits that we can hope to gain
from this exercise in anthropology. For one, it will help us to
appreciate the human diversity that surrounds aging. In some
cases, we may recoil in horror, while in others we may like what
we see. Certainly, we are under no obligation to accept the patterns of aging in any human society as models of what we should
try to copy or avoid. But, if nothing else, the study of aging in
other cultures may temporarily transport us a healthy distance
from our own. This new perspective may help us to look with
fresh eyes at what we now take for granted.

The other benefit is a view of our unity, the flip side of diversity. We are all one species and hence have many things in common. Underlying the dazzling variety of different people growing
old in different places in different ways, we should be able to
detect a oneness, a commonality. If there is an objective reality
to aging in *Homo sapiens,* then by sampling the aging process in
different human cultures, certain patterns, true for all, ought to
emerge eventually. And maybe someday our understanding of

176

aging will be truly "well developed," with an intellectual physique that is both muscular and flexible.

❧

Spring it is cheery,
Winter is dreary,
Green leaves hang, but the brown must fly;
When he's forsaken,
Wither'd and shaken,
What can an old man do but die?

(Thomas Hood)

It is almost a truism that old people in modern societies have a difficult time, especially because society itself seems to be so set against them. It seems no less true, however, that in primitive societies old people also have a difficult time, simply because life is hard, and old life tends to be harder yet, regardless of society's attitudes. Thus, anthropologist Leo W. Simmons estimated that in primitive societies, people over sixty-five rarely make up more than 2 or 3 percent of the population. (Compare that with 10 to 15 percent in modern societies.) A Cree Indian of North America was said to be lucky if he lived to see any gray hairs on his children. Mongol women were reportedly old and wrinkled at forty; and speaking of the Bontoc Igorot, a Philippine group, one anthropologist said, "by forty-five most men are fast getting old. Their faces are seamed, their muscles losing form, their carriage less erect, and their step slower. By fifty-five all are old and most are bent and thin. Probably not over one or two in a hundred live to be seventy."

Of the Eskimos of Point Barrow, Alaska, it was said in the nineteenth century, "They very rarely attain a great age, and the majority by far die under the age of forty years, and a man at sixty becomes very decrepit." Examples of this sort could be multiplied almost indefinitely.

In general, primitive people age fast and die young. If life were easier on them, it seems clear that they would age more slowly and survive longer—witness the higher proportion of elderly people in modernized countries. But as it is, the romantic ideal of happy, healthy old age among the "noble savages" seems rarely to have been realized.

Actually, the status of old people in primitive societies tends to be quite high, but in most cases this lasts only so long as they

177

retain their faculties and a semblance of their previous strength. As they become less able to pull their weight and contribute to the group, they are more likely to be neglected, abandoned, or even killed outright. Although such treatment may seem vicious to us, it really says more about the hardness of primitive life than the hardness of their hearts. When people live balanced on the knife edge of starvation, love for an aged parent often loses precedence to the cruel realities of survival. One generation asks another, "What have you done for me lately?"

Anthropologist John Moffat once found an old Hottentot woman, left by herself in the South African desert. By her own account: "Yes, my children, three sons and two daughters, are gone to yonder blue mountain and have left me to die. . . . I am very old, you see, and am not able to serve them. When they kill game, I am too feeble to help in carrying home the flesh. I am not able to gather wood and make a fire, and I cannot carry their children on my back as I used to." Why was this old woman abandoned by her children? For the same reason a North American might discard a worn-out possession: my television set was no longer working, you see, so I bought a new one. I am old, you see, and no longer working, so I am left to die. Do you see? She did, anyhow.

The ancient Greek historian Herodotus tells us that the Issedones offered sacrifices to their aged parents, whereas the Bactrians fed them to flesh-eating dogs, and the ancient Sardinians tossed their elders from cliffs, laughing as they fell on the rocks below. The Greeks commonly burned their parents' bodies, while the Callatiae were said to eat theirs. Always one to stir up trouble, King Darius of Persia asked representatives of both peoples, gathered at his court, if they would consider exchanging traditions. Both groups were horrified at the prospect. (Herodotus concludes from this, "not Darius, but custom, is the king of all.")

In rural Japan, the elderly were supposedly carried up into the "mountains of death" and left there to die. In some Eskimo groups, old people were expected to commit suicide by abandoning themselves on ice floes or simply by walking off into the snow when times were very hard and famine was upon their people. Even when old people were killed outright, it has typically been with much ceremony and respect, even reverence. Among the Ojibway Indians of North America, while an old man sang a death song and smoked the pipe of peace, his son was expected to kill him with a tomahawk. The Chukchee people of Siberia held a great feast to honor an old man, once he became incapacitated by his age. At the climactic moment, while all sang his praises, the old man's son or younger brother slipped behind him and strangled him with a seal bone. Interestingly, the preferred instrument was often the baculum, or penis bone, symbolic of the strength and vigor that had been lost.

Extraordinary as it may seem, such "geronticide" does not usually imply any lessening of respect—in some cases, quite the opposite. For example, few societies have accorded old people more reverence and heartfelt love than ancient Samoa. Even today, Samoa would appear to be a fine place in which to be old. And yet, it was here that the notorious ritual of "live burial" was practiced. These people were not pushed, protesting, into their graves. Rather, once they felt their death approaching, they would request a funeral. For the old man who had not achieved honor by dying in battle or at sea, what better end to a long life than by attending his own funeral? At these jolly, memorable feasts, respect for the guest of honor was shown by the number of pigs slaughtered in his name. A good time was had by all; and in a way it resembled a classic Irish wake, except that in Samoa the future corpse also joined in the fun.

Ironically, societies that relied heavily on old people may have been especially threatened by an indication of their weakening—either physical or mental. Simone de Beauvoir writes that society "extols the strength and the fecundity that are so closely linked with youth and it dreads the worn-out sterility, the decrepitude of age." Sir James Frazer reports that among some peoples the chief is killed immediately at the first sign of his weakening, especially if his sexual potency begins to flag. Such "regicide" is reported for many African peoples, including the Nemi, the Shilluke of the Nile, and the Chitume, and also in the Congo and in Calicut.

Despite the abundant accounts of the death and dying of old people—or perhaps, because of them—it is very difficult to generalize about the subject. Anthropologist Leo Simmons reported that across different cultures the treatment of the dying elderly varied from "the height of homage to the depth of degradation. Under varying circumstances, and often entirely beyond personal control, an aged person faced with death might be neglected, abandoned, cast out, or killed by his closest of kin; or

179

instead, he might be protected by them and nursed along to the very moment of expiration. In the hour of death the aged might be feared or loved, despised or honored, reviled or even worshiped. And he, in turn, might deny death as a natural necessity, resist it as a curse, submit to it as the hand of fate, embrace it as a golden opportunity or even demand it as a right."

❧

It ought to be lovely to be old
to be full of peace that comes of experience
and wrinkled ripe fulfillment.

. . . .
Soothing, old people should be, like apples
when one is tired of love.
Fragrant like yellow leaves, and dim with the soft
stillness and satisfaction of autumn.

And a girl should say:
It must be wonderful to live and grow old.
Look at my mother, how rich and still she is!—

And a young man should think: By Jove
my father has faced all weathers, but it's been a life!

(D. H. Lawrence)

D. H. Lawrence is considered a modern writer. The same society that was initially scandalized by him has now made a permanent place for Lady Chatterley and her lover. Lawrence's poem on old age positively yearns for respect and peace, for a quiet exaltation no less profound than his stormy glorification of sex. Just as Lawrence's sexuality was initially rejected, his vision of age seems almost obscene in its pious hoping. And yet, Lawrence's earlier writing triumphed because it spoke of something deep and true within us. The same can be said for his poetic view of age.

Furthermore, it is a valid statement about the actual lives of many people, since despite the physical harshness of aging, there is often a "wrinkled ripe fulfillment" about being old—at least for those in our species who are fortunate enough to reach that state among people who respect age and being old.

For many, old equals wise. It is that simple.

In Bali, it is told that long ago, in a remote mountain village, all the old men were rounded up, sacrificed, and eaten. The young people who were left then wanted to build a great house for ceremonial meetings. However, after cutting the necessary trees, none of them could tell the tops from the bottoms, and the house could not be built. Then, a young man arose from among them and said that he would solve their problem, but only if the villagers would promise never to kill old people again. They agreed, whereupon the young man brought out his grandfather, whom he had hidden. The old man proceeded to teach the young men how to tell top from bottom (which, in a manner of speaking, has been the function of old men ever since).

Among the isolated Indian villages of Mexico, where the old traditions still persist, and more people speak ancient Zapotec than modern Spanish, the world "anciano"—or female, "anciana"—means not just old, but old and revered (and also, to be sure, physically weak). English has no equivalent word. When the ancianos tell a story, the traditional beginning is not "Once upon a time," but rather, "Because I am old I tell this story."

A nineteenth-century account of premissionary Samoa speaks of legends and history being passed down by a "hoary headed, toothless, half-blind, wrinkle-faced old man . . . surrounded by his sons and grandsons, and great-grandsons, as they lay together on their mats in the dusk of the evening." It all makes sense, considering that for untold generations all human history and knowledge was limited to the memory of the oldest man. Accordingly, the old were to be trusted, revered, and cherished. This attitude is reflected in the folktales of people around the world, which often portray old people as founts of wisdom and beneficence.

For example, in a Papuan folktale, a man paddled his canoe to the moon, which first appeared to him as a small boy, then a young man, and eventually an old man. The voyager didn't trust the moon until it finally appeared as a very old man, complete with walking stick. Only then did the Papuan leave his canoe and go ashore.

The Crow Indians say that "once an old man was fasting on a mountain top. The stars came down and taught him to sing songs and give him tobacco." The Arawak of South America tell of a time long ago when their ancestors were traveling, led by an old man who warned them not to eat a certain fish. One rash young fellow disobeyed and died. The old man also showed them how to hunt, but one refused to learn and caught nothing. The old man taught them how to build houses so as to be safe from marauding bats. One refused and insisted on sleeping outside on his hammock: in the morning, only a few bones were left of him. The old man told his people not to use a particular canoe; one disobeyed, floated out to the ocean, and was lost. And so it goes.

Not surprisingly, these stories that glorify old age are typically told by people who are themselves old, who probably make the best of the opportunity to embellish them further. An old Polar Eskimo, speaking to explorer K. Rasmussen, explained that "our tales are men's experiences . . . to the words of the newly born none give much credence, but the experience of the older generations contains truth. When I narrate legends, it is not I who speak, but the wisdom of our forefathers."

Gods are often pictured as old, but never as senile. Voltaire suggested that man created God in his own image. If so, it was almost certainly *old* men that did the handiwork. The Jewish and Christian God is usually pictured as ancient, complete with flowing white beard, and "a thousand years in Thy sight are but as yesterday."

Age, experience, and wisdom have been closely bound together in the human psyche. This is tellingly expressed in the following account by anthropologist W. C. Holden, written in 1871. Picture the scene: a young Akamba native had just returned to his East African tribe from a trip to Europe, the first such journey ever made by one of his people. "For some time, the entire party sat in uninterrupted silence, the old men unwilling to admit curiosity." Finally, an elder said, "Well, young man, it is said you are older than we are; you have travelled farther and seen more; you have crossed the sea. Now tell us of your wanderings and what you have seen, but do not pour lies on us." "Yes father," replied the youth deferentially. After the telling, another old man said, "Young man, if you speak the truth, you are old, you have seen much, we are but children." And the aged chief added: "Young man, we thank you for your news. You have made us older than we were, but you are older still, for you have seen with your eyes what we only hear with our ears."

The aged person has seen and done much. He has accumulated many experiences and much knowledge; hence he is wise. Sometimes, society takes an active role in promoting such wisdom. For example, John Hamer, anthropologist at Dalhousie University in Nova Scotia, has studied aging among the Sidamo of southwest Ethiopia. He reports that among these people, the old are exalted. Promotion to "elder" (actually reached during what we would call late middle age—one's fifties) is the most important step in life. At this point, a man no longer makes war or does manual labor; rather, he advises, conducts ritual sacrifices, and so forth. Young people are typically greeted curtly, whereas elders receive lengthy and elaborate greeting. Simple funerals must suffice for the young, whereas complex, time-consuming walls of bamboo are constructed around an elder's grave. The elders live in style and die the same way.

Hamer reports that child-rearing among the Sidamo involves much teasing of children by their parents. As a result, youthful spontaneity is eventually curbed. After a lengthy apprenticeship under these conditions, a Sidamo learns not to act until he or she has considered various alternatives as well as all possible outcomes. This blunting of youthful impetuousness is thought of as true wisdom and uniquely qualifies a world-be elder to join the exalted ranks.

The highland Druze of Israel's Golon Heights treat their unique religion as a kind of conspiracy within Islam. Young Druze are kept from the special secrets; in fact, traditionally they are not even told that they are Druze until they are older. Young men, not yet initiated into the secret books, are called "Jahil," the unknowing ones. By late middle age, they may aspire to being "Aqil," those who know. By this time, they are expected to have purged themselves of emotion and appetites, and to be duly reflective.

The Samoans, as already mentioned, hold the aged in high regard. Their society once was and still is organized by the "matai" system, each matai being the elected leader of his extended family. Generally, the oldest member is chosen. Samoan language also shows the respect accorded age: all male relatives are called "father" so long as they are at least fifteen years older than the person in question. Those within ten to fifteen years in age are known as "brother," and those who are fifteen or more years younger are called "son." A similar age-defined system of respect holds for women, who are called "mother," "sister," or "daughter," respectively. Among the African Bantu-speaking peoples, a comparable pattern is found: someone who is wise and benevolent is known as "grandfather" or "grandmother," regardless of the actual biological relationship.

In some cases, respect for the elderly is simply institutionalized. It is demanded, given, received, and rarely questioned. Among the ancient Incas, the word of the priest-king was law, and the law stated that first, the land of the Sun God was tilled; second, the land belonging to widows, the sick, and the aged; and only then, one's own land. Among the Aztecs, Montezuma II gave the sick, orphaned, and aged an entire city, Calhuacan. There they were fed, clothed, and lodged out of the public coffers. The Iroquois say that "it is the will of the Great Spirit that you reverence the aged, even though they be as helpless as infants." And a common Iroquois prayer begins, "Preserve our old men among us." The Bible is similarly clear: "Days shall speak and a multitude of years shall teach wisdom." Leviticus is no less clear than Proverbs: "Thou shalt rise up before the hoary head and honor the face of the old man." And Deuteronomy states that a disobedient son, who fails to obey his father, shall be brought to the village elders, who will then stone him to death.*

Religion works in various ways to promote the cause of the elderly. Among the Palaung of North Burma, for example, old age is especially revered, since it is believed that a long life is a reward for having been virtuous in one's previous incarnation. Young married women, in particular, try to appear older, not only so as to garner increased respect, but also in the hopes of avoiding hard physical work.

Finally, in addition to being considered valuable and occasionally burdensome, old people also are often considered dangerous. This, too, leads to a position of respect. For instance, among the Aranda of Australia, old men are the most powerful, so long as they remain competent. They are also freed from the usual food and social taboos under which younger persons must live. The elderly, being close to death, contain a special magic of death-in-life, and frequently are seen as mediators between the living and the dead. Given that fear of death is an important cornerstone of most religions, it follows naturally that religious leaders are most often recruited from among the elderly.

Even at death, old people may retain their influence and prestige. A simple and effective technique is to distribute one's prop-

---

*It just may be that the ancient Hebrews protest too much. The vehemence with which disrespect for age is condemned might just as well be seen as indicating a society in which such behavior was rampant—hence the exhortations by Old Testament writers, who were themselves probably quite old.

erty only when dying, and not before. This is true, for example of the Arctic Yakut, the Ashanti of West Africa, the Akamba of East Africa, and the Vedda of Ceylon. A dying Berber of North Africa has messages whispered into his ears, for transmission to dead relatives. In their culture, the elderly gain respect by being sole proprietors of a deathbed messenger service. Among the African Shilluk, one old man is reported to have promised to ensure successful calving of the family's cows, but only if he got his wish and was buried in the cattle kraal. Similarly, an elderly Australian aboriginal might promise to bring rain promptly, on the condition that he be treated well during his final days.

It seems likely that most old people can, in fact, provide the wisdom, experience, knowledge, and balanced good judgment for which they have been respected around the world. On the other hand, we are entitled to be somewhat skeptical about the claim that after death they are capable of interceding with the gods on behalf of their more junior, still-living brethren. But here is a story for the skeptics, related by anthropologist H. G. Lockett. Supela, the old Sun Priest, died on 4 July 1928. His people, living in the arid southwest of the United States, had been suffering from a prolonged drought, and Supela was expected to intercede for them in the spirit world. He even proposed to make the trip in just four days—record time—since his life had been so pious that he wasn't expected to have to pause and work off any sins en route. Sure enough, exactly four days after his death, there was heavy thunder, lightning, and a drenching rainstorm!

❧

When it comes to respect for age, China and Japan seem to be in a class by themselves. Wherever ancestors are honored, so is age, since the older a person, the closer he or she is to being an ancestor. Furthermore, the association of age with wisdom is also deeply ingrained in most Oriental cultures. Confucius wrote the following: "At fifteen, I set my heart upon learning. At thirty, I had planted my feet firmly upon the ground. At forty, I no longer suffered from perplexities. At fifty, I knew what were the biddings of Heaven. At sixty, I heard them with docile ear. At seventy, I could follow the dictates of my heart; for what I desired no longer overstepped the boundaries of right."

Besides Confucianism, the other great Chinese religion was Taoism, founded largely by the teaching of Lao-tzu (literally translated, "Old Master"). Nor surprisingly, Taoist holy men are typically old and, in fact, according to legend, Lao-tzu himself was even born a wise old man, complete with white beard and balding head. Apparently, he had spent many decades *in utero*, and therefore never suffered the indignities and lack of respect and attention that a wet-behind-the-ears, would-be holy man would doubtless receive.*

Writing in 1931, Lin Yu-tang provided an interesting glimpse into prerevolutionary China: "In China the first question a person asks the other on an official call, after the name and surname, is 'What is your glorious age?' " If the respondent says he is young, then the appropriate reply is to murmur something about the future that lies ahead; if old, much more deference is shown.

In America, influenced as we are by the Protestant work ethic, we seem to value independence and self-reliance above all else. One of our proudest boasts is "I made my own way." By contrast, the elderly Chinese were overwhelmingly proud to be cared for by their grown children. Americans are often ashamed of being dependent on the upcoming generation, and will go to great lengths, even living in destitution if need be, so as to avoid "being a burden." By contrast, elderly Chinese used to brag openly of their children's generosity toward them.

On the other hand, if life in traditional China was good for the elderly, it was the younger generation that paid the price. Age ruled in the Confucian days, often despotically. The lives of the young were controlled by the old, from arranged marriages to the organization of domestic chores. When a young man married, his wife moved into her husband's home, where she found herself immediately and entirely under the thumb of her in-laws, especially her mother-in-law. If she was the wife of the eldest son, then at least she had some advantages over the wives of the

---

* In this respect, Christianity is something of a novelty among world religions, nearly all of which are strongly gerontocratic—with both religious leaders and even the gods being typically quite old. What, then, should we make of the baby Jesus? It is worth pointing out, I suppose, that the Father presumably retains authority over His Son (after all, which one got crucified?). Furthermore, orthodox Judaism is strongly gerontocratic, so that Christianity—as a new wrinkle to an old religion—may have found it especially useful to emphasize its youth and promise with a baby king. Imagine an elderly Jesus: he might not have been distinguishable from other competing patriarchal rabbis.

younger sons. Eventually, of course, with the death of her husband's parents, she emerged as the feared mother-in-law, tyrannizing the wives of her own sons. But although it was often a long wait, youth generally went along with the family gerontocracy, perhaps out of piety and with a sense of inner comfort and approval, but also with resignation, and maybe even with a certain measure of despair.

The Maoist revolution was a revolution against old China, and partly at least, this was quite literal: against the old in China. Certain aspects of this revolution have been ongoing—for example, the Cultural Revolution was a direct attack against the old, many of whom remained entrenched despite the political upheaval that culminated in 1949. The extraordinarily young Red Guards became the symbol of a youth-oriented revolution, but not surprisingly, they went too far and had to be restrained. Now, old people still predominate in the Chinese political leadership, although the position of the elderly in everyday family matters remains something of a mystery. We do know, however, that one important function of the elderly in today's China is to serve as government-approved "Teachers of Bitterness," instructing the coming generation in the social evils of prerevolutionary times.

Japan also has a long history of profound reverence for age. Modernization has probably occurred more quickly and more dramatically among the Japanese than among any other people on earth. Within one generation, Japan transformed itself from a feudal society to a major economic power in the world. Nonetheless, respect for the elderly has persisted, as witnessed by the modern tradition of "oya-koko" ("silver seats"), for example. Although not literally made of silver, they are specially reserved for aged railroad passengers—a fine example of incorporating old traditions into an industrialized society. Deference to age continues to permeate Japanese home life, and a person's sixty-first birthday is a profoundly important celebration. Elderly Japanese routinely exaggerate their years rather than disguising them.

And yet, especially as Western values take hold, things may be getting worse for Japan's elderly. A widely read story by the popular Japanese writer Niwa Fumio told about a thoroughly unpleasant, physically obnoxious octogenarian woman. It was titled "The Hateful Age," and became something of a national slogan. Can it be that excess of reverence, as in Japan, or reverence coupled with oppression, as in prerevolutionary China, leads to excess of response? If so, what does this portend for the Pepsi generation?

❦

As we have seen, respect for the elderly is almost universal, so long as the elderly remain competent. (To this we should probably add the likely inverse, suggested by our glimpse of Abkhasia and Vilcabamba: the elderly may well remain competent insofar as they continue to be respected.) As physical and mental powers decline, as eventually they must, so does the status of the elderly. As a general rule, the position of old people varies directly with their ability to occupy a niche in their society. And old people have been adroit at finding ways to keep themselves occupied, important, and therefore secure.

In their battle to retain their status, and often their very survival, the old have several things going for them. For one, the human brain is largely sensitive to dramatic, short-term changes—the appearance of a lion, a thunderstorm, a rival, the cry of a baby, and so forth. We are often unaware of steady processes like changes in our own weight and height, or even the progress of the seasons. This curious tunnel vision is responsible for the sense in which our own age sneaks up on us, since it gives no clear warnings of its approach. Just as we are slow to recognize aging in ourselves, we are often oblivious to its progress in someone else. Herein lies an advantage for the aging individual: there is a type of intellectual inertia that makes us slow to notice and respond to age-related weakening in another. As a result, the old man can rule by reputation, often long after he has surrendered the ability to do so by prowess.

An adult male baboon may spend years as the undisputed boss of his troupe. As he grows older, he will usually retain this august position. His "social longevity" occurs partly because aging baboons often establish alliances with other elderly colleagues, so that when one of them is threatened, all respond. In this way, aging individuals successfully cling to positions of authority over younger ones who would be the victors in one-on-one combat.

But even beyond this, baboons rule by reputation. The aging despot may be merely a shadow of his former self, canines worn down to his gums, nearly blind and hardly able to run, never mind fight; nonetheless, he was once a force to be reckoned with, and since his aging has been gradual and imperceptible, he still commands authority over the younger generation.

Cicero wrote, "Old age, especially an honored old age, has so great authority that it is of more value than all the pleasures of youth."

We don't suddenly sprout wrinkles overnight, or develop a stooped posture, flabby muscles, or cataracts. Not unlike baboons, we age slowly, undramatically, and therefore things probably do not go as badly for us as otherwise they might.

Furthermore, not only is our decline gradual, but we—like baboons—also have good memories. We are impressionable, and the authority, power, and competence of someone else are among the things that impress us. We remember what someone *was*. For quite some time, this memory may cloud our recognition of what someone now *is*. This combination of imperceptible decline plus memory of previous prowess is all the more potent since age weakens us only after we have passed our prime. Having achieved a zenith of power and ability, the old person can often slide down quite some way with relative impunity. Even when the old lion has lost his teeth, the thought of his bite lingers on.

As we have seen, old people may profit by their wisdom, by society's rules that demand obedience and respect, and by certain mental illusions whereby age gets its due and then some. Beyond this, old people often function in specific important ways within their society, thereby assuring themselves a degree of satisfaction as well as security.

It seems that with age, physical weakening occurs long before mental weakening. There are some things that simply cannot be accomplished by brawn, and these, naturally, become the province of the old. As they gradually withdraw from arduous physical labor, the elderly often participate in more household activities: weaving, sewing, making nets and pottery, tatooing and barbering, midwifery, medicine, singing, storytelling, and other forms of entertainment. The tribal elders often become judges, historians, and masters of ceremonies in the most literal sense. Old people often preside over ritual initiations, which also serve to keep the young respectful and fearful. It is the elders who conduct painful circumcisions, direct the fasting, and conduct the ritual mutilations that signify entry into adulthood. Through much of the primitive world, young people are terrified by "Bull-

roarers," devices which make loud roaring, groaning, and whis-
tling noises when spun overhead; the aged speak with a similar
voice, and it is loud, impressive, and long-remembered.

Old people are the masters of taboos, areas of secret knowledge only dimly sensed by the younger generation and therefore
feared. It should not be surprising, of course, that these taboos
work to the benefit of the aged. Food taboos are especially notable: old people are often exempt from strictures that apply to
the young, and, significantly, all reported cases involve nutri-
tious foods that are reserved for the elderly. Here is a partial list.

Polar Eskimo: only the old were allowed to eat eggs, hearts,
lungs, and livers, as well as baby seals, hares, and grouse.

Omaha Indians: the "washna," or tender part of the buffalo's
intestine was considered a delicacy. Young people were told,
"You must not eat the washna, for if you do, the dogs will bark
at you." Similarly, if a young person attmepted to suck the marrow out of bones, he was reprimanded, "You must not do that.
If you do, you will sprain your ankle." Even the broth made from
the buffalo was taboo for the young; they were warned, "Your
ankles will rattle and . . . joints become loose."

Witoto (Colombia): only the aged could cannibalize the flesh
of enemies slain in war.

Aztec: drunkenness was punishable by death, except for those
over seventy, for whom unlimited quantities of alcohol were allowed "to warm the cooling blood of their age."

Lango (Africa): before the eating of any large animal killed in
a hunt, a ram had to be sacrificed. Only the old men were permitted to eat the ram.

Fan (West Africa): tortoise meat made one slow-moving, so it
was acceptable food only for the aged—who, of course, were slow
already.

Xosa (Africa): only the very young or the very old were permitted to eat birds' eggs or to drink fresh milk. Furthermore,
kidney meat caused impotence, so only the very old could eat
it, since it was assumed that they were already impotent.

Iban (Northwest Borneo): venison made young men as timid
as the deer, but old men could still eat it, since presumably they
were already timid (although not too timid to have suggested the
taboo!).

Chukchi (Siberia): certain cuts of reindeer meat caused impotence in men and flabby breasts in women, so only old people could eat them.

Sema Naga (Burma): goat meat made young women too passionate, but old women could deal with it.

Arunta (Australia): eating a female bandicoot would cause one to bleed to death at circumcision (and hence it was taboo for boys), and would result in hemorrhage at menstruation among women (thereby neatly exempting postmenopausal women). Similarly, eating large lizards would cause hypersexuality, and kangaroo tails lead to premature age and baldness.

In the United States, there is a different technique of guaranteeing food for the old and poor: food stamps. With their monthly allocation of stamps, recipients have access to any food in the supermarket. But their special claim to society's resources is limited to this meager monthly allocation, and furthermore they must undergo the humiliation of being "on the dole." By contrast, the food taboos of many "primitive" societies have the effect of roping off a certain section of the supermarket, for the elderly only. Moreover, they are not made to feel like second-class citizens. Rather, they are granted access to certain special foods as a right and privilege, and because of the unique characteristics of the age they have reached.

In general, old people are chosen to officiate at the major events of life: births, deaths, marriages, initiations into adulthood, christenings, baptisms, and so forth. Among certain Bantu peoples, sexual intercourse is forbidden to all during times of crisis. When the emergency has passed, the patriarch and his senior wife have intercourse with solemnity and appropriate ritual. Only then are the others permitted to follow suit. Similarly, the ceremonial role of age is shown during Bantu sacrifice to the ancestors: the eldest man slaughters the animal, while on his right shoulder rest the hands of each of his younger brothers. On their shoulders are the hands of their eldest sons, followed in turn by younger sons, grandsons, and so on.

Religion and magic loom especially large in the repertoire of the old. It is to the old man or woman that the young man goes, seeking potions that will soften a maiden's heart, or stop the heart of a hated enemy. Among the Lapps, certain elderly women would, for a fee, repeat magic formulas that pushed snakes into the bodies of enemies. Whether or not these doughty old ladies

191

were actually successful at this task, they were unquestionably fierce enough in their own right: they were also employed to castrate reindeer, crushing the testicles with their teeth!

The Kiwai Papuans of New Guinea used "strength fluid" from an old woman's vagina to annoint the first yams of the season, thus assuring that they would grow. The Old Testament similarly is filled with old man shamanism, in which God preferentially communicates with the aged Moses, Abraham, or Saul. In such ways, old people doubtless have retained an important, irreplaceable role for themselves. Among the African Lele, medicine men only pass on their secrets when they are very old, thereby keeping themselves in demand. When an old man's incantations, secrets, and magical knowledge are his sole possession, he should not be expected to part with them readily.

Among the Siberian Yakut, the elderly patriarch is said to be treated with "almost slavish respect." And yet, things change dramatically when and if a real decline sets in. The same anthropologist who commented on the Yakuts' "slavish respect" for their elderly, also reported, "The Yakuts treat their own relatives, who have grown stupid, very badly. Usually they try to take from them the remains of their property, if they have any; then constantly, in measure, as they become unprotected, they treat them worse and worse. Even in homes relatively self-sufficient I found such living skeletons, wrinkled, half-naked, or even entirely naked, hiding in corners, from where they creep out only when no strangers are present, to get warm by the fire, to pick up together with children bits of food thrown away, or to quarrel with them over the licking of the dish emptied of food." Such pitiful scenes are the result of old people "growing stupid," or "becoming unprotected"; in other words, losing the ability to retain a useful, important, well-defended place for themselves.

When old people are no longer able to command obedience or respect, they must rely on love—which is OK, so long as it is there, and strong enough. Especially if they relinquish their power and possessions, they may be greatly at risk, like the aged Lear who announced:

> and 'tis our fast intent
> To shake all cares and business from our age,

Conferring them on younger strengths, while we
Unburden'd crawl toward death.

Lear's story, not surprisingly, is tragic.

In rural Scandinavia, the custom of "Flaetfoering" called for the aged parents to make a circuit of their married children, living with each in exact proportion to his or her already-received inheritance. A risky business, as Lear would attest.

Our survey of other cultures suggests that the best form of social security is for the elderly to retain authority and a useful role. Clinging to life in this way may have its liabilities, especially since the advancing generation may feel deprived, and hence resentful. But at least in some cases, things can be resolved, especially when mutual love and respect are strong enough. For example, among the energetic and industrious Ibo of eastern Nigeria, the aged occupy a rarely challenged position of respect. It is generally acknowledged in Ibo society that everyone eventually reaches an age at which he or she no longer is a *provider* and henceforth must be *provided for*. Nonetheless, the elderly retain their authority, controlling the land and other material possessions. When conflicts occur, they are usually mild, as between fathers and sons when the patriarch remains vigorous and refuses to give up his land to his sons, who may be in their thirties or forties, married, and with their own families.

Anthropologist Austin Shelton recounts one case of three sons who were unhappy that their father refused to step down and distribute his land, as they felt he should. For his part, the old man said that his sons were greedy and would just have to be patient. The sons got together to buy a new, young, attractive wife for their father, confiding to the anthropologist, "Our father will be so busy with this woman that he won't feel like planting yams." The result? The old man was very pleased with his sons' generosity, enjoyed his new wife, and also planted all his yams.

So, around the world, the aged are by no means a pitiable lot. They are often tough, resourceful, respected, and—when all else fails, and if they are lucky—loved. The greatest security for old people lies in remaining appreciated and important, either by their material possessions, or the less tangible qualities of wisdom, experience, and spirituality. In nearly all cases, however, the ultimate recourse is to kin. When all else fails, the elderly find security, if they find it at all, in their network of relatives.

Not long ago, a Mozambique native spokesman, Nephtali Mbanzi, pleaded with a missionary:

> Please do not establish an institution to care for the old people here. In our system the aged always has children, sons and daughters (including nephews and nieces, as you call them), and grandchildren. These have first duty to provide for them. Then there are their brothers, their father's brothers, and their families. Beyond these are more remote relatives. No person is without family. Kin are to support each other. Do not destroy our kinship spirit by removing our right and our duty to care for our own elders in love and respect.

※

Clearly, then, there are many ways of growing old, depending not only on the individual but also on the society. Among most nontechnological societies, change has come rapidly (if at all) by sudden contact with the powerful and expansionist West. The United States of America, by contrast, began anew. It was a new land, peopled afresh—but strongly influenced from the beginning by a European Protestant tradition followed successively by two revolutions: one political and one industrial. It seems likely, therefore, that the American attitude toward the aged has changed and evolved over the past two centuries. Let us now turn to aging in America, first a glimpse of history and then a view of the present-day social reality.

13

Aging in America

History

My days are in the yellow leaf;
The flames and fruits of Love are gone;
The worm, the canker, and the grief
Are mine alone!

Lord Byron wrote this in England more than two hundred years ago. One might assume that he was bemoaning an advanced age, that he was at least in his sixth, seventh, or eighth decade. But, incredibly, the poem from which these lines are taken is titled, "On This Day I Complete My Thirty-Sixth Year." In fact, Byron may have been prescient, since he actually died before reaching age thirty-seven. But in his attitude toward aging, Byron resembled a typical modern American.

Our youth-oriented, throw-away society would make an Abkhasian blanch. "Hate that gray? Wash it away!" We demand that our products be "new and improved," and look to teenagers for the latest fashions. Interestingly, this has not always been the case. Our fascination with youth is actually a fairly recent trend, and one that has been ably chronicled by historian David H. Fischer, from whose work this chapter will draw heavily. A yellow leaf may be seen, as Byron saw it, as a symbol of withering. But it is also the culmination of a fruitful life, and autumn can be brilliant with color. The tradition of colonial America was much closer to this perspective than it was to Bryon and the gerontophobia of modern times.

Our brief review of aging in this country involves a foray into an interesting yet rather neglected field: social history. It is easy to associate the study of history with the major events that schoolchildren are expected to learn—the Battle of Hastings, the

195

sailing of Columbus, the signing of the Declaration of Independence, Napoleon's defeat at Waterloo, and so on. However, another part of history, perhaps the most important part, is played out in homes, churches, and places of work, rather than parliaments and battlefields. It takes some detective work to trace down these everyday happenings, since they do not make the newspapers and are rarely recounted by those who chronicle the great events of the day. Nonetheless, the clues are there, and the reward of Professor Fischer's careful sleuthing is a better understanding of how old people used to be treated in the United States.

People did not live especially long in early America. Certainly our colonial forefathers did not enjoy anything like the robust longevity of Abkhasians. Nonetheless, old age was venerated in colonial America, and it was not until the nineteenth century that things began to change, and "elderly" began to mean "washed up," rather than "powerful and revered." At least some of the explanation for the older attitude lies in the role of religion in our early history. The Puritan tradition was strong in colonial America, and part of this tradition derived from Biblical teaching, which, as we have seen, equates age with wisdom and spirituality.

This view is clearly shown in the copious writings of Increase Mather, whose name is a quaint oddity today, but who was one of the most powerful figures in prerevolutionary America. He was a deacon in the influential Congregationalist church and president of Harvard from 1686 to 1701. In his *Dignity and Duty of Aged Servants*, Mather wrote that "if any man is favored with long life, it is God that has lengthened his days." Accordingly, the elderly are the chosen of God, and respect for God demands respect for them as well. Increase's son, Cotton Mather—author of more than five hundred books and articles—put it succinctly: "These two qualities go together: the ancient and the honorable."

In return for their honor, however, the elderly in America were expected to behave with "becoming gravity." Increase Mather again: "Levity in words, and much more in actions, is unsuitable and a shame to them, considering their age, and it stains their glory." Not just levity, but sexuality as well was considered inappropriate in the old. "When the leaves are off the trees," wrote William Bridge in 1679, "we see the birds' nests in the trees and bushes. Now in our old age our leaves are off, then therefore we may see these nests of sin, and lusts in our hearts and lives, which we saw not before, and so be sensible and repent of them." So, just as the Puritan tradition elevated and exalted the elderly, it also set rigid standards. The dutiful son was commended, the rebellious ingrate was condemned. The dignified old person was a model to all; otherwise he was contemptible.

When it came to politics, the preference was clear. "Gray heads are wiser than green ones," wrote Increase Mather. Similarly, in a letter to Thomas Jefferson, John Adams (then eighty-nine years old) maintained that "none were fit for Legislators and Magistrates" except those he called "sad men." Who were those sad men? "Aged men who had been tossed and buffeted by the vicissitudes of Life, forced upon profound reflection by grief and disappointments, and taught to command their passions." Although this attitude was the predominant one—and still seems to prevail in politics—it is worth noting that there were dissenters, even in Puritan New England. Thus, we come to the following complaint, written by one John Wise, in 1713: "It is not how capable a person is, which is the main point. . . . If state policy did consist in Beards, then he-goats would do for ambassadors, as well or better than men. . . . I think it is not how long men have lived, but how wise they have grown." Logical or not, Wise's voice was little heard in the formative days of America.

Instead, old people controlled the young, and not only because the churches required it. Land was wealth, and elderly parents typically retained possession of the land. Sons often were kept landless until they had themselves been married for ten, fifteen, or even twenty-five years. Like serfs, they worked on the land, but it was owned by someone else—the father. The aged father was often austere and tyrannical, and was the undisputed head of his extended household. When love did not suffice to maintain this position, naked power did. "Better it is thy children should seek to thee than that thou shouldst stand to their courtesy," advised Samuel Dexter in 1738. "The honor we owe to our parents and ancestors obligeth us to attend to that spirit of family government and authority which our fathers had; they ruled their houses well, and had their households in good subjection; children and servants knew their places and kept their distances."

In early America, only the rare person lived to enjoy old age

197

and its privileges. Perhaps it is easier to revere the aged when most of them are safely tucked into their graves. It seems clear, nonetheless, that when colonial Americans survived into old age, they were admired and respected, and kept their households "in good subjection." The most frequent complaint about elder parents was not their dependence, but rather the occasional tendency to be overbearing, dictatorial, and miserly.

Early in the twentieth century, Freud proposed that conflict between father and son is basic to the human psyche and therefore somehow "natural." All men supposedly harbor a bit of Oedipus within them, competing aggressively—and even sexually—with their fathers. This may be how things were in upper middle class Vienna around the turn of the century. In early America, however, another assumption was made: youth is "naturally" subservient to age. "The light of nature teacheth men to honour age. The law written in their hearts by nature has directed them to give a peculiar respect and deference to aged men. In most civilized nations they have done so" (Increase Mather).

By the time of the Revolutionary War, a powerful mixture of myth and reality had also developed in the colonies, centered on the "Gray Champion," an elderly man whose strength, courage, and leadership would rescue his people.* This image fits well with the early American attitude toward the aged, and satisfies the best of our longings: if the old are to lead, to hold positions of power and to be obeyed, then it is most comforting to think that they are worthy. And, indeed, often they were.

Perhaps our first gray champion was William Goffe, wanted in England for having been involved in an insurrection against Charles I. By 1675, he was living as a hermit near Hadley, Massachussetts, when an Indian war broke out. The population of Hadley was demoralized, leaderless, and cowering in the meeting house when Goffe mysteriously appeared, with his wild white hair and commanding presence. He showed the frightened townspeople how to use an antique cannon, with which they routed the even-more-frightened Indians with a single shot. He then organized the men in pursuit. When they returned, Goffe had vanished as miraculously as he had appeared. Not surprisingly, he quickly became a larger-than-life myth, reappearing

* The phrase first appeared in Nathaniel Hawthorne's collection of stories, *Twice-Told Tales*.

many times as a saintly apparition, a latter-day savior, endowed with righteousness and years.

There were others. Eighty-year-old Josiah Haynes (a Congregational deacon, no less) marched eight miles with the minutemen to Concord Bridge. When his captain refused to yell "Charge!" with the appropriate vigor, Haynes personally led the pursuit of the British from Concord to Cambridge, chasing twenty-one elite companies of British infantry all the way. This particular gray champion became a posthumous hero, after being killed in battle while reloading his musket.

Samuel Whittemore, a seventy-eight-year-old farmer, made a one-man stand against the British army on the Lexington Road when his patience as a colonist simply ran out. The fierce and ornery Whittemore killed one soldier with a musket, and two more with his brace of pistols. Eventually, he was shot, beaten, and bayonetted by the enraged British, and left for dead. Miraculously, however, he recovered, became a living legend, and died at age ninety-six.

In his effort to trace the social history of old age in America, historian David Fischer has made use of some novel clues, such as family portraits, family trees, old dictionaries, and 200-year-old men's dress suits. They all tell a similar story of reverence for age in the early years of the United States, with a progressive decline in the status of the elderly through the nineteenth century.

Take family portraits, for example. Before 1800, the usual portrait depicted the patriarch looming above the rest of his family, much as the King of Siam was supposed to always have his head higher than any of his subjects. Significantly, this pattern changed after 1800, with a great increase in horizontal arrangement. No one was automatically higher than anyone else, regardless of age. Democracy finally began knocking on the door of America's homes, and the elderly began to lose the special reverence they had enjoyed.

Also, primogeniture (inheritance to the eldest son) declined rapidly after 1800, as did the frequency of children named after their grandfathers. In addition, a new vocabulary of abuse developed around the beginning of the nineteenth century. Words are no more unchanging than are people's attitudes, and indeed, by tracing the changes in words and their meanings, we can trace the changes in people's thinking. "Gaffer" used to be a term of endearment, as a contraction of godfather, but it was changed to one of contempt. A "fogy" was originally a wounded military veteran, but "old fogy" no longer carries any respect at all; in fact, quite the opposite. "Greybeards" once were respected; now they are derided. In addition, new words for old men have been added since 1900, and virtually all of them are critical, condescending, or contemptuous. Take, for example, "codger," "fuddy-duddy," "old-timer," or "pop." Interestingly, negative terms for old women, by contrast, were not innovations of the last century or two. Such words as "crone" and "hag" have very ancient roots. It seems that the Biblical injunction of veneration for age applied generally to old men, not old women. This may help explain why Increase and Cotton Mather, both so stalwart in support of old men, were also major instigators of the Salem witch trials.

Today's American often wears clothes that make him or her look as young as possible, with the exception of adolescents who may seek to add a few years. But in colonial America, up until the 1790s or so, men's dress actually emphasized age. Incredible as it may seem to us today, clothing was designed to make the shoulders appear narrow and rounded, the waist and hips broadened, and the spine bent. Now it is just the opposite: in at the waist, out at the shoulders, and back straight. American men used to wear powdered wigs, basking in the glory of artificially white hair. Now we are bombarded with advertisements showing us how to conceal our gray hair. We are encouraged to submit to hair transplants or hide under a toupee. Ring out the old, ring in the new.

❧

Why did America change? It would be nice to know. While there are many possibilities, there are no sure answers. As we shall see in the following chapter, sociologists believe that urbanization and modern technology nearly always bring along a decline in the status of the elderly. However, America didn't become citified and industrialized until the mid-nineteenth century, by which time old age had already begun to lose favor. Perhaps it is easier to respect elderly people when there aren't very many of them; the percentage of our population over sixty-five has increased dramatically. But again, this is a more recent development. Old age in America began losing status at a time when it was still unusual, and therefore special, to be old.

The best explanation is probably less cut-and-dried, more related to a change of mood that first became evident in the late eighteenth century. Americans had successfully revolted against the Old World and established a brand new country in the New World. Interestingly, although the United States is now the world's oldest continuously democratic republic, we still like to fancy the country as somehow young and new. By contrast, before the revolution, Americans strove to picture themselves as old: Plymouth was known as the "Old Colony," and Virginia was proudly called "Old Dominion." But then came a dramatic change; the cutting of the colonial apron strings. As revolutionary upstarts and apostles of a newly implemented democracy, Americans found themselves obstreperous, impatient, and more than a little brash. They had fired the shot heard around the world. The frontier was about to open and the future belonged to those who dared to break with the past.

As we saw earlier, Henry David Thoreau was no respecter of age. Neither was Emerson: "Nature abhors the old, and old age seems the only disease." And again: "Frankly face the facts and see the result. Tobacco, coffee, alcohol, hashish, prussic acid, strychnine are weak dilutions; the surest poison is time." For a nation on the move, no longer just working the family farm under the thumb of a venerated patriarch, old people were to be tolerated rather than revered.

In 1875, on the fiftieth anniversary of his graduation from Bowdoin College, Longfellow wrote a poem about being old. In it he expresses some hope for old age, although his ambivalence is readily apparent from the title, "Morituri Salutamus" (the gladiators' motto of ancient Rome: "We who are about to die salute you"). As historian Fischer points out, "The exaltation of elders which had come so easily to the Puritans was uphill work for a poet in nineteenth-century New England." Here is Longfellow's effort:

Whatever poet, orator, or sage
May say of it, old age is still old age.
It is the waning, not the crescent moon;
The dusk of evening, not the blaze of noon:
It is not strength, but weakness; not desire,

But its surcease; not the fierce heat of fire,
The burning and consuming element,
But that of ashes and of embers spent,
In which some living sparks we still discern,
Enough to warm, but not enough to burn.

What then? Shall we sit idly down and say
The night hath come; it is no longer day?
The night hath not yet come; we are not quite
Cut off from labor by the failing light;
Something remains for us to do or dare;
Even the oldest tree some fruit may bear;
Not the Oedipus Coloneus, or Greek Ode,
Or tales of pilgrims that one morning rode
Out of the gateway of the Tabard Inn,
But other something, would we but begin;
For age is opportunity no less
Than youth itself, though in another dress,
And as the evening twilight fades away
The sky is filled with stars, invisible by day.

Walt Whitman felt even worse about aging. In fact, it made him downright miserable. Unlike his earlier robust celebrations of life (for example, "The Song of Myself") Whitman's later works were filled with a whining self-pity. In Herman Melville's great American novel *Moby-Dick* (1851), Captain Ahab is powerful with purpose and authority, yet fatally weakened by his inflexibility. He goes down tied hopelessly to his white whale, just as whole generations of old people in America have been doing ever since.

Something new in American letters developed in the late nineteenth century: a "literature of consolation." Books proliferated with such titles as *Looking Toward Sunset, Light at Evening Time, After Noontide, Sunset Hours of Life,* and *Old Age: Its compensations and rewards.* They reeked condescension. And although seemingly supportive of old age, Americans distilled their real attitudes into new proverbs: no fool like an old fool; you can't teach an old dog new tricks; and age before beauty (to which, incidentally, Dorothy Parker is said to have appended, "and pearls before swine!").

Old age becomes almost pathetic in American literature of the last hundred years, justifying Emerson's remark that "the creed of the street is, old age is not disgraceful, but immensely disadvantageous." In T. S. Eliot's "Gerontion" (1920), the narrator is a helpless old man, "in a dry month/ Being read to by a boy,

waiting for rain." Even when old people are treated as heroes—
and this is very rare—the emphasis seems to be on their *over-coming* age, just as a one-legged skier wins our admiration for
overcoming his disability. In Hemingway's *The Old Man and
the Sea* (1952), the dauntless old man is unquestionably heroic,
but look at his description: "Everything was old except his eyes
and they were the same color as the sea and were cheerful and
undefeated." To be cheerful and undefeated, it seems, is to be
young, not old.

This growing anti-aging bias was not limited to North America. Susan Tamke, a professor of "Popular Culture" at Bowling
Green State University in Ohio, recently analyzed the treatment
of old people in nineteenth-century English children's poems and
stories. She concluded that the elderly appeared largely as pious,
wise, but flat and dimensionless figures who delighted in teaching the young or simply watching them. But they almost never
did anything. If good, they were passive. When they had active
roles, however, they were nearly always bad: wicked witches,
evil hags, or nasty stepparents. It seems that the most heroic
portrayal of an old person was reached by Red Riding Hood's
grandmother, who at least ran out of her house to summon aid—
from a young woodsman!

In late nineteenth-century England, Gilbert and Sullivan were
particularly scathing in their treatment of old age. In fact, Gilbert's prime target, in addition to the smug arrogance of the rich
and titled, was old age, which was seen as nothing less than
contemptible. Consider this sequence from *The Mikado:*

Ko-Ko: There is beauty in extreme old age.
          Do you fancy you are elderly enough?
          Information I'm requesting
          On a subject interesting:
          Is a maiden all the better when she's tough?

Katisha: Throughout this wide dominion
          It's the general opinion
          That she'll last a good deal longer when she's tough.

Ko-Ko: Are you old enough to marry, do you think?
          Won't you wait till you are eighty in the shade?
          There's a fascination frantic
          In a ruin that's romantic.
          Do you think you are sufficiently decayed?

Katisha enthusiastically agrees that she is.
Generations of English schoolchildren memorized Robert

203

Southey's poem "The Old Man's Comforts and How He Gained Them" (1799). Although it rings rather "corny" to modern ears, it was taken quite seriously for a very long time. In fact, it was so well known that Lewis Carroll, in his *Alice's Adventures in Wonderland* (1865), felt free to assume that his readers knew it, and to write a parody, which is now better known than the original. Here is Southey's original:

"You are old, Father William," the young man cried;
"The locks which are left you are gray;
You are bald, Father William—a hearty old man:
Now tell me the reason, I pray."

"In the days of my youth," Father William replied,
"I remembered that youth would fly fast,
And abused not my health and my vigor at first,
That I never might need them at last."

"You are old, Father William," the young man cried,
"And pleasures with youth pass away;
And yet you lament not the days that are gone:
Now tell me the reason, I pray."

"In the days of my youth," Father William replied,
"I remembered that youth could not last;
I thought of the future, whatever I did,
That I never might grieve for the past."

"You are old, Father William," the young man cried,
"And life must be hastening away;
You are cheerful, and love to converse upon death:
Now tell me the reason, I pray."

"I am cheerful, young man," Father William replied;
"Let the cause thy attention engage;
In the days of my youth, I remembered my God,
And He hath not forgotten my age."

Compare it with Lewis Carroll's version, which begins as follows:

"You are old, Father William," the young man said,
"And your hair has become very white;
And yet you incessantly stand on your head—
Do you think, at your age, it is right?"

"In my youth," Father William replied to his son,
"I feared it might injure the brain;
But now that I'm perfectly sure I have none,
Why, I do it again and again."

204

"You are old," said the youth, "as I mentioned before
And have grown most uncommonly fat;
Yet you turned a back-somersault in at the door—
Pray what is the reason of that?"

"In my youth," said the sage, as he shook his grey locks,
"I kept all my limbs very supple
By the use of this ointment—one shilling the box—
Allow me to sell you a couple? . . ."

Two centuries earlier, Shakespeare made his attitude toward old age quite clear: "Age, I do abhor thee; youth, I do adore thee." Shakespeare's old people tend to be either buffoons, such as Falstaff or *Hamlet*'s Polonius, or tragically failing, such as King Lear. However, this viewpoint was not widely shared until the nineteenth century, when it sprang forth in both North America and Britain. By the mid-twentieth century, it had become firmly entrenched. Thus, in Samuel Beckett's *Krapp's Last Tape* (1958), old age is used as a symbol for all life: empty, miserable, absurd in its certainty of impending death.

On the other hand, age has retained its high status in the military, where rank and years typically go together. The white-haired enlisted man is as incongruous as the pimply-faced general, and "the old man" is still a term of endearment mixed with respect. Of course, "Old soldiers never die, they just fade away."

But even in the military, the new American attitude toward aging can be found, sometimes in unlooked-for places. William Manchester's biography of Douglas MacArthur, *The American Caesar*, contains the following epigrams from that old soldier:

People grow old only by deserting their ideals. Years may wrinkle the skin but to give up interest wrinkles the soul. . . .
    . . . You are as young as your faith, as old as your doubt; as young as your self-confidence, as old as your fear; as young as your hope, as old as your despair. . . .
    . . . In the ventral place of every heart there is a recording chamber; so long as it receives messages of beauty, hope, cheer and courage, so long are you young. . . .
    . . . When . . . your heart is covered with the snows of pessimism and the ice of cynicism, then and only then are you grown old.

These MacArthurisms were undoubtedly intended to be uplifting. An unintended message, however, is also clear: to be old can sometimes mean to be fearful, despairing, pessimistic, cynical, and cheerless. The solution? Keep young.

How about retirement, that great two-edged sword of aging? To many, retirement offers the hope of leisure and the well-earned rewards of a life spent in hard work. To many others, however, retirement (especially when mandatory) is one of the great bugaboos of life. It is society's way of saying that one is no longer wanted or appreciated. It is often a cruel and painful blow, devastating both financially and personally, bringing with it an enormous loss in self-esteem. Americans in particular tend to derive their identity from their jobs; once deprived of them, not much remains.

In early America, retirement was rarely an issue. Certainly, mandatory retirement was virtually unheard-of, and only partly because not very many people lived long enough to attain "retirement age." The position of the elderly, as we have already seen, was so secure that pushing them out of power was almost inconceivable. The issue of retirement arose, not because old people were being forced into inactive low-prestige roles that they did not want, but rather when the elderly clung too long to their near-tyrannic power. The ancient church deacon who insisted on retaining his postion when he was no longer competent, or the patriarch who refused bitterly to relinquish any of his land holdings, even to his middle-aged, long-married sons—these occasionally threatened the fabric of colonial society. In his *Good Old Age*, Cotton Mather had this to say:

> Old age is often very loth to be laid aside from stations and services. Old folks often can't endure to be judged less able than ever they were for Publick Appearances, or to be put out of Offices. But, Good Sir, be so wise as to disappear of our own Accord, as soon and as far as you lawfully may. Be glad of a dismission. . . . Be pleased with the Retirement which you are dismissed into.

But organized retirement was still a long time coming. It may have been exasperating when old people clung tenaciously and overlong to their "stations and services." However, there was little to be done. Such was the power of age in those times.

Eventually, for reasons that we still don't clearly understand, old age lost its favored position in America and in much of the Western world. And when retirement came to America, it was intended more as a social benefit to the elderly (as well as providing more work opportunities for the next generation) than as

206

a relief from the tyranny of the old. Indeed, as the elderly lost power and prestige, they were ripe to become the subjects of oppression, and had long stopped being the oppressors.

In the United States, old age was finally acknowledged to be a "social problem" in the early twentieth century, with the first state pension plans, industry plans, the medical specialty of geriatrics, and, of course, Social Security. (Private organizations concerned with the welfare of the elderly began long before this, however. For example, on 7 February 1814, New York witnessed the founding of the A.R.R.A.I.F.—the Association for the Relief of Respectable, Aged and Indigent Females.)

Along with the decision that old age was a problem and something that the government had to "do something about" came a definition of old age itself. To most Americans, especially younger Americans, a person becomes old at sixty-five. Why sixty-five? Why not sixty-eight or seventy-four or sixty-one or ninety-two? The answer is quite simple: sixty-five was arbitrarily set as the primary age for receiving Social Security benefits. Hence, it became the most common age of retirement, and therefore, since we equate "work" with "useful," and "useful" with "young," it came to be accepted that old age begins on our sixty-fifth birthday.

There is absolutely nothing magic about age sixty-five, nothing in our biology that marks this age as the portal of oldness. In fact, the selection of sixty-five has a little-known history that does not speak well for its legitimacy. As it happens, sixty-five was chosen by the Social Security Administration simply because Bismarck chose that age for the first modern old age pension system, in Germany nearly a century ago (1881). Now, Bismarck was no "bleeding-heart" or "do-gooder"; he was not especially concerned with providing relief for aged and indigent Germans, respectable or not. Rather, along with many other European leaders and aristocrats, he was alarmed by the spread of Marxism in the latter half of the nineteenth century. Bismarck simply wanted to forestall any chance of a revolution in his own country. In his own words: "Whoever has a pension for his old age is more content and easier to manage than one who has no such prospect." The answer, then, according to Bismarck's advisers, was a pension guaranteed by the government. The only problem was to set the pension age sufficiently high that most people would not reach it, thereby easing the strain on government coffers. Bismarck's statisticians assured him that in nineteenth-century Germany few of his people lived more than sixty-five years. So age sixty-five was chosen. And it was kept because of tradition alone, by the United States more than fifty years later. Interestingly, if Bismarck's criteria were to be employed today, the age at retirement would probably be ninety or more.

❧

As we look across the sweep of American history, the pendulum has swing far. Americans used to revere and emulate the old; now we idolize and copy the young. Professor Fischer laments:

> This historian observed a Boston matron on the far side of fifty, who might have worn a graceful palla in ancient Rome, dressed in a mini-skirt and leather boots. He saw a man in his sixties, who might have draped himself in the dignity of a toga, wearing "hip-hugger" jeans and a tie dyed T-shirt. He witnessed a conservative businessman, who in an earlier generation might have hesitated each morning, wondering whether to wear black or charcoal gray, going to the office in white plastic shoes, chartreuse trousers and cerise shirt, purple aviator glasses and a Prince Valiant haircut. Most astonishing were college professors who put aside their Harris tweeds and adopted every passing adolescent fad with an enthusiasm out of all proportion to their years. One season it was the Nehru jacket; another, dashikis; the next railroad overalls. In the early 1970's it was love beads and leather jackets. Every twist and turn of teen-age fashion revolutionized their costumes. But always, old was out and young was in. There was pathos in those scenes— because the worshippers of youth succeeded only in displaying their age.

But who can blame the old for seeking to be young? Elderly people are given short shrift in today's America. There is even an "ism" to join the pantheon of racism and sexism: ageism, the discrimination against people because of their age. As with the other "isms," some progress is finally being made. For example, the Age Discrimination in Employment Act of 1967 prohibits discrimination in hiring workers forty to sixty-five years of age, but not older. This law has been amended further so that as of 1 July 1982 it is now illegal to force anyone to retire because of his or her age, up to seventy years. In other words, it is illegal to discriminate because of age, except against those who are oldest.

Imagine civil rights legislation that prohibited discrimination against most blacks, except for the very blackest!

We are accustomed to using the number of one's years as a measure of something significant. And yet, we forget that aging is a very individual thing; it doesn't occur in the same way for any two people, and it certainly doesn't happen on a particular date. Are we youthful on the last day of our sixty-fourth year, then automatically ready for retirement one day later? Except for chronological age itself, all measures of aging are quite variable from one person to the next: graying or loss of hair, changes in height, skin texture, memory function, muscular power, kidney efficiency, and so forth. There are youthful octogenarians, and there are those who are "old before their time" at forty-five. *Because* of this variability, the argument goes, we need a measure that applies equally to all people; hence, years of life. But variability is just the point. Aging *is* variable, just as people are. To say that all people are ready to retire when they turn sixty-five is to insist that we can all be fitted onto a Procrustean bed whose dimensions were decreed by outmoded Prussian actuarial tables.

At a certain age (also variable from one person to the next) we "erupt" teeth, pubic hair, wet dreams, menstruation, pregnancy, birth, graduations, and other life events—even death. But aging doesn't work that way; there is no sudden instant when we become "old." Rather, it is a gradual development, with experts unable to agree even when it starts. There is a special absurdity in arbitrarily dividing the continuum of human life into "young" and "old" segments. Of course, society makes other arbitrary age-related decisions: we can vote at eighteen, drink in taverns at either eighteen or twenty-one (depending on the locale), and can serve as president of the United States once we pass thirty-five. These, also, are violations of our personal uniqueness, but at least in such cases the issue revolves around when to grant new responsibility. It is very different, and far more hurtful, when something is arbitrarily being taken away.

Of all our "isms," ageism is perhaps the most illogical. The racial bigot is woefully misguided, but (if white) at least he knows that he will not wake up someday to find himself black, and vice versa. The same applies to sexists (at least in most cases!). But as for ageism, the indignities that we visit on our mothers and fathers shall someday be visited upon ourselves. *We* are tomorrow's old. And the future of aging in America is ours to write.

209

14

Aging in America

Sociology

> That is no country for old men. The young
> In one another's arms, birds in the trees . . .
>
> —W. B. Yeats, "Sailing to Byzantium"

Until recently, only poets, philosophers, and aristocrats thought much about aging and the aged. Old people were so rare in human societies that they were usually treated with great deference and respect. But all that is changing, largely because there are so many old people today. As we have already seen, this is not because the human life-span has been increased, but rather because more people are reaching the Biblical three score and ten. In 1789, a sixty-year-old male American could expect to live another fifteen years or so; in 1963, he could look forward to about sixteen! On the other hand, life expectancy *at birth* has increased dramatically, from about forty to seventy years. In addition, as society becomes urbanized and industrialized, there is almost invariably a decrease in the number of babies born—the so-called "demographic transition." The precise reason for this reduction in the birthrate is not known, but it provides some hope that our world may eventually achieve a state of zero population growth. It also increases the proportion of older people in the population.

Those who were supposed to be "greening" North America in the late 1960s and early 1970s—the postadolescent products of the postwar baby boom—will be graying it in the early twenty-first century. And they will be doing so in the greatest numbers ever. As of the 1980 census, persons sixty-five and over constituted more than 10 percent of the U.S. population. Estimates vary, but it appears that by the next century, the percentage may well be closer to 20 percent. The ten countries with the highest percentage of persons over age sixty-five are (in order) East Germany, Austria, Sweden, West Germany, France, Belgium, England, Norway, Scotland, and Denmark. The United States ranks nineteenth, Canada ranks twenty-first, and, significantly, all of the top eighteen are European and their people have a long life expectancy—averaging about sixty-eight years for men and seventy-three years for women. They also have relatively low birth rates. A lot of babies means not only more people, but a proportionately younger population as well; conversely, a low birth rate typically results in a population with a relatively larger number of older people.

On the other end of the list, we find the African nation of Mali with the smallest proportion of people over sixty-five, followed by Kuwait, Zambia, Greenland, Honduras, Venezuela, Ecuador, Niger, and Nicaragua. Not surprisingly, the life expectancy at birth in Mali is about thirty-seven years (close to what it was in colonial America), and averages about fifty for the other "youthful" countries. When and if these nations undergo their own demographic transition, with fewer births and longer average survival, they can expect to increase the proportion of old people in their population. What will be in store for them? A mixed bag, judging from the American experience.

Nature deals us the cards, but we play our own hand—according to the rules set by society instead of Hoyle. And as we have already seen, society's attitude toward the aged in North America has varied greatly during our history. As members of the species *Homo sapiens*, we are intensely social creatures. Our behavior is strongly influenced by the behavior of others around us, and accordingly we must look toward society to understand how old people are viewed, and also how they view themselves.

When an Englishman reaches his or her one hundredth birthday, a royal message of congratulations arrives from Buckingham Palace. In the United States, there is a telegram from the president. We honor the super-old and respectfully ask them their secret for living so long. ("Not dying," is one good answer.) In *Jean Valjean*, Victor Hugo wrote, "When grace is joined with wrinkles, it is adorable. There is an unspeakable dawn in happy old age." On the other hand, we would rather not hear about old age when it is unhappy. Old age ultimately brings frailty, susceptibility to disease, and closeness to death; thus, it carries with it its own unhappiness. But some of the most serious problems of aging may well lie not so much in the process itself, but in society's response to it. Two thousand years ago, Cicero suggested, "It is not old age that is at fault, but rather our attitude toward it."

The Nambikwara Indians of South America have a word for "young"—significantly, it also means "beautiful." They have another for "old," which also means "ugly." We have different words but a similar attitude. Wordsworth looked for the silver lining, and even he almost came up empty:

Though nothing can bring back the hour
Of splendour in the grass, of glory in the flower;

But he consoled himself with:

We will grieve not, rather find
Strength in what remains behind . . .

"What remains behind" may still possess great reserves of strength, mixed with all-too-human weaknesses as well. Our even-more-human reliance on society, however, has an enormous bearing on what life is like for us as we grow old.

The study of modern society is known as "sociology." Unlike other disciplines, like biology, medicine, history, psychology, or anthropology, each of which involves an area of specialized expertise generally removed from our daily experience, the sociologist seeks to explain to us that which we already know. Accordingly, one might begin reading the prestigious sociological compendium *Handbook of Aging and the Social Sciences* with some skepticism. This would scarcely be relieved upon encountering the following profundity in a chapter on "Death and dying in a social context": "The process of dying obtains its unique qualities because it eventuates in the irreverisible state of being dead." And if that is not enough, earlier in the same chapter, we are informed that "death is the transition from the state of being alive to the state of being dead."

Of course, not all sociology belabors the obvious, and whatever we may think of sociologists, we must admit that they study something important.

For starters, let us consider what I call the "Satchel Paige Principle."* suggested by his question, "How old would you be if you didn't know how old you was?" Like it or not, we are not free simply to be ourselves, because our own perception of "ourselves" is based in large part on how others respond to us. As Satchel Paige pointed out, we know how old we are, and we behave accordingly. Nearly always, we "act our age," and Lord help us if we don't. At the turn of the century, Charles Horton Cooley proposed the concept of the "looking glass self," an earlier statement of the Satchel Paige Principle: we form an image of ourselves based on how others act toward us. We use this image to see and know ourselves, as in a looking glass. At retirement, for example, we are made to feel that we have outlived our usefulness. All too often, we believe this reflection of ourselves, seen in the behavior of others toward us.

Without a doubt, modern society devalues the elderly person. When the elderly person accepts that assessment and downgrades his own expectations of himself, then his competence, his vitality, and even in a sense his worth tend to go down proportionately. It is an example of what sociologist Robert Merton called a "self-fulfilling prophecy," a prediction that, if believed, tends to make itself true. To illustrate the principle, let's look at an example unrelated to aging. Urban planners and others periodically claim that the New York City region requires an additional airport. JFK, LaGuardia, and Newark, it seems, are not enough. The argument is plausible, given the current increase in air passengers in that area. And certainly if an additional airport is built, it will be used, thereby justifying its construction. (In fact, once built, a fourth airport will undoubtedly increase air traffic so much that developers will soon be calling for a fifth.) The point is that the prophecy of increased air travel in the New York area becomes self-fulfilling if we listen to it. On the other hand, if we do not listen and instead decide to route additional European flights elsewhere on the eastern seaboard, then New York City air traffic will not increase, and an additional airport will not be needed there. A similar argument applies to building additional highways: if we accept the prophecy that there will be more cars and more demand for roads, then clearly, more roads

* Satchel Paige was one of the greatest baseball players of all time. A black, he was kept out of the major leagues until well past his prime, but even then played until nearly fifty years old.

213

must be made. And if more roads are made, then there will be cars to ride on them. But if we plan for mass transit instead, then *that* will become our future.

Aging may also be like this. If we are told certain things about growing older, and if we believe them, then whatever we are told about our aging selves may actually become true. A self-fulfilling perception, as well as prophecy.

"What you see is what you get." Modify that to, "What others see in you is what you think you are," and also, "what you are actually likely to become." It is a type of social placebo effect: if we are persuaded that a sugar pill, or a billy goat testicle, is going to rejuvenate us, then to some extent it actually does. Similarly, if we are told that we are old and useless, then all too often we just roll over and prepare to die. Perhaps the biological theory of "running out of program" has its painful parallel in the social phenomenon of "running out of useful role." We are programmed by our own training and by our society to serve useful, productive roles during the ages of about twenty-five through sixty-five. After that, the program is often finished and the sense of mission is withdrawn. In a sense, the abandoned satellite has a better chance than the overage human; at worst, it is adrift without instructions and therefore at the mercy of breakdowns and unforeseen events. But the human is actually directed to *stop functioning*. We are told how old we are, and what that is supposed to mean.

In modern America, we are also told that age is undesirable. Sports figures, for example, are over the hill at thirty-five—this is certainly true for football, baseball, and basketball, the big three of American spectator sports. George Blanda was a celebrated "grand old man," still playing football at forty. The same was true of Archie Moore in boxing. No one who watched Mohammed Ali at thirty-six can doubt that he would have been defeated easily by the Ali of ten years before—that is, when he was "in his prime." But prime for what? Power and quick reflexes count for something, but they are only one dimension of life. The point is that our sports superheroes are typically two-dimensional characters anyhow. By age forty, they become pathetic figures, and then they seem to disappear. Millions of Americans grow up with the message that the aging person self-destructs as he grows older.

Modern industry has also fostered this delusion. The fashion business provides a good example. In order to generate sales, garment manufacturers succeed in hoodwinking us into discarding perfectly functional articles of clothing long before they are worn out, simply because they are hopelessly "old fashioned" and out of style. And style, of course, is the newest and latest. We take this all for granted, and yet life does not have to be this way. There are many societies whose people wear the same traditional garb they have worn for centuries. Not surprisingly, their attitudes toward "new" and "old" are quite different from ours. A society that plans the obsolescence of its things would not be inconsistent in programming its own people for the trash heap as well.

And what of those people? If they are sufficiently accepting of the phenomenon, and desensitized to the process, they may even go along with it when turned upon themselves.

The General Motors Corporation was faced with a real dilemma when Ford came out with its highly successful and reliable Model T. The problem was solved, and with typical ingenuity: it was decreed that different models would come out annually, making the previous year's obsolete. Science had already made believers of us all, so what was "new and improved" was "in." We craved, and still crave, the latest scientific and engineering advances, this year's model, or if we are really lucky, *next* year's. In a rapidly changing society, we are very much aware that we cannot swim in the same river twice. In fact, we are discouraged from even trying. A throw-away society that looks eagerly ahead to this year's advances can hardly be expected to retain much interest in last year's models. Tragically, this often happens to last year's people too.

We live by the clock, and—less obviously—by the calendar as well. Bernice Neugarten, a social psychologist at the University of Chicago, has emphasized the importance of "social timetables" in our own life cycle. Although rarely stated out loud, nearly all of us are aware of whether our behavior at any time is "age-appropriate." We see ourselves as either on time or not, early or late for our various appointments with life: graduation, marriage, parenthood, grandparenthood, widowhood. We consult our timetables to know if we are early or late, often being pleased with the former and distressed with the latter. Death of a spouse is nearly always stressful, but much less so when it is recognized as "on time." Conversely, failure of our life cycle trains to run on time can be highly stressful, as when a couple, in their late middle age, find themselves with an orphaned grandchild. Similarly, an even greater trauma than children leaving home is when our calendar tells us that they should, but they don't!

How old would we be if we didn't know how old we really are? We'll probably never know.

❧

A frequently mentioned goal for our society is to eliminate distinctions based on race, sex, and age. Yet, we have also witnessed—and welcomed—the rise of ethnic consciousness, feminism, and gerontology. No one would claim that black and white are indistinguishable, or that they should be. The same holds true for man and woman, and for differences in age as well. Distinctions can be hurtful when they result in inequality of opportunity, but when used as simple descriptions of reality, they serve a useful function. Thus, people are not undifferentiated blobs of sameness, like a huge glop of tapioca pudding. They come in different shapes and sizes, different abilities and inclinations, and different ages as well. Can we accept differences in age as being not intrinsically better or worse, but just *different* and hence worthwhile and even exciting?

Psychoanalyst Carl Jung wrote: "Being old is highly unpopular. Nobody seems to consider that not being *able* to grow old is precisely as absurd as not being able to outgrow child-sized shoes. A still infantile man of thirty is surely to be deplored, but a youthful septuagenarian—isn't that delightful? And yet *both* are perverse, lacking in style, psychological monstrosities." The person who cannot age is a monster, but so is a society that cannot accept aging and is unable to profit from what age has to offer.

There may be other, hidden costs as well. Dr. Maurice Linden, writing in the *American Journal of Psychiatry*, suggested that "arogance and willfulness in the young" follow from lack of respect for the old. Without revered senior figures, young people may develop an exaggerated and headstrong impression of their own importance. As evidence, Dr. Linden points to the low rate of juvenile delinquency among Hebrew, Chinese, and Indian cultures—societies that traditionally hold their elderly in high esteem.

Whether esteemed or not, most people are acutely aware of their own age and that of others around them. Sociologist

Mathilda White Riley has emphasized the concept of "age stratification" in the analysis of American society. She suggests that
individuals treat each other more as members of the same age
group (technically referred to as a "cohort") than as individuals.
Furthermore, each age group is different, since members of each
generation have shared experiences with others of the same generation that differ significantly from those of other generations.
Some of us experienced the Depression as part of childhood, others went through World War II. The Sputnik kids grew up with
a fascination for science, especially physics. They also grew up
with DDT in their fat and strontium-90 in their bones. Another
generation came of age with civil rights marches, LSD, and the
Vietnam War. Perhaps the next generation will distinguish itself
by halting our current drift toward nuclear war, thereby giving
all of us (themselves included) the chance to grow old in the first
place.

Social scientists regularly make pronouncements about "the
elderly," and yet in a surprising number of cases they are mistaken, simply because they have failed to consider these "cohort
effects." For example, persons sixty years old during the 1970s
have more in common than the number of years they have lived.
They also share having been grade-schoolers during World War
I, teenagers during prohibition, young adults during the Depression, and so on. They might be very different from the sixty-
year-olds of the year 2000, who have lived most of their lives in
the atomic age and are in their forties today. A full understanding of the effects of aging *per se*, separated from the effects of
having lived through the same history, would therefore require
something more than just studying people of a given age: there
must be "longitudinal" studies, which follow people for many
years, noting changes along the way and looking for common
patterns. Some longitudinal studies are currently under way, most
of them concentrating on changes of medical interest, such as
blood pressure. But so far we know surprisingly little about
"normal aging," either medically or socially.

Beyond the Satchel Paige Principle, there is one other general
social theory that applies to aging: the theory of "disengagement," first proposed in a book that appeared in 1961, written
by Elaine Cumming and William Henry. In *Growing Old: The*

Process of Disengagement, Cumming and Henry presented the results of a lengthy study of aging in Kansas City and also extended their findings to aging in general. Their theory is just what the name implies: growing old, according to them, is accompanied by social disengagement of the elderly person from his or her surroundings. It is a two-stage theory. In the first place, society tends to exclude the aging individual, largely because it is awkward and disruptive for people to occupy crucial roles when they will shortly be dying. Secondly, the old person is said to be a partner to this process, actively withdrawing from society just as society withdraws from him or her.

Engagement, on the other hand, is defined as the "interpenetration of the person with the society to which he belongs." The degree of engagement is roughly revealed by the effect on society if the individual dies while engaged in that society. Hence, society protects itself by reducing the engagement of those who are likely to die. Furthermore, the aging individual, sensing his approaching death, is supposed to shift his concerns to other things, thereby disengaging himself. "If the individual becomes sharply aware of the shortness of life and the scarcity of time remaining to him, and if he perceives his life space as decreasing . . . then readiness for disengagement has begun" (Cumming and Henry).

Psychologist Robert Kastenbaum of Wayne State University has identified what he calls "psychological loss of the future," a foreshortened perspective on life as people recognize that they have more past accumulated and less future available to them. Pioneer sociologist Emile Durkheim opined that "society has retreated from the old person, or what amounts to the same thing, he has retreated from it." Thomas Jefferson gave personal testimony to disengagement theory when he wrote, "It is reasonable that we should drop off and make room for another growth. When we have lived our generation out, we should not wish to encroach upon another." Jefferson even went so far as to suggest that the U.S. Constitution should be rewritten every nineteen years. As the previous generation withdrew, the next one could literally write its own rules. We have not carried disengagement that far. In fact, disengagement theory seems especially inappropriate when applied to politics, since it is precisely in this realm that elderly people seem to be unusually involved. The list of "senior statesmen" is long and impressive: De Gaulle, Tito, Mao

Tse-tung, Chiang Kai-shek, Brezhnev, Franco, Khomeini, Reagan. Aged politicians do not often disengage willingly, and despite the troublesome instability often generated by the death of a political leader, societies do not seem to withdraw from elderly leaders simply because of their age.

Yet, perhaps the aged politician is an exception. In most cases, aging does seem to bring with it an increase in contemplation, quiet, and an appreciation of solitude that even surprises the person's juniors. There is often a turning inward upon oneself. The French writer Jouhandeau put it this way: "Never have I felt myself attached to life by so slender a thread, so slender that it might snap at any moment. It is this that crowns my joy in still being." Another Frenchman, François Mauriac, also said it clearly: "I do not feel detached from anyone or any thing. But from now on living will be enough to keep me occupied. This blood which still flows in the hand I lay upon my knee, this sea I feel beating within me, this transitory, not eternal ebb and flow, this world so close to its end—all these insist upon being watched every moment, all these last moments before the very last: that is what old age is."

Maybe there is a special zen of aging, a delicate art of growing old gracefully, with a unique appreciation of one's present, closely tied to disengagement from other aspects of life. Just as winter causes us to gather more often around the fireplace and to spend less time in over-the-fence transactions with neighbors, age may bring its own special hunkering down into one's self. Interpreted by others as disengagement, is it really a very special, personal kind of *engagement*? "Some sigh for yesterday! Some for tomorrow!" wrote French diplomat and poet Paul Claudel, at age 80. "But," he continued, "you must reach old age before you can understand the meaning—the splendid, absolute, unchallengeable, irreplaceable meaning of the word *today!*"

Disengaged need not be the same as discarded. Elaine Cumming writes: "The fully engaged man is, in essence, bound; the disengaged man is free—if he has resources and health enough to allow him to exercise that freedom. The ability to enjoy old age may be the ability and the opportunity to use freedom." There are interesting differences between men and women in this respect. Since men are more likely to be "engaged" outside the family circle—in their work—retirement and its ensuing disengagement is typically more abrupt and difficult for them. Among the elderly, men adapt to loss of a spouse less well than do women. For men, remarriage is the major way to reestablish any form of social intimacy with another; often, it is the only way. Women, by contrast, are more able to find satisfying companionship via friends and their extended family. In a sample of several hundred elderly persons seeking public assistance, 22 percent of the men were homeless, as opposed to only 6 percent of the women.

Although the elderly are often seen as the custodians of tradition, they may also possess a curious social immunity that allows them to do things that would be taboo for younger people. Part of this results from a relaxation of sexual mores, since the elderly are often seen as being somehow "less sexual." But part of it also seems to emanate directly from the elderly themselves, presumably as a result of their disengagement. In Bertolt Brecht's play "The *Un*worthy Old Lady," the heroine, widowed at age seventy-two, behaves scandalously—and loves it. Movies, from "The Over-the-Hill Gang" to "Harold and Maude," have lately been extolling the unconventional, geriatric hero. And Shakespeare's Lear tears off his hypocritical clothes in his "madness" when nothing is left to him and—tragically disengaged— he finally sees pretense for what it is.

Disengagement may be encouraged by rapid social change. Like Jonathan Swift's Struldbruggs, who were unable to keep up with the daily changes in their own language, old people come to feel more and more isolated as things change, because they are often unable or unwilling to keep up. As modernization proceeds, the social status of the aged usually declines. In the United States, at least, this has been the case. With improved health care, more people survive into old age, thereby leading to more competition with those who are younger. In addition, modernization itself has brought automation in its wake, with fewer total jobs. The knowledge and experience of the elderly have become obsolete more quickly with the rapid pace of change in our society. Retirement is encouraged, even required. Change is hard, and harsh.

Certainly one of the most important of such changes is the death of friends and relatives. The aged Chateaubriand once commented: "My too-long life is like those Roman roads, lined with monuments to the dead." The loneliness of the long-lived person may be as much a cause of his disengagement as a result.

What about political and religious attitudes? Most people believe that the aged are more religious, disengaged from this world and looking toward the next, and also more conservative. Recent studies have shown, however, that neither of these stereotypes is true. Any differences appear to be the result of "cohort effects" rather than a "longitudinal" result of aging itself. A study by the E. P. Andrus Gerontology Center at the University of Southern California found that whereas middle-aged persons ranked personal success and achievement high, the old (and the young) considered that service to humanity, world peace, and racial equality were more important. Similarly, the Methodist Church polled its members during the early 1970s, asking their opinions regarding future directions for the church. The most conservative responses came from those forty-five to fifty-four years old. The young and the old agreed with one another once again, ranking aid to minorities as number one, and working for world peace a close second.

As a general principle, nonetheless, disengagement seems to be real enough. That is, it is an accurate *description* of what happens to many people as they grow older. But this should not necessarily be taken as a *prescription*, a recommendation of what ought to be. In fact, evidence is accumulating that people who remain actively engaged also remain happier, healthier, and possibly even live longer. (Remember the Abkhasians.) At eighty, veteran actor George Burns was asked if he worried about dying. His instant reply: "Me? I can't die. I'm booked!" In fact, as long as he remains "booked," and thereby engaged, he may be less likely to die.

Despite the common assumption that most old people in America live in nursing homes or other institutions, the facts are otherwise: only about 4 percent of those over sixty-five live in this way. The remaining 96 percent live by themselves, with each other, or with family. The great fear of institutionalization expressed by many old people is only partly a result of the nursing homes' reputation for poor care; the main issue is that going to a "home" means forced disengagement from family, friends, and community. Significantly, surveys have shown that old people who live close to their grown children and see them regularly are consistently happier than those who live farther away. They are probably healthier as well. Furthermore, when it comes

221

to nursing homes, the best ones are invariably those that provide the most opportunities for engagement in local activities.

Given the choice, most people—whether young or old—prefer engagement to disengagement. As we have seen in chapters 11 and 12, there is good reason to believe that prior to urbanization and technology, most human societies treated their elderly better than North Americans do today. And in most cases, old people did not "disengage", as the theory would have it. Theory is useful if it makes sense out of what would otherwise be confusing, and if it suggests new ways of looking at things. Disengagement theory does all this. But it also has many shortcomings, not the least of which is that it may become its own self-fulfilling prophecy: if we all agree that old people "naturally" disengage, then the next step is to encourage the process. When the expectation gets strong enough and old people see it mirrored in those around them, the Satchel Paige Principle begins to work, and lo and behold, disengagement theory becomes true!

❧

When Sigmund Freud was asked what people must learn in order to be happy, he replied, "to work and to love." The working, loving person is hardly disengaged. When asked to divulge his secret, Gabriel Chapnish, at 117 years, was a bit more specific: "Active physical work and a moderate interest in alcohol and the ladies." Tennyson's "Ulysses" complained:

How dull it is to pause, to make an end,
To rust unburnished, not to shine in use!
As though to breathe were life!

Ulysses had been a leader during the Trojan War. He had survived an adventurous, ten-year odyssey back to his home kingdom where he once more validated his heroism and apparently was then expected to live out his days in a state of suitable disengagement. But by the end of Tennyson's poem, our hero had decided differently:

. . .—you and I are old;
Old age hath yet his honour and his toil.
Death closes all; but something ere the end,
Some work of noble note, may yet be done,
Not unbecoming men that strove with Gods.

> . . . Come, my friends,
> 'tis not too late to seek a newer world.
> . . . .
> Though much is taken, much abides; and though
> We are not now that strength which in old days.
> Moved earth and heaven; that which we are, we are;
> One equal temper of heroic hearts,
> Made weak by time and fate, but strong in will
> To strive, to seek, to find, and not to yield.

Of course, we are not all Ulysses. Striving to be an aged hero may prove as chafing as the expectation of being "disengaged." Heroism, by definition, is only for a few. The real heroes may be those who can organize a society within which all people, of all ages, can choose their own life course, free of expectation from society, poets . . . or sociologists.

In her book *The Coming of Age,* French writer Simone de Beauvoir gave her opinion of aging, society, and the responsibility of each individual:

> Morality teaches a serene acceptance of those ills which science and technology are powerless to abolish—pain, disease, old age. It claims that the courageous endurance of that very condition which lessens us is a way of increasing our stature. If he lacks other projects, the elderly man may commit himself to this. But here we are playing with words. Projects have to do only with our activities. Undergoing age is not an activity. Growing, ripening, ageing, dying—the passing of time is predestined, inevitable. There is only one solution if old age is not to be an absurd parody of our former life, and that is to go on pursuing ends that give our existence a meaning—devotion to individuals, to groups or to causes, social, political, intellectual, or creative work.

No less than the theorizing sociologist, Ms. de Beauvoir has her own axe to grind, predictable from her long association with existential philosopher Jean-Paul Sartre. To the existentialist, life is absurd—because of the inevitability of death—and therefore, we must all define ourselves by what we *do.* When we are young, there is enough to *do* in simply growing up. As adults, however, this changes and we are expected to *do* something more, if only to support ourselves and our children. The question is: What is appropriate in old age? (What is appropriate in middle age? At any age?)

British-born gerontologist Alex Comfort (best known in North

America for his advocacy of the joy of sex) tells an appropriate story. It seems that a well-meaning young senator was taking a group of retired persons on a tour of the Capitol Building. Trying to show interest, he asked one old man, "And what used you to be?" The old man fixed the senator with a steady gaze and replied, "I still am."

15

Bon Voyage

What can we say in conclusion? This has been a wide-ranging tour. Our itinerary was vast, for an exploration of aging is nothing less than an exploration of life. Time's arrow flies on, carrying us along with it—changing us, making us wise, foolish, serene, anxious, hopeful or hopeless, exalted or tragic, each in his or her own way, or all these at once. Rue it or revel in it, we cannot avoid it, and in these pages at least, we have not done so. Life goes on and so—for a time—do we.

To age is to enter the future, and by definition the future is unknown and therefore somewhat frightening. Perhaps now, having finished this book and completed our promised intellectual exploration (and a little older as well!), you can continue on your own trip with less fear, more understanding, and possibly even some real enthusiasm. Or, if you are one of those people for whom only *others* grow old, at least you may be able to view their aging in a new perspective.

Part of this book has been a preview, what the movie theaters optimistically call "coming attractions": changes in your body, your mind, your sex life. Something will have been gained if tomorrow, you do not take yourself by surprise, if you don't exclaim as Stephen Vincent Benét did:

When I was young, I slept like stone,
When I was young, I grew like tree.
Now I lie, abed, alone
and I wonder if 'tis me.

We have also sampled both the history and the sociology of aging in America, as well other ways of growing old, including a close look at some places where old age appears to be less a burden than a privilege, and extreme old age less a "believe-it-or-not" curiosity than a regular part of everyday life. There may have been lessons learned. At minimum, we can appreciate the range of variation on the biological theme; at maximum, perhaps we can choose from among these variations, thereby making life not just longer, but better as well.

We have passed through time, reviewing the persistent and often peculiar efforts at rejuvenation, from ancient history to modern quackery. We have peered into the modern science of gerontology, finding that age is unlikely to be prevented or "cured" like some dread disease, but neither is it to be ignored, or treated with indifference or fatalism, like the ultimate burnout of the sun. Rather, it cries out to be understood and, within certain limits at least, tinkered with.

This exploration started with a reminder: you have an appointment with age, as we all do. The clock is still ticking. Time is not running *out*, however; it is running *on*. So don't worry: however far you get, and however you seek to arrange it, this is one appointment that you cannot miss (unless, of course, you cease your journey altogether). And while you are meeting that appointment, the passing of time itself may insure some exciting and creative changes, in you and in society as a whole. Thus, Nobel Prize–winning author Czeslaw Milosz, in his collected essays *Vision From San Francisco Bay* (1982), suggested that "by changing civilizations, time continually liberates new souls and bodies in man, and thus time is not a serpent devouring its own tail." Instead, time is a liberating matrix, in which we grow, develop, and change.

We have met no end of commentary and advice on growing old, from Dante's acquiescent cheerfulness to Dylan Thomas' admonition, "Do not go gentle into that good night / Rage, rage against the dying of the light." However you choose to go, at least you will not go uninformed. Having completed our intellectual exploration, you are not only an armchair adventurer, but also a seasoned traveler in your own right, and for better or worse, your personal expedition is still proceeding. We return you now to your own life. Bon voyage.

References and Notes

"Whoever quotes his sources," it says in the Talmud, "brings redemption to the world." Herein you shall find some sources; as for redemption, I decline responsibility. In fact, even the sources cited here must be incomplete. The literature of gerontology (both technical and popular) is now immense, and far beyond my goals and ability to review in the next few pages. Surprisingly, however, there have been very few efforts to combine the two—to explicate technical findings for a popular audience. This has been my goal in writing the present book, and in these references and notes I shall present some further suggestions for readers who might want to continue their personal, intellectual explorations.

There are three important volumes, each one massive, relatively current, scrupulously thorough, and professionally impeccable, that provide heavy-duty, state-of-the-art compendiums of technical detail and numerous additional references. They are the fruits of a laudable publishing effort by Van Nostrand Reinhold (New York), and all three were published in 1977. These volumes are: *Handbook of the Biology of Aging* (C. Finch and L. Hayflick, eds.), *Handbook of the Psychology of Aging* (J. Birren and K. Schaie, eds.), and *Handbook of Aging and the Social Sciences* (R. Binstock and E. Shanas, eds.). The reader who wants more, on any topic related to gerontology, will find these handbooks most useful, if he or she is not overwhelmed. In the notes to follow, I shall simply refer to these indispensable volumes by the names of the editors.

1. Appointment with Age

The Walt Whitman epigraph is from his poem "Youth, Old Age and Night," which appears in volume 1 of *Leaves of Grass*. The selection by Proust ("At first I could not understand . . .") comes, as one might expect, from his *Remembrance of Things Past*. Menander's opinion that "a long life is a painful thing . . ." comes from *The Principal Fragments*, trans. F. G. Alinson (London: Heinemann, 1930). Dante's advice is contained in *The Convivio of Dante Alighieri* (London: J. M. Dent & Sons, 1903). Byron's derision of age appears in his "Stanzas Written on the Road Between Florence and Pisa," and Mimnermos' words are taken from fragment 2 (Diehl edition, 1964). Victor Hugo's paean to an old man comes from his "Booze endormi," part of the collection *La légende des siècles* (Boston: D. C. Heath Co., 1909). The Chateaubriand quotation, as with others presented in chapters to follow, comes from his memoirs, *Mémoires d'outre-tombe* (Paris: Garnier Frères, 1910). Freud's observation on old age is contained in his *On Narcissism: An Introduction* (London: Hogarth Press, 1914).

The old woman's plaintive comment on her old age is taken from "An Old Woman Speaks," in B. K. Smith's *Aging in America* (Boston: Beacon, 1973). Thoreau's disparaging view of the elderly is made abundantly clear in his famous *Walden*, and the Goethe reference to oak trees is quoted in an article by L. Edel which is as fascinating as its title: "Portrait of the Artist as an Old Man" (*The American Scholar*, 1977/78). For additional information on Luigi Cornaro, see J. Burkhardt, *The Civilization of the Renaissance in Italy* (London: Phaidon, 1955), and also E. Trimmer, *Rejuvenation: The History of an Idea* (London: Robert Hale, 1967). Garson Kanin's delightful anecdote about the retired electrician is from his equally delightful defense of age, *It Takes a Long Time to Become Young* (New York: Doubleday, 1978).

Victor Hugo's observation is from *Les misérables*, and André Gide's is from his *Journal, 1939–1942* (Paris: Gallimard, 1946). The poet Aragon's question and answer come from his *Les chambres* (Paris: Editeurs Français Réunis, 1969), and the melancholy comment of Ninon de Lenclos, noted French libertine and salon figure of a bygone era, can be found in C. Austin's fascinating biography, *The Immortal Ninon* (London: G. Routledge & Sons, 1927).

W. B. Yeats' complaint about his own aging is found in his *Letters*, ed. R. J. Finneran, G. M. Harper, and W. M. Murphy (New York: Columbia University Press, 1977), and Voltaire's sadness about dwelling among ruins is recounted in *Voltaire's Correspondence*, ed. Theodore Besterman (Paris: Gallimard, 1975). Finally, Dylan Thomas' advice "do not go gentle into that good night" is from his poem with that title, published in 1952.

2. Rejuvenation, Part I

For further detail on the Gilgamesh epic, see A. Heidel, *The Gilgamesh Epic and Old Testament Parallels* (Chicago: University of Chicago Press, 1946), and for a very readable introduction to historical, literary, and cross-cultural aspects of rejuvenation, see O. Segerberg, *The Immortality Factor* (New York: E. P. Dutton, 1974). The standard reference among historians has been G. Gruman, *A History of Ideas about the Prolongation of Life*, a technical monograph published in 1966 by the Transactions of the American Philosophical Society (volume 56, part 9). Its description of Ponce de Leon and "hyperborean" myths is especially useful. In *Rejuvenation: A History of the Idea*, E. Trimmer provides an excellent account of the water cures, Prester John, and Taoist efforts. For a good source on alchemy and rejuvenation, see M. Eliade,

The Forge and the Crucible (New York: Harper, 1956). The Lucretius quotation is from *De Rerum Natura* 3 ("On the Nature of the Universe"). The reader intrigued by Shunamitism might want to consult the following report dealing with mice: O. Muhlbock, "Factors Influencing the Life Span of Inbred Mice" (*Gerontologia* 3 [1959]: 177).

The life-span of British clergy is discussed in Alex Comfort's *The Biology of Senescence* (New York: Elsevier, 1979), in which the quotation by Herman Boerhaave also appears as an epigraph. The words of Ibn Sina are recounted in P. McGrady, *The Youth Doctors* (New York: Coward McCann, 1968), and the Taoist Chin P'ing Mei speaks to us in *The Golden Lotus* (London: Routledge, 1939). Benjamin Franklin's delightful preference for Madeira wine can be found in *Mr. Franklin: A Selection of His Personal Letters*, ed. L. W. Larabee and W. J. Bell, Jr. (New Haven: Yale University Press, 1956).

3. Rejuvenation, Part II

Probably the best, most readable discussion of rejuvenation quackery is found in E. Trimmer, *Rejuvenation: A History of the Idea*. Readers wanting more on early medical efforts (Metchnikoff, Voronoff, Steinach, and especially Niehans) would probably do best with P. McGrady, *The Youth Doctors*, an engaging and chatty account. Additional material on Brown-Séquard, including the quotations attributed to the good doctor, are taken from O. Segerberg, *The Immortality Factor*. Metchnikoff's own work, *The Prolongation of Life* (London: Heinemann, 1907), is still available in many libraries. Subtitled "Optimistic Studies," it gives the upbeat flavor of biologic thinking on the subject during the early twentieth century. Serge Voronoff's *Testicular Grafting from Ape to Man* (London: Brentano, 1927) was a sensation in its day, and makes an interesting period piece in the 1980s. Finally, Anna Aslan fans might want to consult her paper on "Theoretical and Practical Aspects of Chemotherapeutic Techniques in the Retardation of the Aging Process," appearing in M. Rockstein, ed., *Theoretical Aspects of Aging* (New York: Academic Press, 1974). This same volume also contains the paper by T. Yau, as well as a valuable compendium of review articles detailing biologic theories of the aging process.

4. What If?

For a useful review of world population and demographic trends, see "Aging and World-wide Population Change," a chapter by P. Hauser in Binstock and Shanas. For a moral and philosophical view of life extension, I recommend D. Juniper, *Man against Mortality* (New York: Charles Scribner's Sons, 1973). A few social scientists, occasionally even with government support, have begun investigating the likely implications of increased longevity in American society: in particular, P. Uhlenberg's chapter on "Demographic Change and Problems of the Aged,"

229

References and Notes

in *Aging from Birth to Death,* the proceedings of a symposium sponsored by the American Association for the Advancement of Science, and published by Westview Press, in Boulder, Colorado (1979), and also an important report titled "Extending the Human Life Span: Social Policy and Social Ethics," edited by B. Neugarten and R. Havighurst, and published by the National Science Foundation (Washington, D.C., 1977). Finally, for a sober, realistic, and practical appraisal of longevity prospects and the most clearheaded, useful advice I have seen, consult J. Fries and L. Crapo, *Vitality and Aging* (San Francisco: W. H. Freeman, 1981). A good collection of responsible geriatric futurism can be found in L. Jarvik, ed., *Aging into the 21st Century* (New York: Gardner Press, 1978).

5. The Biology of Aging, Part I

For two readable treatments of sociobiology—the new view of life in general and social behavior in particular, illuminated by evolution—I recommend Richard Dawkins' *The Selfish Gene* (Oxford: Oxford University Press, 1976) and my own book *The Whisperings Within* (New York: Penguin, 1981). Sir Peter Medawar's evolutionary theory of aging was first described in his remarkable *The Uniqueness of the Individual* (New York: Basic Books, 1957), and the error theory of the unique Leo Szilard made its debut, I believe, in his technical paper "On the Nature of the Aging Process" (*Proceedings of the National Academy of Sciences* 45 [1959]: 30). Australian Nobelist Macfarlane Burnet discusses xeroderma pigmentosum in his book *The Endurance of Life* (New York: Cambridge University Press, 1978), and Leslie Orgel's theory of error catastrophe is well recounted in his article "The Maintenance of the Accuracy of Protein Synthesis and Its Relevance to Aging" (*Proceedings of the National Academy of Sciences* 49 [1963]: 517). The differing longevity of male and female flies is detailed in M. Rockstein and H. Lieberman, "A Life Table for the Common House Fly, *Musca domestica*" (*Gerontologia* 3 [1959]:23). Raymond Pearl's pioneering but statistically dense work is available in his still accurate *The Biology of Population Growth* (New York: Knopf, 1930), and Hans Selye's discussion of the relation between stress and aging can be found in his article "Stress and Aging" (*Journal of the American Gerontological Society* 18 [1970]: 660). George Sacher's work on brain size and longevity is reviewed in his important book *Aging and Levels of Biological Organization* (Chicago: University of Chicago Press, 1965). G. P. Bidder's speculations regarding deterministic growth and aging appear in his article titled "Senescence" (*British Medical Journal* 115 [1932]: 5831), and C. McKay describes his skinny rats in detail in his chapter "Chemical Aspects of Aging and the Effect of Diet upon Aging," appearing in E. V. Cowdry, *Problems of Aging* (Baltimore: Williams & Wilkins, 1952). Lastly, anyone interested in the biology of aging should encounter the summarizing genius of a remarkable man, British-born polymath Alex Comfort—philoso-

pher, novelist, anti-nuclear activist, psychotherapist, and biological gerontologist. His book *The Biology of Senescence* (New York: Elsevier,
1979) is crammed with references and lucid summaries of all the major
theories.

"The Blind Men and the Elephant" is found in *The Poetical Works of
John Godfrey Saxe* (Boston: Houghton, 1892). The evolutionary view of
August Weismann is expressed in his *Essays upon Heredity and Kindred
Biological Problems*, ed. E. P. Poulton, S. Schonland, and A. Shipley
(Oxford: Clarendon Press, 1892); and Alexander Graham Bell's study of
longevity was published by the now extinct Genealogical Records Of-
fice (Washington, D.C.) in 1918, under the title "The Duration of Life
and Conditions Associated with Longevity: A Study of the Hyde Ge-
nealogy." Max Rubner's original work on energy quotas in living things
appeared as "Probleme des Wachstums und der Lebensdauer" (*MittGes.
Inn. Med.*, Vienna, 7 [1908]: 58).

6. The Biology of Aging, Part II

The awful but instructive diseases of premature aging are discussed
technically in W. Reichel, R. Garcia-Bunel, and J. Dilallo, "Progeria and
Werner's Syndrome as Models for the Study of Normal Human Aging"
(*Journal of the American Geriatric Society* 19 [1971]: 369). Leonard
Hayflick's pioneering work on cell division is ably recounted in his article "The Cell Biology of Human Aging" (*Scientific American* 242
[1980]: 58). Alexis Carrel's original claim for the immortality of tissue
culture cells appears in "On the Permanent Life of Tissues" (*Journal of
Experimental Medicine* 15 [1912]: 516). It is interesting to note that he
also coauthored a book, *The Culture of Organs* (New York: P. B. Hoe-
ber, 1938), with Charles A. Lindbergh.

P. L. Krohn's work on mouse skin transplants is technically presented
in his report "Heterochronic Transplantation in the Study of Ageing"
(*Proceedings of the Royal Society of London* 157 [1962]: 128). An early
and now-classic reference to J. Bjorksten's cross-linkage theory is his
report "A Common Molecular Basis for the Aging Syndrome" (*Journal
of the American Geriatric Society* 6 [1958]: 740), and for a good discussion of collagen, see R. Kohn, *Principles of Mammalian Aging* (Engle-
wood Cliffs, N.J.: Prentice-Hall, 1971). Denham Harman has written
many convincing papers on his free radical theory; for example, see "Free
Radical Theory of Aging: Effect of Amount and Degree of Unsaturation
of Dietary Fat on Mortality Rate" (*Journal of Gerontology* 26 [1971]:
451). If you are intrigued by the prospects for vitamin E as an anti-
oxidant, you might want to investigate A. L. Tappel's "Will Anti-
oxidant Nutrients Slow Aging Process?" (*Geriatrics* 23 [1968]: 97). The
most accessible discussion, to my knowledge, of Donner Denckla's work
is found in A. Rosenfeld, *Prolongevity* (New York: Knopf, 1976). R.
Walford, *The Immunologic Theory of Aging* (Baltimore: Williams &
Wilkins, 1969), discusses just that, and anyone seriously interested in

biology and aging could easily become immersed in Finch and Hayflick, for days or even weeks. Finally, for a nonbiologic note, the observation by Gaius Manilius is from his *Astronomica*, vol. 4, part 16.

7. *Of Tortoises and Trees*

Once again, Alex Comfort's *The Biology of Senescence* is a goldmine of information on longevity in other living things. The Francis Bacon quotation is from his *Historia Vitae et Mortis* (1645). The reader wanting a good lay-person's introduction to aging and longevity in animals and plants could do no better than the following book by a remarkable husband-and-wife team of biologist-writers: L. and M. Milne, *The Ages of Life* (New York: Harcourt, Brace & World, 1968). Surprisingly little is available on aging in animals, especially behavioral changes; an interesting exception is D. Bowden, ed., *Aging in Non-human Primates* (New York: Van Nostrand Reinhold, 1979).

8. *Aging and the Individual: Body*

Yeats' view that "an aged man is but a paltry thing . . ." appears in his renowned poem "Sailing to Byzantium," and the Corneille poem fragment is quoted in Simone de Beauvoir's detailed and literate study *The Coming of Age* (New York: G. P. Putnam's Sons, 1972). The Galen quote may be found in his ancient *On the Natural Faculties* (London: Heinemann, 1916), and the somber observation of pharaoh Ptah-hotep, in *The Instruction of Ptah-hotep and The Instruction of Ke'gemni* (London: J. Murray, 1918).

The Gompertz equation is described accurately yet understandably in Milne and Milne's *The Ages of Life,* and Nathan Shock's work on whole systems and aging is well described in his chapter "System Integration," in Finch and Hayflick. Indeed, just about everything biological in chapter 8 comes, in one way or another, from what I have learned by reading Finch and Hayflick! Fries and Crapo, with their *Vitality and Aging,* offer good advice for those who seek it, as does another useful manual by Alex Comfort, *A Good Age* (New York: Touchstone, 1976).

9. *Aging and the Individual: Mind*

Birren and Schaie's remarkable compendium on aging and the mind is a must. The Chateaubriand quotation is from the preface to his *Mémoires d'outre-tombe,* and the Simone de Beauvoir quotations are lifted from *The Coming of Age.* The concepts of fluid and crystallized intelligence are reviewed in K. Riegel, "History of Psychological Gerontology" (in Birren and Schaie), and virtually everything else you might want to know about aging and memory can also be found there. When it comes to age and achievement, try H. Lehman, *Age and Achievement*

(Princeton: Princeton University Press, 1953), and for a concise treatment of the growing field of geriatric psychiatry, you might want to turn to yet another book by the amazing Alex Comfort, this one titled *The Practice of Geriatric Psychiatry* (New York: Elsevier, 1980). Erik Erikson's eight stages of human mental development are presented in his *Childhood and Society* (New York: Norton, 1963), and for Robert Butler's concept of the "Life Review," see his article by that title in the journal *Psychiatry* (26 [1963]: 65). Butler was director of the National Institute on Aging—it will be difficult to find a more articulate, responsible, and devoted advocate.

Hans Christian Andersen's lament is from *Correspondence of Hans Christian Andersen*, ed. F. Crowford (London: Dean, 1891), and the conversation between Roosevelt and Holmes is recounted in Kanin's *It Takes a Long Time to Become Young*. David Gutmann's work "Toward a Species Psychology of Aging" is ably summarized in his chapter in Birren and Schaie, and also in his report of the highland Druze appearing in J. Gubrium, ed., *Time, Roles and Self in Old Age* (New York: Human Sciences Press, 1976). Mauriac's anthill analogy comes from his *Nouveaux mémoires intérieurs* (Paris: Flammarion, 1965), and the study of old people and school yearbooks is by H. Bahrick, "Maintenance of Knowledge: Questions about Memory We Forgot to Ask" (*Journal of Experimental Psychology* 108 [1979]: 296). The observations by Bernard Berenson, noted art historian and essayist, are found in *The Selected Letters of Bernard Berenson*, ed. A. K. McComb (Boston: Houghton Mifflin, 1964).

For aging and psychoses, such as Alzheimer's, try E. Busse and D. Blazer, eds., *Handbook of Geriatric Psychiatry* (New York: Van Nostrand Reinhold, 1980.) For biofeedback and other physiologic aspects of aging and psychology, see Diana S. Woodruff's chapter "A Physiological Perspective on the Psychology of Aging," in D. S. Woodruff and J. E. Birren, eds., *Aging: Scientific Perspectives and Social Issues* (New York: Van Nostrand, 1975). Samuel Johnson's observation on our view of memory in old and young appeared in A. Comfort, *A Good Age*, and for M. A. Liebermann's research on a Jewish old age home, see his "The Relationship of Mortality Rates to Entrance to a Home for the Aged" (*Geriatrics* 16 [1961]: 515), as well as his "Adaptive Processes in Late Life," in N. Datan and L. H. Ginsburg, eds., *Life-Span Developmental Psychology* (New York: Academic Press, 1975).

10. Aging and the Individual: Sex

"You think it horrible . . ." is from Yeats' poem "The Spur," and the Sophocles quotation is recounted in Plato's *Republic*, 329C. Seneca's observation about his newfound separation between soul (or mind) and body comes from *Epistulae Morales*, 26.2, although the translation is not literal. The quotation from Charles de Marguetel de Saint-Denis, Seigneur de Saint-Evremond, is contained in *The Letters of Saint-Evremond* (London: G. Routledge & Sons, 1930), and André Gide's account of his personal lust comes from his *Journal.* The now-classic Kinsey reports are *Sexual Behavior in the Human Male* (1948) and *Sexual Behavior in the Human Female* (1953), both published by W. B. Saunders & Co., Philadelphia. (How many people know that before turning his professional attention to sex, Alfred C. Kinsey was a noted entomologist, specializing in the taxonomy of butterflies?) For basic, clinical details on sex—although with very little on the elderly—see W. Masters and V. Johnson, *Human Sexual Response* (Boston: Little Brown, 1966) and *Human Sexual Inadequacy* (Boston: Little Brown, 1970). Perhaps the best, most informative, commonsense guide to sex and aging is R. Butler and M. Lewis, *Sex after Sixty* (New York: Harper & Row, 1976). Finally, Benjamin Franklin's famous advice on loving an older woman is reprinted in many places; my favorite, however, is *Dr. Benjamin Franklin and the Ladies: Being Various Letters, Essays, Bagatelles and Satires to and about the Fair Sex* (Mt. Vernon, N.Y.: Peter Pauper Press, 1939).

11. Aging in Other Places: Shangri-la in Three Parts

The primary source on the Abkhasians—and virtually the only one available in English—is Sula Benet, *Abkhasians: The Long-Living People of the Caucasus* (New York: Holt, Rinehart and Winston, 1974). The Abkhasian poets cited in this chapter are to be found in Benet's book as well. For the Vilcabambans, a comparable introduction is David Davies, *The Centenarians of the Andes* (New York: Doubleday, 1975). Very little has been written on the Hunzas, but some useful information appears in an article by the eminent physician Alexander Leaf, titled "Every Day Is a Gift When You Are over 100" (*National Geographic*, January 1973).

12. Aging in Other Places: A Selected Anthropology

Thomas Hood's poem ("Spring it is cheery . . . .") is titled "Ballad." A landmark study of aging in cross-cultural perspective is the work of anthropologist Leo Simmons, *The Role of the Aged in Primitive Society* (New Haven: Yale University Press, 1945). In this book, Simmons not only compiles an impressive array of ethnographic accounts, many of them first-person, but he also seeks correlations among hundreds of societies, including the Eskimos of Pt. Barrow, with regard to their treatment of the elderly. The physical condition of the Bontoc Igorot is taken from an account by A. Jenks, appearing in volume 1 of *Ethnological Survey Publications* (Manila, 1905). The matter-of-fact statement by an aged Hottentot woman of her own expendability is quoted from R. Moffat in Simmons, *The Role of the Aged in Primitive Society.* Simone de Beauvoir, in *The Coming of Age,* also does an admirable job of reviewing aging in other lands, especially ancient customs and modern-day practices in Japan and the South Pacific. The D. H. Lawrence quotation is from his poem, aptly titled "Beautiful Old Age." K. Rasmussen's conversation with the old Eskimo is recounted in his *The People of the Polar North*, cited in Simmons, *The Role of the Aged in Primitive Society*; and anthropologist W. C. Holden's account of the Akamba is from his *The Past and Future of the Kafir Races* (1871), also cited by Simmons. Confucius' advice is found in his *Analects* (New York: Dover, 1981).

An excellent source for the anthropology of aging is D. Cowgill and D. Holmes, eds., *Aging and Modernization* (New York: Appleton-Century-Crofts, 1972). It includes J. Hamer's account of the Ethiopian Sidamo, "Aging in a Gerontocratic Society." H. G. Lockett tells the Supela rain story in his "The Unwritten Literature of the Hopi" (*University of Arizona Social Science Bulletin* 2 [1933]: 110). The Cicero quote is from *De Senectute*, 61. The description of aging among the Yakut of Siberia comes from W. Sieroshevski, *The Yakut*, published in St. Petersburg in 1896, and quoted in Simmons. Austin Sheldon's description of "The aged and eldership among the Ibo" of Nigeria can be found in Cowgill and Holmes, eds., *Aging and Modernization*. For "growing old in Samoa," see L. Holmes, *Samoan Village* (New York: Holt, Rinehart and Winston, 1974). Some excellent and recent accounts of cross-cultural aging include P. Amoss and S. Harrell, eds., *Other Ways of Growing Old: Anthropological Perspectives* (Stanford: Stanford University Press, 1981), and C. Fry, ed., *Dimensions: Aging, Culture and Health* (New York: Praeger Scientific, 1981). Lin Yu-tang's observation about telephone manners in pre-revolutionary China comes from his *The Importance of Living* (London: Heinemann, 1931). Binstock and Shanas also provide some views of aging in other human societies, although their focus is largely on Westernized societies, especially the United States.

13. Aging in North America: History

In preparing this chapter, my most useful source was David Fischer's *Growing Old in America* (New York: Oxford University Press, 1978) and the numerous references therein, including the quotations from Increase and Cotton Mather, William Bridge, John Wise, and Samuel Dexter. The reader should note, however, that Fischer's interpretations— and my own—are not universally accepted by historians. For a rather different view, one that emphasizes continuity in certain aspects of aging in America combined with change in others, read W. Achenbaum, *Old Age in the New Land* (Baltimore: Johns Hopkins University Press, 1978). Then make up your own mind.

14. Aging in North America: Sociology

Binstock and Shanas is the basic reference. Among other important chapters, it includes one by B. Neugarten and G. Hagstead on the concept of social timetables, another by M. W. Riley on age stratification, and several useful sections dealing with social intervention, its opportunities and effects. The classic, original statement of disengagement theory can be found in E. Cumming and W. Henry, *Growing Old: The Process of Disengagement* (New York: Basic, 1961). Since publication of that work, many sociologists have been busy refuting it; see, for example, A. Hochschild, "Disengagement Theory: A Logical, Empirical and Phenomenological Critique," in J. Gubrium, ed., *Time, Roles and Self in Old Age* (New York: Human Sciences Press, 1976). A good collection of essays and evocative accounts is B. Hess, ed., *Growing Old in America* (New Brunswick: Transaction Books, 1980); and for superb, straightforward advice, read Alex Comfort's *A Good Age.*

Paul Claudel's poetic engagement is recounted in his *Oeuvres en prose* (Paris: Gallimard, 1927); Jouhandeau's similar feelings are from his *Réflexions sur la vieillesse et la mort* (Paris: B. Grasset, 1956); and Mauriac's engagement with his own functioning body is vividly described in his *Nouveaux mémoires intérieurs.* Chateaubriand's "too-long life" is mourned in his *Mémoires d'outre-tombe.* For Cicero, see *De Senectute,* and Wordsworth's lament over his loss of "splendor in the grass" comes from his poem "Ode: Intimations of Immortality from Recollections of Early Childhood." Yeats' view that "This is no country for old men . . ." is expressed in his "Sailing to Byzantium." Carl Jung's observation about acting one's age can be found in *Modern Man in Search of a Soul* (New York: Harcourt, Brace, Jovanovich, 1933).

For Robert Kastenbaum's concept of the "psychological loss of the future," see his work in *New Thoughts on Old Age* (New York: Springer, 1964), and Thomas Jefferson's suggestion that old age and political creativity don't usually go together is contained in *The Family Letters of Thomas Jefferson,* ed. E. M. Betts and J. A. Bear, Jr. (Columbia, Mo.: University of Missouri Press, 1966).

Finally, for ringing critiques of Society's attitude toward aging in present-day America, you cannot do better than J. Levin's *Ageism, Prejudice and Discrimination against the Elderly* (Belmont, Ca.: Wadsworth, 1980), and R. Butler's *Why Survive?* (New York: Harper & Row, 1975) for an equally troubling description of society's economic failings.

15. Bon Voyage

The S. V. Benét poem fragment comes from his plaintive yet funny "Old Man Hoppergrass."

Index

Abderhalden, Emil, 47
Abishag the Shunamite, 17-18
Abkhasia, 154, 155, 172-75; physical life in, 156-61; social life in, 161-65
Alchemy, 19-20, 23-24
Alzheimer's disease, 123-25
Andersen, Hans C., 121
Andrus, Ethel P., 8
Antediluvian theme, 25-26
Aragon, Louis, 4
Aristophanes, 146
Aristotle, 120, 174
Arteriosclerosis, 110
Aslan, Anna, 49-51
Aurora, 52-53
Avicenna. *See* Ibn Sina

Baruch, Bernard, 4, 48
Beauvoir, Simone de, 136, 179, 223
Bell, Alexander G., 69-70
Benét, Stephen V., 161-62, 225
Benet, Sula, 155-66 *passim*
Berenson, Bernard, 133
Bergman, Ingmar, 139
Bidder, G. P., 79-80
Bismarck, Otto von, 207-8
Bjorksten, Johan, 95-96
Boerhaave, Hermann, 18, 24
Boulding, Kenneth, 174
Brain, 125-26
Brain cells, 58
Bridge, William, 196
Brinkley, John R., 42-43
Brodum, William, 37
Browning, Robert, 6-7, 152
Brown-Séquard, Charles E., 39-41

Burnet, Macfarlane, 72-73, 101-2
Burns, George, 221
Butler, Robert, 136-37
Butler, Samuel, 71
Byron, George Gordon, Lord, 6, 195

Cancer: immortality, 88
Cannon, Walter, 35
Carrel, Alexis, 85-86
Carroll, Lewis, 204-5
Cells: doubling of, 86-90; cycling of, 92-95
Cellular therapy, 45-49
Chateaubriand, François René, Vicomte de, 8, 120-21, 220
Chevalier, Maurice, 3
China, 185-88
Cicero, 10, 126, 189
Claudel, Paul, 219
Cognitive dissonance, 35-36
Cohort effect, 217
Collagen, 95-98
Comfort, Alex, 223-24
Congreve, William, 146
Cooley, Charles Horton, 213
Cornaro, Luigi, 10, 32
Corneille, Pierre, 108-9
Cranach, Lucas, 30
Creativity, 131-32
Cross-linkage theory, 95-98
Cumming, Elaine, 217-19
Cureton, Thomas, 116
Curtin, Sharon, 8-9

Dante Alighieri, 5-6
David, King, 17-18
Davies, David, 155, 166-70 *passim*

237

Index